DELIBERATION AND DEVELOPMENT

DELIBERATION AND DEVELOPMENT
Rethinking the Role of Voice and Collective Action in Unequal Societies

Patrick Heller and Vijayendra Rao, Editors

WORLD BANK GROUP

Washington, DC

ISBN (paper): 978-1-4648-0501-1
ISBN (electronic): 978-1-4648-0502-8
DOI: 10.1596/978-1-4648-0501-1

Cover design: Critical Stages

Library of Congress Cataloging-in-Publication Data

Deliberation and development : rethinking the role of voice and collective action in unequal societies.
    pages cm
 Includes bibliographical references and index.
  ISBN 978-1-4648-0501-1 (alk. paper) — ISBN 978-1-4648-0502-8 (ebook)
 1. Debates and debating. 2. Discussion.
 PN4181.D398 2015
 808.53—dc23

                                                              2015007883

Titles in the Equity and Development Series

The Equity and Development Series addresses the distributional consequences of macroeconomic policies and showcases techniques for systematically analyzing the distributional consequences of policy reform. Titles
in this series undergo internal and external review under the management
of the Research Group in the World Bank's Development Economics Vice
Presidency.

Free access to titles in the Equity and Development Series is available at
https://openknowledge.worldbank.org/handle/10986/2160

Contents

Tables

Preface

This book brings together two fields that rarely converse with one another: deliberative democracy and development studies. The study of deliberation—which explores normative and practical questions around group-based decision making via discussion or debate, particularly as an alternate or supplement to voting or bargaining—has emerged as a critical part of the debate on democracy over the last two decades. Concurrently, the field of development has seen a spurt of interest in community-led development and participation premised on the ability of groups to arrive at decisions and manage resources via a process of discussion and debate. Despite the growing interest in both fields, they have rarely engaged with one another.

Studying the intersection between deliberation and development can provide valuable insights into how to incorporate participation into development across a variety of arenas. Moving beyond broad theoretical claims, close examination of specific cases of deliberation and development allows scholars and practitioners to evaluate actual processes and to pose the question of how deliberation can work in the twin conditions of extreme inequality and low educational levels that characterize the developing world.

This book brings together new essays by some of the leading scholars in the field. Our hope is that it will deepen the understanding of participatory decision making in developing countries while initiating a new field of study for scholars of deliberation. In the process, we hope it will shed light on how to best design and implement policies to strengthen the role of participation in development.

Patrick Heller and Vijayendra Rao

Acknowledgments

This book emerged (slowly) from a conference held at the World Bank in November 2010. The conference was co-organized by the Communications for Governance and Participation (CommGAP) program in the World Bank's External Affairs Vice-Presidency and the Poverty and Inequality Unit in the Bank's Development Research Group. We would like to thank Sina Odugbemi, who led CommGAP at the time, for his intellectual engagement and steadfast support of this effort, and Anne-Katrin Arnold, who helped manage the conference and whose careful notes of the proceedings proved immensely useful to us in writing the introductory chapter and providing feedback to the contributors. The conference was funded by a grant from the Department for International Development (DFID) to CommGAP, for which we are extremely grateful. Publication of the book was funded by a grant from the South Asia Food and Nutrition Security Initiative (SAFANSI) to the Social Observatory unit in the World Bank's Research Department, which is tasked with improving the implementation of participatory and deliberative approaches to address poverty and food insecurity. We appreciate its support.

We are also immensely grateful to Michael Woolcock, who reviewed the manuscript for publication and gave us several constructive suggestions, and to the other participants in the 2010 conference, particularly Anis Dani, Karla Hoff, and Ghazala Mansuri, who contributed in many ways to the development of ideas in this book. Finally, we would like to thank Patricia Katayama, the acquisitions editor; Susan Graham and Deborah Appel-Barker, who handled production and printing; and Barbara Karni, whose superb skills as an editor were put to good use.

About the Contributors

Editors

Patrick Heller is professor of sociology and international studies at Brown University and the director of the graduate program in development at the Watson Institute at Brown. His main area of research is the comparative study of social inequality and democratic deepening. He has published on urbanization, comparative democracy, social movements, development policy, civil society, and state transformation. He has also studied urban transformation in South Africa and built a database on spatial transformation of the postapartheid city. He is the author of *The Labor of Development: Workers in the Transformation of Capitalism in Kerala, India* (1999) and coauthor, with Richard Sandbrook, Marc Edelman, and Judith Teichman, of *Social Democracy and the Global Periphery* (2006). His most recent book, *Bootstrapping Democracy* (2011), coauthored by Gianpaolo Baiocchi and Marcelo Silva, explores politics and institutional reform in Brazilian municipalities. He holds a PhD in sociology from the University of California, Berkeley.

Vijayendra Rao is a lead economist in the Research Department of the World Bank, where he leads the Social Observatory, an effort to improve the implementation of large-scale participatory projects. He is a "radical interdisciplinarian," integrating his training in economics with theories and methods from anthropology, sociology, and political science to study the social, cultural, and political context of extreme poverty in developing countries. His research has spanned several subjects using this approach, including the rise in dowries in India, domestic violence, sex work, gender discrimination, public celebrations, culture and development policy, mixed methods, participatory development, and deliberative democracy. His most recent book, coauthored with Ghazala Mansuri, is *Localizing Development: Does Participation Work?* He serves on the editorial boards of several journals and is a member of the Successful Societies program at the Canadian Institute for Advanced Research (CIFAR). He holds a PhD in economics from the University of Pennsylvania.

Contributors

Arjun Appadurai is the Goddard Professor of Media, Culture and Communication at New York University, where he is also senior fellow at the Institute for Public Knowledge. He is the author or editor of more than a dozen books and numerous scholarly articles on India, globalization, urban studies, and development. His most recent book is *The Future as Cultural Fact: Essays on the Human Condition* (2013). His book *Banking on Words: The Failure of Language in the Age of Derivative Finance* will be published in 2015. He holds a PhD in anthropology from the University of Chicago.

Gianpaolo Baiocchi is an associate professor of individualized studies and sociology at New York University, where he also directs the urban democracy lab. His most recent book, *The Civic Imagination* (2014), coauthored with Elizabeth Bennett, Alissa Cordner, Stephanie Savell, and Peter Klein, examines the contours and limits of the democratic conversation in the United States. He previously worked on participatory budgeting in Brazil. He holds a PhD in sociology from the University of Wisconsin-Madison.

Peter Evans is professor emeritus in the department of sociology at the University of California, Berkeley and a senior fellow in international studies at the Watson Institute for International Studies at Brown University. He is best known for his work on the comparative political economy of national development, exemplified by his 1995 book *Embedded Autonomy: States and Industrial Transformation*. He holds a PhD in sociology from Harvard University.

Archon Fung is the academic dean and Ford Foundation Professor of Democracy and Citizenship at the Harvard Kennedy School. His research explores policies, practices, and institutional designs that deepen the quality of democratic governance. He focuses on public participation, deliberation, and transparency. He co-directs the transparency policy project and leads the democratic governance programs of the Ash Center for Democratic Governance and Innovation at the Kennedy School. His books include *Empowered Participation: Reinventing Urban Democracy* (2004) and *Full Disclosure: The Perils and Promise of Transparency* (2007), coauthored by Mary Graham and David Weil. He holds a PhD in political science from MIT.

Varun Gauri is senior economist with the Development Research Group of the World Bank and co-director of the *World Development Report 2015: Mind, Society, and Behavior*. His current research examines why public agencies comply with human rights court rulings and why individuals support public goods. His publications include *School Choice in Chile* (1998) and *Courting Social Justice: The Judicial Enforcement of Social and Economics Rights in the Developing World School* (2010). He has been a visiting lecturer in public and international affairs at Princeton University and a visiting professor in the department of economics at ILADES in Santiago, Chile. He holds a PhD in public policy from Princeton.

Hollie Russon Gilman is a fellow in technology and public policy at Columbia University's School of International and Public Affairs. She is an expert on technology, civic engagement, innovation, and governance. She served as Open Government and Innovation Advisor in the White House Office of Science and Technology Policy. She holds a PhD in government from Harvard University.

Gerry Mackie is associate professor of political science and co-director of the Center on Global Justice at the University of California, San Diego. He is a political theorist interested in contemporary democratic theory and problems of collective action. His main area of interest is democracy, particularly the conceptual and normative problems of democratic voting. His first book on voting, *Democracy Defended* (2003), received the Gladys Kamerer Prize from the American Political Science Association. He has worked with the NGO Tostan in West Africa since 1998 and UNICEF since 2004 on ending harmful social practices, including female genital cutting. He holds a PhD in political science from the University of Chicago.

Jane Mansbridge is the Charles F. Adams Professor of Political Leadership and Democratic Values at the Harvard Kennedy School and a recent past president of the American Political Science Association. She is the author of *Beyond Adversary Democracy* (1980) and other works on deliberation, deliberative systems, feminism, self-interest, oppositional consciousness, social movements, participation, political representation, and accountability. She holds a PhD in government from Harvard University.

Paromita Sanyal is an assistant professor in the department of sociology at Cornell University. Her research focuses on development, gender, and economic sociology. She has studied how microcredit programs affect women's agency and public deliberation at the *gram sabha* (village forum/meeting), a key institution in India's system of decentralized governance. She is the author of *Credit to Capabilities: A Sociological Study on Microcredit Groups in India* (2014). She holds a PhD in sociology from Harvard University.

Jennifer Shkabatur is an assistant professor at the Lauder School of Government, Strategy, and Diplomacy at the Interdisciplinary Center (IDC), in Herzliya, Israel, and a consultant on social development and information and communication technology (ICT) at the World Bank. She studies governance innovations in developed and developing countries and the effects of ICT on public sector reforms. She holds a PhD from Harvard Law School.

J. P. Singh is professor of global affairs and cultural studies at George Mason University. His book *Globalized Arts: The Entertainment Economy and Cultural Identity* (2011) won the American Political Science Association's award for best book on information technology. Two new books—*Sweet Talk: Racism and Collective Action in North-South Trade Negotiations* and *Development 2.0: How Technologies Can Foster Inclusivity in the Developing World*—will be published in 2015. He has advised UNESCO, the World Bank, and the World Trade Organization. In 2006–09 he was the editor of *Review of Policy Research*, the journal specializing in the politics and policy of science and technology. He holds a PhD in political economy and public policy from the University of Southern California.

Ann Swidler is professor of sociology at the University of California, Berkeley. Her influential work on culture, religion, and American society includes *Organization without Authority* (1979), the now-classic article "Culture in Action" (1986), and *Talk of Love* (2001). She is the coauthor of *Inequality by Design* (1996), *Habits of the Heart* (2007), and *The Good Society* (2011). Her recent research explores how culture shapes institutions by analyzing global and local responses to the AIDS epidemic in Sub-Saharan Africa. She analyzes how the massive international AIDS effort interacts with existing African cultural and institutional patterns, examining how cultural models and institutional logics intersect in chieftaincies, NGOs, and religious congregations in Africa. She holds a PhD in sociology from the University of California, Berkeley.

Susan Cotts Watkins is a visiting scientist at the California Center for Population Research at UCLA and professor emerita in the department of sociology at the University of Pennsylvania. Her early work was on the historical declines in fertility in Europe and the United States. Since the mid-1990s, she has been studying the role of social networks in demographic and cultural change in Sub-Saharan Africa. She directed a study on social networks and fertility in western Kenya between 1994 and 2000. Since 1998 she has been director or codirector of a longitudinal study of responses to the AIDS epidemic in rural Malawi (www.malawi.pop.upenn .edu). She is currently collaborating with Ann Swidler on a book on AIDS altruism in Africa. She holds a PhD in sociology from Princeton University.

Abbreviations

CAME	Conference of Allied Ministers
CBO	community-based organization
DSM	dispute settlement mechanism
EU	European Union
FNPP	National Forum on Popular Participation in Democratic and Popular Administrations
GATS	General Agreement for Trade in Services
GATT	General Agreement on Tariffs and Trade
GVH	group village headman
ICT	information and communication technology
INCD	International Network for Cultural Diversity
INCP	International Network on Cultural Policy
ITO	International Trade Organization
KDP	Kecamatan Development Project
MFN	most favored nation
NGO	nongovernmental organization
NICE	National Initiative for Civic Education
OBC	other backward caste
PT	Partido dos Trabalhadores
SC	scheduled caste
SDI	Slum/Shackdwellers International
SMAG	Seed Multiplication Group
SME	small and medium-size enterprise
TA	traditional authorities
TRIPS	Trade-Related Aspects of Intellectual Property Rights
UNDP	United Nations Development Programme

UNESCO   United Nations Educational, Scientific and Cultural
            Organization
UNICEF   United Nations International Children's Emergency Fund
USAID   U.S. Agency for International Development
WIPO   World Intellectual Property Organization
WTO   World Trade Organization

CHAPTER 1

Deliberation and Development

Patrick Heller and Vijayendra Rao

Deliberation is the process by which a group of people can—through discussion and debate—reach an agreement. Ideally, agreement is achieved by both persuading people of a different way of thinking (usually by changing their preferences) and engaging in a process of reasoned compromise.

Agreement is rooted in the perceived legitimacy of the process. When it is effective, deliberation can be transformative, empowering poor communities, enhancing the capacity for collective action, and harnessing the capacity of communities to manage their own affairs.

There are two broad types of deliberation: formal deliberation, in which the process is deliberative but the final outcome may rest on a vote or negotiation, and substantive deliberation, in which the outcome directly reflects deliberation. In principle, deliberation can be part of any decision-making process, but in development policy circles it has generally been thought of in the context of local participatory development, where deliberative elements are in principle incorporated within a system of community management and control. The record of local participation in development projects has been mixed (Mansuri and Rao 2013), largely because such projects, induced as they are from the outside through donor-funded projects, have generally failed to tackle the challenges of high inequality and low capabilities, which make deliberation difficult.

This book does two things. First, it rethinks the role of deliberation in development and shows that it has potential well beyond a narrow focus on participatory projects. Deliberation can have a transformative effect on many if not all aspects of development. Building a deliberative system (described by Jane Mansbridge in chapter 2) is a potentially valuable way

We are indebted to Varun Gauri, Jane Mansbridge, Paromita Sanyal, Ann Swidler, and Michael Woolcock for valuable comments.

of addressing inequality. Breaking persistent inequality, or inequality traps, requires one to think beyond inequality of opportunity to recognize inequality of voice and agency (Rao and Walton 2004), and think about how effective deliberative processes can equalize agency. Deliberative processes also have the potential to solve many types of coordination failures that are increasingly seen as the central challenge of development (Sen 2000; Hoff and Stiglitz 2001; Basu 2010). These possibilities for equalizing voice and solving coordination problems have broad implications at both the extremely local level (see chapter 5, by Gerry Mackie) and the global level (see chapter 3, by Peter Evans, and chapter 9, by J. P. Singh).

Second, the book attempts to demonstrate that taking deliberation seriously calls for a different approach to both research and policy design, with a much greater emphasis on the processes by which decisions are made rather than an exclusive focus on outcomes. Chapters in the book extend the analysis of modes by which deliberation is conducted, moving from a focus on consensus-building speech acts to "performative failures" (see chapter 4, by Arjun Appadurai) and emotional expressions (see chapter 8, by Paromita Sanyal). Other chapters (chapter 6, by Gianpaolo Baiocchi, and chapter 7, by Ann Swidler and Susan Cotts Watkins) show how efforts to promote deliberative decision making sometimes fail. In this sense, the book contributes to a broader literature that seeks to understand the role of communicative processes in development (Odugbemi and Jacobson 2008).

This chapter lays out what deliberation means, places it in historical context, and draws on political and social theory to outline its challenges and potential. It highlights the relationship between deliberation and inequality and shows how deliberative democracy differs from and complements electoral democracy. It underscores the potential of truly empowered deliberation for development and identifies the challenges involved in making it a viable process. It then draws on other chapters to show how deliberation works in various contexts related to development.

The link between deliberation and development?

Deliberation is a very old idea. Humans, as social beings, have to make collective decisions. Across a range of settings, argument, discussion, compromise, and consensus often drive those decisions.

Cultures have evolved various ways of engaging in deliberative decision making; these processes are active around the world (Mansuri and Rao 2013). In chapter 7, Swidler and Watkins argue that "traditional" deliberative forums—in their case the practice in Malawi of community members discussing issues with chiefs and asking chiefs to bring people together to reach a consensus—may provide more genuine deliberation than deliberation "induced" by a nongovernmental organization (NGO) or donor. The development challenge is to harness such intrinsic deliberative capacity, make it equitable, and give it teeth—by, for instance, incorporating it within a formal system of government. A good example is the *gram sabha* system in Indian village democracies, where "traditional" forms of discourse have been harnessed to new modes of more equitable debate and discussion within a formal system of government (Rao and Sanyal 2010; Heller, Harilal, and Chaudhuri 2007).

The idea of deliberation experienced a dramatic revival in political theory and social theory in recent decades. Through much of the postwar period, definitions of collective decision making were associated with the Schumpeterian notion of "representative democracy," which focuses on the simple and elegant notion of representation through competitive elections and rests on the idea that democracy is fundamentally about aggregating heterogeneous preferences. In contrast, the idea of deliberation, which harks back to classic normative conceptions of democracy, derives from the premise that "democracy revolves around the transformation rather than simply the aggregation of preferences" (Elster 1998, 1). Renewed interest in deliberative democracy has animated almost all major modern political theorists, from John Rawls and Jürgen Habermas to Amartya Sen. It has also become increasingly central to contemporary debates on development, in particular democratic governance.

This revival is a response to several complex and interrelated changes in post–World War II democracies. First, there has been a perceived decline in both the capacity and legitimacy of political parties. For much of the postwar period, political parties in established democracies provided reliable and effective vehicles of mass politics, more or less aggregating interests into programmatic platforms and stable policy regimes, in both Western polities and the older democracies of the global South, most notably India. Programmatic parties are now in decline across electoral democracies. Whether measured in terms of the rise in populist or ethnonationalist parties or in declining trust in representative institutions and political elites, there is clearly a crisis of representation.

Second, the shortcomings of traditional electoral politics—most notably the failure to deal with the new issues of postindustrial society—have been associated with the rise of "new social movements" and renewed interest in the role of civil society in the process of forming and organizing preferences and interests.

Third, the postindustrial period has witnessed a dramatic pluralization of social identities, which has presented new challenges to the traditional system of party representation and to democratic governance in general. Party politics once reliably aligned along class cleavages and could be addressed through various social compacts. Today "identity politics" have become increasingly salient.

Taken together, these developments have triggered a crisis of democratic governance. The two great institutional pillars of modern capitalist society—representative democracy and bureaucratic governance—are suffering from increasing deficits of effectiveness and legitimacy, as Fung and Wright (2003) note.

The response to these deficits in policy thinking and contemporary politics has taken one of two forms. The first—which Prabab Bardhan (1999) labels the technocratic response—sees the problem as one of increasing complexity and in particular an excess of demand-making. Following the line of thought most closely associated with the work of Samuel Huntington (1968), it argues that societal pressures are overloading contemporary institutions. The prescription involves insulating institutions—in particular the market and the bureaucracy—from politics. Many current versions of "good governance" follow this logic, placing enormous faith in the virtues of self-regulating markets and insulated expert-run administrative bodies.

The second response is less focused on the institutions of democracy and more concerned with the practices of democracy. It has taken the form of an explosion of interest in various forms of participatory, associational, and deliberative democracy, as well as calls for new forms of democratic governance. Expanding on these ideas, Keane (2009) argues that democracy, wherever it exists, is becoming increasingly "monitory," with greater emphasis on the active participation of citizens in monitoring the everyday practices of democracy rather than exclusive reliance on elections. This shift toward monitory democracy has led to calls to revitalize politics outside of traditional political institutions by providing new avenues and forums for citizens to exercise their political and civil rights and deliberate issues in the public sphere.

There is another reason why interest in deliberation in the context of development policy has increased. Over the past three decades, the very understanding of development has shifted from a narrow focus on economic transformation (summarized by either growth rates or industrialization) to a more holistic view (Sen 2000). This concern has come to include democracy itself, as well as a broader conception of development that includes social development, justice, and environmental sustainability. Such a preoccupation is not simply a recalibration of what development means—a shifting of the goalposts—but a shift from a traditional preoccupation with ends to increased sensitivity to processes and means. Indeed, this new concern can be seen as a direct outgrowth of the failures of modernization theory: the presumption that forces of technological and/or economic growth (or in the left-wing variant, the rationality of planning) could provide an evolutionary and encompassing solution to the challenges of development.

The very idea of "development" as something that is directed, planned, or orchestrated has come in for criticism, including a body of literature that rejects the entire concept as a form of discursive power. The prevalent discourse in many academic and policy circles is to reject magic pills, one-size-fits-all solutions, or, in Evans's (2004) colorful terminology, "institutional monocropping."

But this rejection is also associated with a new recognition that if development is a complex process of transformation that comes with difficult choices and must attend to a multiplicity of interests and identities, the need for active coordination is all the more essential. The gist of this new approach is to argue that neither experts nor markets can get it right, that solutions have to fit the context, that the tradeoffs are enormously complex and the resulting need for experimentation is best supported by careful democratic deliberation (Sabel 1995; Rodrik 2007).

Defining deliberation

At the most general level, deliberation refers to a process of decision making based on discussion. Gutmann and Thompson (2004, 7) define *deliberative democracy* as "a form of government in which free and equal citizens (and their representatives) justify decisions in a process in which they give one another reasons that are mutually acceptable and generally accessible, with the aim of reaching conclusions that are binding in the present on all citizens but open to challenge in the future."

Deliberation represents one of three decision-making mechanisms in a democratic society: voting, bargaining, and arguing (deliberation) (Elster 1998). Voting is a one-shot game in which the outcome is the aggregated expression of *predetermined* preferences. The act of voting is an isolated, individual event that does not involve interaction, though it can be preceded by either implicit bargains (as in horse trading or patronage); persuasion (through campaigning, for instance); or deliberation. Bargaining is an iterated process between two actors who engage in an exchange process in which the outcome is the adjustment of conflicting preestablished preferences to a compromise position. The compromise itself is generally interpreted as reflecting the balance of power. It is important to underscore that for both voting and bargaining, actors' preferences are seen as exogenous to the process itself. In contrast, deliberation relies on the endogenization of preferences.

The idea of deliberation is based on two premises. The first is that preferences are not given but are rooted in meanings that are by definition "intersubjective." In contrast to voting or bargaining, deliberation can be transformative, in that it can result in changes in the constitutive meanings that guide action and inform preferences—or at a minimum lead to greater (intersubjective) understanding (Gauri, Woolcok, and Desai 2012).

The second is that collective decisions can be justified only through the public use of reason. The more a decision is secured through a process of rational discussion, the closer it comes to a "common good" and hence carries greater legitimacy than the arithmetic fiat of voting (majority rule) or the competitive power play of bargaining.

The first premise is a theoretical claim, the second a procedural one. In deliberative theory, preferences are understood as constructed. In this view, the democratic process does not begin with elections but with "opinion and will formation" (Habermas 1996). This position is rooted in a core theoretical claim that in addition to being driven by interests and passions, individuals also respond to reason and communication. In theory, communicative practices involve presenting and debating both factual and normative claims; the more this process is open and gives all speakers equal voice, the more it approaches the deliberative ideal of decision making through reason-giving. In sum, people are open to having their preferences shaped through deliberation, and the closer the process comes to creating an "ideal speech situation" of unburdened debate, the closer the outcome resembles a social good.

The problem with this theoretical claim is that all too often deliberative theorists, more or less, presume basic civil and political equality and then turn their focus to the dynamics of preference formation through deliberation. But associational inequalities are the norm rather than the exception, especially in the developing world; one has to begin with the premise that preferences are formed in real social contexts that are rife with asymmetrical power relations. The "revealed preference" of a vote may be less an expression of the individual's free will than the outcome of manipulation, coercion, acute dependency, or deprivation. An empirically grounded theory of deliberative democracy consequently demands that one carefully examine the conditions under which preferences are formed rather than taking them for granted as expressions of free will.

There has been much debate about what constitute acceptable conditions in which reason-giving may prevail (see chapter 3). Dryzek (2005, 224) develops a useful frame that involves three key tests: the communicative process must be noncoercive, capable of inducing reflection, and "capable of linking the particular experience of an individual or group with some more general point or principle."

Critics argue that this situation can never be attained. This chapter addresses this point at length, because it is invariably the first point of critique of deliberative theory. Suffice it to say here that this ideal of reason-giving citizens stands as an important "regulative ideal" (to use the term Mansbridge uses in chapter 2) against which all real-world cases of democratic decision making should be evaluated.

The procedural case for deliberation rests on the assumption that by giving and taking arguments, citizens can adapt or change their preferences—and in doing so can be nudged toward positions that are more mutually accommodative. A strong version of this argument sees deliberation as the path to consensus or the "common will." Weaker forms see deliberation as a critical preliminary step to more conventional decision-making processes of voting or bargaining.[1]

The idea here is that although extended argument may not yield a spontaneous consensus, it can narrow the grounds of disagreement in several ways. First, because deliberation requires that all participants reveal their preferences and invites public scrutiny of all claims, it can reduce the degree to which manipulation, deception, and propaganda inevitably seep into any communicative situation. Deliberation can help expose or secure participants' credibility. Second, deliberation can provide new information that may change the parameters of an individual's decision making. Third, to the extent that deliberation can reveal new information as well as build trust, it can facilitate coordination. Indeed, sustained dialogue is the basis for cooperative solutions emerging from iterative game theory (see, for example, Ostrom 1990; Dasgupta 2009). Fourth, deliberation can have "other-regarding" effects: as participants gain greater understanding of others, they are more likely to take others' preferences or moral worldviews into account.[2] This effect is the basis for the broader claim in sociology that deliberation can promote social solidarity (Cohen and Arato 1992; Habermas 1996).

In some respects, these claims are far less controversial than is generally assumed. The literature and policy prescriptions tend to construct representative and deliberative (or participatory) democracy as mutually exclusive. More careful theories of deliberation show that ideally they are complementary processes. For Habermas (1996), deliberation, as it takes place in the many associational settings of civil society, is largely about problematizing social issues, making public arguments about new norms, and then influencing—but not directing—the institutional process of decision making. The democratic complex of representative structures, routine administration, and judicial review is the sluice gates through which the deliberations of civil society must necessarily be processed. These institutions themselves can include specific deliberative elements, such as parliamentary debates and courtroom discussion, but their final decision-making authority is rooted in legal powers based on electoral sanction.

Indeed, both Habermas and Rawls view courts as the paradigmatic institutions of public reason-giving, or deliberation. Ideally, respect for legal authority arises from the persuasive power of judicial communication; in Habermas's terms, it must be possible for individuals to respect the law on the basis of insight, not only because they are coerced. That understanding of the normative basis of law generates criteria for effective and normatively sound deliberation in the legal sphere, criteria that include publicity and dialogical interaction (Gauri 2012; Gauri and Brinks 2012; chapter 8 of this volume).

Once one recognizes that democracy is a complex, dynamic amalgam of deliberative process and institutionalized sanction (what one can call the "procedural view"), it becomes clear that deliberation as such is not a substitute for electoral democracy but a necessary condition for deepening democracy. And there is no reason to believe that the messy process of deliberative decision making is necessarily less efficient than electoral democracy. Indeed, recent research on deliberative forums in rural India finds that discourse within them reflects the preferences of the median voter, much like an efficient electoral system (Ban, Jha, and Rao 2012).

Mackie (1998, 71) sums up the procedural view succinctly: "Democracy involves both voting and discussion, and discussion is obviously at least as important to democracy, descriptively and normatively, as voting." As Fraser (1992, 51) argues in writing about Habermas, democracy holds out the possibility of "individuals socialized to demand rational, normative legitimations of social authority."

These debates are somewhat esoteric; remarkably, the arguments have been mainstreamed. No evolution in the understanding of politics has been of greater significance than the renewed interest in civil society. The strains of this debate are vast and complex, but the renewed interest in civil society—whether in the context of the postauthoritarian societies of Eastern Europe or the struggling democracies of the global South—stems from a shared disappointment with the unforgiving logic of interest-based politics. Increased concern about the extent to which the state and political parties can be held accountable exclusively through periodic elections in a world marked by increasing organizational complexity has generated new interest in the countervailing power and influence of civil society. In the more celebratory versions of this argument, civil society is associated with the virtues of pluralism, tolerance, transparency, other-regardingness, trust, and more generally normatively based action—all virtues that are considered in short supply in political society. Setting aside the obvious rejoinder that actual civil societies can be monolithic, intolerant, exclusionary, and in some cases very uncivil—subject to the very same failures that beset markets and states—the point remains that the new faith in civil society reflects in effect concern with the need to supplement the aggregative and bargained logics of formal politics with deliberated inputs.

 Under what conditions can deliberation actually take place, and under what conditions can it have substantive effects? Answering these two questions lies at the heart of this book. Every chapter deals directly with both questions. This introduction sets out some general parameters by which one might evaluate these two questions. But before we get into the devilish details, we want to lay out clearly how and why we believe deliberation matters and what kind of outcomes it might ideally have, especially in promoting development as democracy.

Deliberation and unequal citizenship

Theories of representative democracy tend to take citizenship for granted. They assume that once endowed with basic rights, in particular the right to vote, subjects are transformed into citizens who all enjoy the same basic rights and associational capacities. Of course, the exercise of these rights is predicated on the proper functioning of a host of institutions, putatively measured by various indexes, such as the Freedom House index. But even democracies that score high on these indexes—India, for example, falls just short of the highest score—are still marked by what O'Donnell (1993) calls "low-intensity citizenship."

Undercapacitated citizenship is pervasive in developing countries. Classical and contemporary theories of democracy take for granted the decisional autonomy of individuals as the foundation of democratic life. This capacity of rights-bearing citizens to associate, deliberate, and form preferences in turn produces the norms that underwrite the legitimacy of democratic political authority. But this view conflates the status of citizenship (a bundle of rights) with the practice of citizenship (Somers 1993). Given the highly uneven rates of political participation and influence across social categories that persist in advanced democracies (especially the United States), the notion of citizenship should always be viewed as contested. In developing democracies, where inequalities remain high and access to rights is often circumscribed by social position or compromised by institutional weaknesses (including the legacies of colonial rule), the problem of associational autonomy is so acute that it brings the very notion of citizenship into question (Fox 1994; Mamdani 1996; Mahajan 1999).

A high degree of consolidated representative democracy should not be confused with a high degree of effective citizenship. Closing this gap between formal legal rights in the civil and political arena and the actual capability to meaningfully practice those rights is the key challenge of democratic deepening (Heller 2012). Sen's argument in *Development as Freedom* might be reinterpreted to say that deliberation is the metacapability and that individuals are free only when they can effectively deliberate:

Public debates and discussions, permitted by political freedoms and civil rights, can also play a major part in the formation of values. Indeed, even the identification of needs cannot but be influenced by the nature of public participation and dialogue. Not only is the force of public discussion one of the correlates of democracy . . . but its cultivation can also make democracy itself function better. . . . Just as it is important to emphasize the need for democracy, it is also crucial to safeguard the conditions and circumstances that ensure the range of and reach of the democratic process. Valuable as democracy is as a major source of social opportunity . . . there is also the need to examine ways and means of making it function well, to realize its potentials. The achievement of social justice depends not only on institutional forms (including democratic rules and regulations), but also on effective practice. . . . This is a challenge that is faced both by well-established democracies such as the United States (especially with the differential participation of diverse racial groups) and by new democracies (2000, 158–59).

The problem is one not simply of associational inequalities (highly unevenly distributed capacities to participate in the system) but also of outright exclusion. Exclusion can take the form of categorical exclusions enforced through coercive societal practices such as untouchability, racism, and much more insidious processes of rendering subalterns invisible, delegitimizing their claims, or creating a general environment in which their voices are not only not heard but systematically disparaged. In a world where such inequalities are pervasive, insidious, and self-reproducing, the idea of a deliberative setting or public sphere does seem utopian.

Moreover, one needs to recognize (with Foucault) the importance of discourse as power, particularly in thinking about theories of deliberation, where the idea of free and open communication is central. If discourses are constituted within a "regime of truth" that legitimizes, values, and rewards certain forms of speech while delegitimizing others, then discourse itself becomes an instrument of power.

If discourse is constituted by and constitutive of power, then how is deliberative democracy—decisions based on public reason-giving—at all possible? The rejoinder from Habermas is that while all forms of action may be conditioned by power, deliberation (or more specifically, "communicative action") is not oriented to power per se. If action within the formal polity or the market is steered by the objective of gaining more power (respectively, legal authority and money), the *telos* of communication is mutual understanding: when we communicate, we aim to make the other share an understanding with us. That understanding can be expressive (conceptions of beauty), normative (agreement on what is "right"), or objective (agreement on facts). Speech can, of course, be motivated by ulterior goals, such as making money or gaining votes. But even in such instances, all speech acts involve making a validity claim, and all validity claims are subject to evaluation. Arguments themselves (rather than self-interest or power distributions) become the basis of agreement when, through a process of discussion and debate, participants intersubjectively recognize "criticizable validity claims." As (Habermas 1984, 17) notes:

> Thus all arguments, be they related to the questions of law and morality or to scientific hypotheses or to works of art, require the same basic form or organization, which subordinate the erisitc [debating] means to the end of developing intersubjective conviction by the force of the better argument.

Recognizing that collective decision making can be guided by the "force of the better argument" has two interrelated implications. First, recognizing the validity of arguments, which can be expressive, normative, or objective, binds participants together. Because they accept the legitimacy of the final decision, the decision assumes the status of a new norm and the basis for stable cooperation. Institutions built on the strength of a deliberative process are far more stable, legitimate, and likely to command loyalty (Goodin 2003).

Second, Habermas argues that the complex coordination problems of modern societies need not be resolved only through the instrumental-strategic forms of action that steer the market economy and the rational-legal bureaucratic state. At the heart of deliberative theory is his claim that rational agreement based on the giving of public reasons can also be the basis of social action.

Can deliberation make a difference?

Critics of deliberation often dismiss it as little more than talk. They have a point. Unless deliberative systems have teeth and can be tied to specific binding decisions, they run the risk of being ephemeral and even masking power relations.

Most immediately, this concern points to the problem of the "chain of sovereignty," the series of steps through which a deliberated preference is translated into action. In modern societies, such chains are long and can be broken or hijacked at many different points. The biggest challenge of Brazilian municipalities' experiments with participatory budgeting—arguably the most renowned form of instituted deliberation—has been ensuring that decisions made in deliberative forums are translated into budgeted projects and actually implemented (Baiocchi, Heller, and Silva 2011). In this respect, making deliberation work puts an enormous premium on institutional design. We return to this point later. For now we want to bracket the problem of the chain of sovereignty to make the case for why the process of deliberation itself might be intrinsically valuable.

 If the poor and the excluded lack power, they lack the power to freely form their preferences. In his famous theory of power, Stephen Lukes identifies the capacity to shape the ideological terrain—the terrain of acceptable interpretations, values, and preferences—as one of the most important and also most pernicious forms of power. "Is it not the supreme and most insidious exercise of power to prevent people, to whatever degree, from having grievances by shaping their perceptions, cognitions, and preferences in such a way that they accept their role in the existing order of things, either because they can see or imagine no alternative to it, or because they see it as natural and unchangeable, or because they value it as divinely ordained and beneficial?" (1974, 28).

The issue of constrained preferences leads directly to the role of culture in shaping public action (Rao and Walton 2004). In a seminal article,

Appadurai (2004) argues that most treatments of "culture" presume a certain pastness, a lock-in of beliefs, habits, traditions, or norms that in effect reproduce the status quo. But he also points to new developments in anthropology that present a more forward-looking, or transformative, vision of culture. First, it is now widely recognized that rather than being the guarantors of consensus, cultures are laden with disensus and may even harbor elaborated "counter-hegemonic" elements of discourse (Fraser 1992). Second, the "boundaries of cultural systems are leaky, and . . . traffic and osmosis are the norm, not the exception" (Appadurai 2004, 65). Taken together, the implication is that the "voiceless" in fact have both internal and external resources for resisting and challenging dominant ideologies.

Appadurai goes on to argue that a key resource to cultivate for the poor is the "capacity to aspire"—that is, the cognitive ability to define the parameters of the possible and to link means and ends. The capacity to aspire is unevenly distributed, because "the better off, by definition have a more complex experience of the relation between a wide range of ends and means, because they have a bigger stock of available experiences of the relationship of aspirations and outcomes, because they are in a better position to explore many opportunities to link material goods and immediate opportunities to more general and generic possibilities and options" (2004, 68). The capacity to aspire then becomes a building block for all capacities: only if one can imagine a better life and identify the necessary course of action to securing it will other capacities come into play. Reconceived in this manner, "culture"—and specifically the capacity to imagine and represent the world—is indeed a source of power, but it is dynamic, actively reproduced, and, as such, subject to contestation and transformation.

In chapter 4 of this volume, Appadurai extends these ideas to show that "failure" in deliberative contexts can be a powerful tool for the poor and disadvantaged to change the unequal contexts in which deliberation often occurs. Effective deliberation, he argues, is about not just "context-legibility" (the ability to engage within a given deliberative structure) but "context-change" (the capacity to shift the nature of context so that the terms of engagement are more favorable to the poor). With rehearsal and repetition, "performative failures," in which the disadvantaged purposely violate the rules of speech acts to gather attention to their interests, can be strung into success. Deliberation can permit a form of linguistic civil disobedience to take place that can make the terms of engagement between the rich and the poor more equal. Appadurai calls such strings of performative failures "deliberative chains."

The problem is not simply one of empowering the poor, however. Poverty and exclusion don't happen to people; they are done to people. Inequality in general is produced through the operation of durable categories such as race, class, ethnicity, and gender (Tilly 1998), leading to "inequality traps" (Rao 2006; World Bank 2006). Empowering the poor certainly means hearing and cultivating the voices of the poor (Narayan and others 2001), as well as recognizing, exposing, and critiquing the barriers and exclusions that limit their aspirations. Making public debate more inclusive is precisely where deliberation can matter.

In a democracy, the poor have three possible levers of empowerment: voting, bargaining, and arguing. Voting can and has been a source of empowerment for lower-class and marginalized groups, but this empowerment effect has been effective only after a long process of actively forming collective interests. More generally, voting tends to simply lock in existing preferences. As Gutmann and Thompson pointedly remark, "By taking existing or minimally corrected preferences as given, as the base line for collective decisions, the aggregative conception fundamentally accepts and may even reinforce distributions of power in society" (2004, 16). Bargaining may be the basis for organizing compromises, but this interlacing of interests cannot by definition change the existing distribution of power.

In contrast, even absent a chain of sovereignty, a process of deliberation can be transformative in two respects. First, if the voiceless are given an opportunity to have voice, they almost invariably express collective demands for recognition. As in the case of so many social movements, demands for recognition imply not only assertions and strengthening of an identity but also explicit critiques of the norms, ideas, structures, and institutions through which exclusion has been historically produced. These demands and challenges, following the social movement literature (Snow, Soule, and Kriesi 2007), address the problem of the fallacy of inevitably, exposing the natural, the preordained, or the given as the made, imposed, and reproduced. When the status quo is brought into question, the possibilities for collective action, including new patterns of voting, expand. Moreover, when the voiceless are made part of the public discussion, new normative and factual views are injected into the discussion that can transform the terms of the debate. Social movements and many civil society organizations generally problematize and popularize issues that for various reasons are outside mainstream political discourse; when successful, they inject new norms and perspectives into public debate. In both respects, deliberation can create spaces for the "hidden texts" of the voiceless. The resulting engagements can at a minimum provide some dignity and new capacity to the poor and even push culture, and more explicitly normative frameworks, into a more self-reflective mode.

Second, if deliberation can counteract power and domination, it can also help resolve, or at least moderate, contentious or complex societal problems. It can help resolve coordination problems through four mechanisms: valuation, proportionality, integration, and commitment.

Developmental choices are by definition complex bundles of decisions marked by delicate tradeoffs. Some tradeoffs can be evaluated in fairly utilitarian terms, including cost-benefit analysis or technical considerations. But many tradeoffs raise core questions of what people value and what is just. Neither voting nor bargaining lends itself to developing appropriate evaluative frames. Preserving the Amazon River has a cost-benefit logic that can in principle be measured and subject to an instrumental calculation, but it also has aesthetic, cultural, and even spiritual value that is best weighed through public discussion. Deliberation in this sense can serve as a powerful tool of valuation, as clearly illustrated by the evolution of the debate on the environment. A massive expansion of technical knowledge has fed the environmental debate. But new norms of sustainability, justice, conservation, solidarity (including intergenerational solidarity), and aesthetic concerns that a surge of movements, NGOs, foundations, and global networks, all operating largely on the strength of making public arguments, have generated have also driven new policy positions.

Some of the most contentious issues in development involve compensation and proportionality. How much should a community be compensated for giving up its rights to land for some other use (mining, highway construction)? What constitutes a community, and who within the community should be compensated? Why should a community be resettled, who should be resettled, and how should they be resettled? Deliberation can provide an airing of views around these issues and attempt to reach some form of understanding. Resolutions arrived at in a truly deliberative way— where the government, private interests, and the rich and poor within a community are all given equal voice—may also be considered fairer.

Deliberation also facilitates coordination through integration. Extended deliberation can facilitate trust and collective agreement. Microcredit schemes do not simply pool the resources of participants and collectively enforce collection, they link participants to one another through discussion and collective decision making. Such iterated interactions and discussions can directly expand marginalized women's associational capabilities, as Sanyal (2014) shows. Ostrom (1990) and others point to shared norms as the basis for successful coordination, but they generally underplay the extent to which these norms evolved out of deliberative practices among stakeholders. Summarizing Dryzek's (2006) work on the notion of ecologically rational deliberation, Lockie points out that "what distinguishes situations where natural resources have been managed sustainably over long periods of time from those that have not is that the agencies and stakeholders involved have developed ways to communicate and interact with each other" (2007, 790).

Finally, deliberation can secure greater commitment not only from participants but also from elites. The legitimacy of a deliberative process hinges on all participants revealing their preferences as well as their stakes in the outcome. The resulting publicity increases the costs, in both social and strategic terms, of exiting, hijacking, or blocking the process. It is extremely difficult to support purely self-interested proposals in a public debate. The very willingness to participate in a deliberative process carries a commitment to doing what is in the public interest and the attendant pressure to "do the right thing." Any commitments that emerge from the process carry greater sanction, because they are backed by the force of a deliberated agreement. Unlike in a bargained outcome or an election, in which commitment is thin, in the sense of deriving only from acceptance of the process, a deliberative process can in principle produce an outcome that is both procedurally and normatively legitimate. It does so not because all participants believe the outcome is best for them but rather because there are reasonable grounds for accepting the substance of the outcome. The resulting degree of commitment is not just a matter of acceptance but a recognition that one has a responsibility to seeing the decision through.

Making deliberation work

Definitions of deliberation invariably identify a rough form of equality as a necessary precondition. But even if formal political equality prevails in many democracies in the developing world, inequalities of agency and associational capacity remain the norm. In thinking through the possibilities for deliberation, one has to begin from a position of skepticism: making deliberation work calls for specific processes, practices, and institutional designs that can level or at least neutralize associational inequalities.

Yet one also needs to recognize that the process of deliberation may have some comparative advantages. First, the ideal of deliberation is hardly an invention of modern democracies. In both a general sense and more specific institutional senses, the practice of deliberation is widespread. Sen (2006) argues forcefully that there is a long tradition of argumentation in India. Even if this practice was confined to elites, it was nonetheless one in which claims from below held a particularly strong appeal. Scholars of Africa often note that traditional forms of chieftainship involved extended deliberations with village elders and that most of the chiefs' authority and legitimacy lie in their capacity to align their decisions with community values and norms (Swidler 2014). Throughout the world, scholars have documented a range of community-based deliberative institutions that predate industrialization, most notably various structures for common resource management (Ostrom 1990). Indeed, as Mansbridge reminds us in chapter 2, the Westminster notion of democracy as an adversarial system of competing interests is a relatively new idea, which in many cases supplanted more consensus-driven approaches to conflict resolution.

Second, disadvantaged groups are often less disadvantaged in deliberative arenas than in other forms of politics. As Gutmann and Thompson note:

> The lack of political success of marginalized groups does not stem from a lack of deliberative competency, but rather from a lack of power. To the extent that the political struggles take place on the basis

of deliberation rather than power, they are more evenly matched. Because moral appeals are the weapons of the weak, a deliberative playing field is more level. . . . Compared to bargaining or other purely aggregative methods of politics, deliberation can diminish the discriminatory effects of class, race, and gender inequalities that rightly trouble critics (2004, 50).

The normative claims of subordinate groups—to recognition, status equality, fairness, basic needs—are all claims that resonate powerfully in the public sphere. Because they are claims that are of universal significance behind Rawls's veil of ignorance, a society that deliberates is one that is particularly sensitive to the claims of the poor and excluded.

Many organized religions explicitly place the poor on a higher moral ground. When conservative Catholic doctrine was challenged from below in the 1960s by the "base communities" in Brazil, the result was a new doctrine of "preferential bias" toward the poor. Habermas argues that the discursive repertoires of new social movements are particularly forceful in constitutional democracies because they invariably frame their demands in terms of the "unredeemed claims of bourgeois society"—that is, rights promised but never delivered in elite-dominated democracies.

In sum, it is possible to argue that far from being a utopian ideal, the practice of deliberation is widespread and has a long history. But expanding both the scope and the influence of deliberation raises a host of practical challenges.

Scales and settings

The challenge of identifying the conditions under which deliberative processes are most likely to take hold is daunting, particularly in contexts of pervasive inequality. No comprehensive model or framework has been proposed, for good reason. The two necessary conditions for deliberation—reason-giving and rough associational equality—are difficult to meet. The problem is made only more acute when one takes into account the fact that deliberation has been identified as a decision-making or decision-shaping process at different scales and in different settings.

This section begins by identifying four conceptually distinct settings. The first two—the public sphere and voluntary associations—in effect constitute civil society, but are analytically distinct from it. The third looks to governance institutions that are specifically located in the state. The fourth, deliberative forums, are a hybrid of state and society.

The public sphere

For deliberative theorists, the public sphere is the privileged site of opinion and will formation. Habermas defines the public sphere as a medium through which the communicative practices of civil society are processed.

Civil society organizations (NGOs, advocacy groups, movements, the media, universities, think tanks) problematize and publicize certain issues, exerting influence on the political process. In a well-functioning public sphere, problematized issues are fully deliberated and those that carry the force of the better argument are eventually taken up by the "constitutional-parliamentary complex." Political parties did not initiate debates on civil rights, feminism, or the environment, but the public sphere's communicative processing eventually influenced them to take up positions on these issues. Similarly, courts often reinterpret the law on the strength of evolving public opinion. What distinguishes a deliberative public sphere is the extent to which communicative action—the force of the better argument—prevails over strategic or coercive forms of action.

Two conditions buttress a deliberative public sphere. The first is a vibrant civil society or organized, pluralistic civil society organizations that are autonomous from the state and market and can effectively exercise voice. Ideally, the voices that are heard are representative of the full spectrum of societal issues, not just a reflection of economic or political power. The second is the quality of the political-administrative system and other institutional sensors through which communicative practices are translated into legislative or administrative action.

On both these criteria, established democracies have their problems, but the global South appears to be severely deficient. The political-administrative system there is more likely to be dominated by patronage or populism than citizen engagement, and civil society is either very weak or dominated by parochial and clientelistic interests.

Such a generalization masks extraordinary variation both across and within nations. As Baiocchi's account in chapter 6 shows, Brazilian civil society has not only developed extraordinary capacities, it has also directly projected itself into the state. Within India there is tremendous variation across states in the degree to which civil society organizations have influenced state policy. Over the past decade, civil society initiatives have resulted in transformative legislation, most notably passage of the Right to Information Act. As Appadurai comments in chapter 4, "Shadow publics, counter-publics, partial publics, and aspirational publics are certainly a major feature of India's story in the second half of the 20th century." If anything, decentralization reforms have opened up significant new spaces of civil society engagement (Rao and Sanyal 2010; Heller 2012). And as Varun Gauri shows in chapter 10, courts in much of the developing world have become increasingly proactive in giving voice to issues generally ignored or obscured by political parties; they are giving greater standing to subordinate groups, advancing both the reason-giving and inclusionary logic of deliberation.

As a concept, the public sphere is much like nationalism: it clearly matters but remains hard to define and even harder to measure.

Three observations about the public sphere are important. First, open spaces of discussion and debate coupled with a multiplicity of publics ensure that some communicative practices join the contest of interests and power in shaping opinions. Second, there are clear instances when the deliberated opinions of the public sphere and its many publics directly affect governance outcomes, either by directly shifting electoral alignments (for example, the rise of Green parties in Europe) or more diffusely by influencing the agendas and commitments of politicians and state agents (for example, new attitudes about gender). Third, the degree to which the debates of the public sphere are actually deliberative and the extent to which they make a difference can be determined only empirically. Much closer examination is needed of the constellations of interests and reasons that constitute existing civil societies and the nature of their engagement with the parliamentary-institutional complex.

Deliberation and associational life

Associations are the building blocks of civil society; a long line of democratic theorists have argued that associational life is critical to the health of democracy.

Associations can promote deliberation in two ways, which are not necessarily compatible. First, going back to John Stuart Mill, democratic theorists have argued that associations can serve as "schools of democracy," teaching participants the skills and norms of democratic engagement. Many organizations explicitly promote deliberative decision making as an intrinsic objective. Second, associations can aggregate and effectively project a multiplicity of voices into the public sphere. There may, however, be a tradeoff between these two deliberative effects of association: the demands of internal deliberation may come at the expense of organizational efficiency, limiting the capacity of associations that are internally deliberative to intervene successfully in the public or governance spheres. Alternatively, some associations are not internally deliberative, and indeed, especially in cases where the participants have strong shared interests and identities, hierarchical decision making may be viewed as more effective than deliberation. Even if such organizations are not schools of democracy, they may nonetheless promote deliberation, simply by raising and defending issues, identities, or interests that might not otherwise be heard in the broader public debate. Such hierarchical organizations may, in fact, be more effective in that debate precisely because they do not have to rely on internally deliberative procedures.

It is also possible that associations may simply reflect existing social and institutional structures, amplifying existing inequalities of voice, or, as Warren (2001, 11) puts it, translating "pluralism into parochialism." Associations can threaten or undermine deliberation in civil society in two scenarios. First, associations can be little more than extensions of social or economic power. They may represent the "convening" power of landlords, caciques, chiefs, and assorted bosses or forms of "traditional" authority, such as a caste or communal association, in which the organizational principle of the association is more hierarchical than participatory. If subordinate groups belong to or support an association because of various social or economic dependencies from which they cannot afford to exit, then their associational autonomy—and hence capacity for internal deliberation—is fatally compromised.

Second, forms of "voluntary" association can be little more than extensions of state or political power. This dependency is the defining problem of authoritarian societies; it is also the problem of many unions, NGOs, and neighborhood associations in democratic societies. When these associations depend so much on the state (or an external funding agency) for resources or for authority that they cannot act autonomously, they are not deliberative. This problem also affects "participation" in development projects, as Mansuri and Rao (2012) highlight. The conditions under which civil society spaces and associations can nurture deliberation are highly contingent and call for careful analysis of how civil society is positioned with respect to both the state and society/the economy.

In its ideal typical democratic incarnation then, civil society is characterized by voluntary forms of association that are constituted by and protective of communicative power and seek to exert their influence by engaging with and seeking support in the public sphere. Taken together, these attributes will trend toward the production of the very types of universalizing norms that undergird the democratic ideal of collective deliberation.

Governance institutions

Institutions of governance are not generally given much consideration in the literature on deliberation and democratic participation because most scholars treat complex organizations as Weberian bureaucratic ideal types (hierarchical command-and-control systems). Yet an emerging literature on new governance shows that modern bureaucratic agencies can and do benefit from deliberative structures. Certain expert bodies—notably academic institutions, where principles of peer review and open deliberation prevail over hierarchical fiat—have always benefited from such structures to some extent. But increasingly scholars have pointed to highly diffused epistemic networks, including professional networks of international jurists, scientists, and others, as well as forms of new governance, particularly in the European Union (EU), where the emphasis is on horizontal and deliberated rather than vertical and commanded forms of accountability. A body of new work on "experimentalist governance" (Búrca, Keohane, and Sabel 2013) points to the advantages of positive feedback and learning by doing that flow from more deliberative bureaucratic structures. In chapter 3, Evans revisits the traditional Weberian understanding of the

---

developmental state. He argues that given the extraordinary challenges of coordination and co-production that confront the developmental state of the 21st century, success will depend on building deliberative structures of governance.

Deliberative processes matter for governance institutions in two respects. The first is the extent to which internal decision-making processes involve some form of deliberation. Within some agencies and institutions, dialogue, argumentation, and persuasion can be critical to decision making. Such internal deliberation is more likely to prevail when the body is highly meritocratic and norms of performance predominate; when members share similar training and expertise and have accordingly been socialized into adjudication criteria that involve making reasoned arguments (governed by the terms of their shared profession); and when the body is highly insulated from external pressures. All three of these conditions—institutional logic, professional norms, and insulation—can also result in deliberation without accountability. Central banks and academic institutions may come to mind.

The second key dimension of deliberation for governance institutions is their degree of embeddedness in society (see chapter 3). To what extent are governance institutions sensitive to external communicative influences? Or, as Singh puts it in chapter 9, to what extent does the deliberative structure of the institution allow only strategic interests to be heard?

Examples abound. The World Commission on Dams linked policy making at the World Bank to a wide range of nonstate actors and the judiciary (which according to Gauri has, in some cases, become more sensitized to civil society); new "neo-corporatist" structures, such as sectoral councils in Brazil, have brought government actors and civil society together in decision-making bodies. Warren (2009) takes the argument a step further. Reviewing the case literature from the United States and Canada, he identifies instances of what he calls governance-driven democratization, in which state actors and agencies actively seek to build deliberative partnerships with stakeholders.

Deliberative forums

The fourth type of deliberative setting explored here is the deliberative forum—institutional settings that have been explicitly designed to promote deliberation, such as participatory budgeting, juries, Deliberative Polling (Fishkin and Luskin 2005), and other decentralized forms of participation, such as *gram sabhas* in India. This category overlaps most with Fung and Wright's empowered participatory governance. These forums are in effect hybrid institutions, designed specifically to facilitate deliberative interfaces between the state and civil society.

Public discussion is often poorly linked to the learning, problem solving, and sustained attention necessary for policy decisions. This limitation can be mitigated by designed "minipublics" that are delinked from "both the strategic elements of electoral politics and the unfocused elements of broad publics" (Warren 2009, 10).

Deliberative forums directly address these problems through a number of mechanisms.

First, they have a much more targeted logic of engagement. Rather than relying on the diffuse representation of the public sphere or the information-poor representation of elections, these forums are designed to either randomly sample a small group that can deliberate for the larger public (juries and Deliberative Polling) or target the groups most directly affected by the issue area. Second, forums are directly linked to a specific problem and a specific decision, such as making a budget or providing election materials to voters in a contentious referendum. Third, forums have well-defined and carefully delineated procedures for specifically maximizing deliberation, including procedures to ensure transparency of interests, mechanisms to encourage historically marginalized groups to have more input, and procedures to reduce barriers to individuals for changing their preferences. Fourth, forums are generally information rich, because the selected participants are knowledgeable to begin with or systematically exposed to relevant information.

Conclusion

This introduction provides an overview of the relationship between deliberation and development. It explores its meaning, value, and relationship to poverty and inequality. It examines how deliberation can be made to work and explores its links to institutions of government and civic associations.

Deliberation done at scale requires collaboration between what Mansuri and Rao (2012) call "induced" and "organic" participation. Any large-scale intervention is necessarily induced, in that it is promoted by donors and governments and implemented by large bureaucracies. Such interventions are not spontaneous expressions of civic power driven by intrinsically motivated actors. They are attempts to promote bottom-up participation by actors acting from the top. If the incentives and motives of decision makers at the top are not aligned with the desires and incentives of people at the bottom, any attempt to induce participation is bound to fail.

Deliberative governance requires social partners. Hybrid institutions that interface between the state and civil society can function properly only if given adequate support from the state. In particular, promoting deliberative decision making in situations of significant inequality requires paying close attention to the structures and actors of the settings identified; the ways in which these varied settings—the public sphere, civic associations, governance institutions, and deliberative forums—interact with one another; and the broader institutional settings in which they operate.

The chapters in this volume show that, if done right, deliberation has great potential for contributing to diverse and difficult development challenges. Deliberation can address important social problems, such as female genital mutilation, that require a collective approach to shifting social norms (see chapter 5). It can help direct and empower the voices of the poor and thus help address the linked challenges of poverty and inequality (see chapter 8). It can help resolve intrinsically complex coordination problems by bringing diverse interests to the table (see chapters 2 and 3). But doing deliberation right is challenging because it requires a significantly different approach to development, an approach that is tolerant of, and able to learn from, messiness and failure. Deliberative governance can have unpredictable consequences, but it allows the sausage-making process of government to be visible to all interested parties and gives the disempowered the ability to participate in those decisions.

In seeking and incorporating the views of beneficiaries, deliberation can have both intrinsic and instrumental value. Instrumentally, it can be important as a community-based monitoring tool. Whether substantive or formal, deliberation provides information to concerned citizens, incorporates their views into decision-making processes, and gives them a say in tracking whether those decisions are effectively implemented. If done right, it can supplement traditional systems of bureaucratic or representative accountability with a continuous self-contained system of decision making and monitoring of action.

Intrinsically, deliberation can promote a process of learning by doing. It is a cooperative and communicative activity that can allow new information to be quickly incorporated into decisions and mistakes to be efficiently addressed. As a learning tool, it becomes central to the view of development as a process-based activity, in which planning and execution are just as important as learning by doing. As Singh shows in chapter 9, deliberation has value not just for local communities but also for international organizations, because it can allow less powerful countries to participate in the process of decision making.

The challenge lies in institutionally facilitating deliberation in contexts of sharp inequalities. How, in particular, does one create a deliberative system within a development intervention? As Swidler and Watkins point out in chapter 7, done incorrectly, "deliberation" can result in something akin to a rote-learning-based school system, where development professionals lecture beneficiaries about how to deliberate, defeating the entire purpose of the exercise. There is a danger that this type of intervention can give rise to a version of Gresham's Law: project-driven deliberation drives out real deliberation. Given the asymmetries of power that accompany any development intervention, aligning institutional facilitation with genuine community engagement calls for careful consideration of how power, authority, and resources are allocated.

Only then does it become possible to set up structures in which a deliberative "system" can flourish. A deliberative system can happen, as in the Indian case, as the result of a constitutional process that empowers deliberative forums and gives them funds and decision-making authority (Rao and Sanyal 2010; Heller 2012). It can also happen by building effective deliberation into a project-based decision making, as the Kecamatan Development Project did in Indonesia (Barron, Diprose, and Woolcock 2011). As Evans argues in chapter 3, a necessary requirement for setting up deliberative systems is cooperation and commitment from higher levels of government—that is, the state has to be embedded in civil society. Technology can play an important role in expanding the scale of the conversation and improving access to deliberative forums, as Archon Fung, Hollie Russon Gilman, and Jennifer Shkabatur show in chapter 11.

At an intrinsic level, deliberative decision making can give voice to the voiceless and help shift the terms of engagement for the poor by giving them the tools to draw attention to their concerns. As Appadurai argues in chapter 4, when the voices of the marginalized and disadvantaged are first heard, they may seem discordant and out of the norm. However, it is precisely this discordance that forces others to pay attention and give recognition to neglected social realities.

Notes

1. The political theorist Ian Shapiro (2003) presents a third, and even more diluted, argument by making the case that deliberation matters not so much because it can transform preferences but because it can block elite domination.
2. It is important to emphasize that deliberation is not about reaching a consensus. "Deliberation cannot make incompatible values compatible, but it can help participants recognize the moral merit in their opponents' claims when those claims have merit" (Gutmann and Thompson 2004, 11).

References

Appadurai, Arjun. 2004. "The Capacity to Aspire: Culture and the Terms of Recognition." In Culture and Public Action, ed. V. Rao and M. Walton. Stanford, CA: Stanford University Press.

Baiocchi, Gianpaolo, Patrick Heller, and Marcelo K. Silva. 2011. Bootstrapping Democracy: Transforming Local Governance and Civil Society in Brazil. Stanford, CA: Stanford University Press.

Ban, Radu, Saumitra Jha, and Vijayendra Rao. 2012. "Who Has Voice in a Deliberative Democracy?" Journal of Development Economics 99 (10): 428–38.

Bardhan, Pranab. 1999. "The State against Society: The Great Divide in Indian Social Science Discourse." In Nationalism, Democracy and Development, ed. Sugata Bose and Ayesha Jalal, 184–95. Delhi: Oxford University Press.

Barron, Patrick, Rachel Diprose, and Michael Woolcock. 2011. *Contesting Development: Participatory Projects and Local Conflict Dynamics in Indonesia.* New Haven, CT: Yale University Press.

Basu, Kaushik. 2010. *Beyond the Invisible Hand: Groundwork for a New Economics.* Princeton, NJ: Princeton University Press.

Búrca, Gráinne, Robert Owen Keohane, and Charles Sabel. 2013. "New Modes of Pluralist Global Governance." *New York University Journal of International Law and Politics* 45 723–86.

Cohen, Jean L., and Andrew Arato. 1992. *Civil Society and Political Theory.* Cambridge, MA: MIT Press.

Dasgupta, Partha. 2009. "Trust and Cooperation among Economic Agents." *Philosophical Transactions of the Royal Society* 364 (1533): 3301–9.

Dryzek, John S. 2005. "Deliberative Democracy in Divided Societies Alternatives to Agonism and Analgesia." *Political Theory* 33 (2): 218–42.

———. 2006. *Deliberative Global Politics: Discourse and Democracy in a Divided World.* London: Polity.

Elster, Jon. 1998. *Deliberative Democracy.* New York: Cambridge University Press.

Evans, Peter. 2004. "Development as Institutional Change: The Pitfalls of Monocropping and the Potentials of Deliberation." *Studies in Comparative International Development* 38 (4): 30–52.

Fishkin, James S., and Robert C, Luskin. 2005. "Experimenting with a Democratic Ideal: Deliberative Polling and Public Opinion." *Acta Politica* 40 (3): 284–98.

Fox, Jonathan. 1994. "The Difficult Transition from Clientalism to Citizenship." *World Politics* 46 (2):151–84.

Fraser, Nancy. 1992. "Rethinking the Public Sphere: A Contribution of the Critique of Actually Existing Democracy." In *Habermas and the Public Sphere,* ed. Craig Calhoun, 109–43. Cambridge: MIT Press.

Fung, Archon, and Erik O Wright. 2003. *Deepening Democracy: Institutional Innovations in Empowered Participatory Governance.* London: Verso.

Gauri, Varun. 2012. "The Publicity 'Defect' of Customary Law." In *Legal Pluralism and Development: Dialogues for Success,* ed. Caroline Sage, Brian Tamanaha, and Michael Woolcock. Cambridge: Cambridge University Press.

Gauri, Varun, and Daniel M. Brinks. 2012. "Human Rights as Demands for Communicative Action." *Journal of Political Philosophy* 20 (4): 407–31.

Gauri, Varun, Michael Woolcock, and Deval Desai. 2012. "Inter-subjective Meaning and Collective Action Developing Societies: Theory, Evidence, and Policy Implications." *Journal of Development Studies* 49 (1): 109–19.

Goodin, Robert E. 2003. *Reflective Democracy.* Oxford University Press.

Gutmann and Thompson 2004. *Why Deliberative Democracy?* Princeton, NJ: Princeton University Press.

Habermas, Jürgen. 1984. *The Theory of Communicative Action.* Boston: Beacon Press.

———. 1996. *Between Facts and Norms: Contributions to a Discourse Theory of Law and Democracy*. Cambridge, MA: MIT Press.

Heller, Patrick. 2012. "Democracy, Participatory Politics and Development: Some Comparative Lessons from Brazil, India and South Africa." *Polity* 44, 643–65.

Heller, Patrick, K. N. Harilal, and Shubham Chaudhuri. 2007. "Building Local Democracy: Evaluating the Impact of Decentralization in Kerala, India." *World Development* 35 (4): 626–48.

Hoff, Karla, and Joseph Stiglitz. 2001. "Modern Economic Theory and Development." In *Frontiers of Development Economics*, ed. G. Meir and J. Stiglitz, 389–459. New York: Oxford University Press.

Huntington, Samuel P., and Harvard University Center for International Affairs. 1968. *Political Order in Changing Societies*. New Haven, CT: Yale University Press.

Keane, John. 2009. *The Life and Death of Democracy*. New York: W.W. Norton and Company.

Lockie, Stewart. 2007. "Deliberation and Actor–Networks: The 'Practical' Implications of Social Theory for the Assessment of Large Dams and Other Interventions." *Society & Natural Resources* 20 (9): 785–99.

Lukes, Steven. 1974. *Power: A Radical View*. London: Macmillan.

Mackie, Gerry. 1998. "All Men Are Liars: Is Democracy Meaningless?" In *Deliberative Democracy*, edited by John Elster, 69–96. Cambridge Studies in the Theory of Democracy. Cambridge, UK: Cambridge University Press.

Mahajan, Gurpreet. 1999. "Civil Society and Its Avtars: What Happened to Freedom and Democracy." *Economic and Political Weekly* 34: 1188–96.

Mamdani, Mahmood. 1996. *Citizen and Subject: Contemporary Africa and the Legacy of Late Colonialism*. Princeton, NJ: Princeton University Press.

Mansuri, Ghazala, and Vijayendra Rao. 2012. *Localizing Development: Does Participation Work?* Washington, DC: World Bank.

Narayan, Deepa, Robert Chambers, Meera Shah, and Patt Petesch. 2001. *Crying Out for Change: Voices of the Poor*. Washington, DC: World Bank.

O'Donnell, Guillermo. 1993. "On the State, Democratization and Some Conceptual Problems: A Latin American View with Glances at Some Postcommunist Countries." *World Development* 21 (8): 1355–59.

Odugbemi, Sina, and Thomas Jacobson. 2008. *Governance Reform under Real World Conditions*. Washington, DC: World Bank.

Ostrom, Elinor. 1990. *Governing the Commons: The Evolution of Institutions for Collective Action*. New York: Cambridge University Press.

———. 2000. "Collective Action and the Evolution of Social Norms." *Journal of Economic Perspectives* 14 (3): 137–58.

Rao, Vijayendra. 2006. "On Inequality Traps and Development Policy." *Development Outreach* 8 (1): 10–13. http://www-wds.worldbank.org/external/default/WDSContentServer/WDSP/IB/2010/11/04/000334955_20101104060008/Rendered/PDF/372500NEWS0REP10Box311126B01PUBLIC1.pdf.

Rao, Vijayendra, and Paromita Sanyal. 2010. "Dignity through Discourse: Poverty and the Culture of Deliberation in Indian Village Democracies." *Annals of the American Academy of Political and Social Science* 629 (May): 146–72.

Rao, Vijayendra, and Michael Walton. 2004. "Culture and Public Action: Relationality, Equality of Agency and Development." In *Culture and Public Action.* ed. V. Rao and M. Walton. Stanford, CA: Stanford University Press.

Rodrik, Dani. 2007. *One Economics, Many Recipes: Globalization, Institutions, and Economic Growth.* Princeton, NJ: Princeton University Press.

Sabel, Charles F. 1995. "Bootstrapping Reform: Rebuilding Firms, the Welfare State, and Unions." *Politics & Society* 23 (1): 5.

Sanyal, Paromita. 2014. *From Credit to Capabilities: A Sociological Study of Microcredit Groups in India.* Cambridge: Cambridge University Press.

Sen, Amartya. 2000. *Development as Freedom.* New York: Knopf.

———. 2006. *Argumentative Indian.* London: Picador.

Shapiro, Ian. 2003. *The State of Democratic Theory.* Princeton University Press.

Snow, David A., Sarah A. Soule, and Hanspeter Kreisi, eds. 2007. *Blackwell Companion to Social Movements.* Malden, MA: Wiley-Blackwell.

Somers, Margaret R. 1993. "Citizenship and the Place of the Public Sphere: Law, Community, and Political Culture in the Transition to Democracy." *American Sociological Review* 58(October): 587–620.

Swidler, Ann. 2014. "Cultural Sources of Institutional Resilience: Lessons from Chieftaincy in Rural Malawi." In *Social Resilience in the Neo-Liberal Era*, ed. P. Hall and M. Lamont, eds., Cambridge University Press.

Tilly, Charles. 1998. *Durable Inequality.* Berkeley, CA: University of California Press.

Warren, Mark. 2001. *Democracy and Associations.* Princeton, NJ: Princeton University Press.

———. 2009. "Governance-Driven Democratization." *Critical Policy Studies* 3 (1): 3–13.

World Bank. 2006. *Equity and Development: World Development Report 2006.* Washington, DC: World Bank.

CHAPTER 2

A Minimalist Definition of Deliberation

Jane Mansbridge

This chapter provides a brief conceptual elaboration of the meaning of deliberation, the standards for good deliberation, the concept of a deliberative system, and the functions of such a system. It is intended as a guide for practitioners to the philosophical background and controversies regarding the concept of deliberation and as an invitation to join the process of developing appropriate standards for good deliberation.

I suggest defining deliberation in the public sphere minimally and broadly as "mutual communication that involves weighing and reflecting on preferences, values and interests regarding matters of common concern" (adapted from Dryzek 2000, 76). The breadth, minimalism, and relative neutrality of this definition mark the beginning, not the end, of analysis. The next analytic step is to apply a set of standards for relatively good or bad deliberation. Both analysts and practitioners can use these standards, while acknowledging their contested status and assisting in their evolution.

The minimalist definition of deliberation that I advance is intended to both improve analytic clarity and make sense in the field. It easily captures the discussions that led to the socially, although not governmentally, binding decisions to end genital cutting in Senegal, on which Gerald Mackie reports in chapter 5 of this volume. It captures the reflective and weighing aspects of formal church committees and trainings by nongovernmental organizations in Malawi, which Ann Swidler and Susan Watkins cautiously describe in chapter 7 not as representing deliberation per se but as having the potential for deliberation. It captures the weighing and reflection that take place in the discussions that led to decisions for conflict resolution, such as the chief's courts and village meetings in Malawi that Swidler and Watkins describe. The definition even captures significant parts of informal interactions, such as the argument about AIDS that

Swidler and Watkins report among passengers on a bus, where many passengers reflected on and weighed, at least minimally, the arguments of the others.

Although minimalist, this definition of deliberation does not encompass some forms of talk or expression on matters of common concern. The term *deliberation* has at its root the idea of weighing alternatives. Thus, by the definition suggested here, everyday talk that is unreflective and does not attempt to weigh the aspects of an issue does not count as deliberation. One-way talk in which no one disagrees or presents another possibility does not count as deliberation. One-way expressions of solidarity—such as the song and dance performance at UN headquarters by advocates for the homeless that Arjun Appadurai describes in chapter 4—do not count as deliberation or deliberative. The incident that Swidler and Watkins describe in chapter 7—in which one group of spectators urges on two women beating a girl who has slept with the husband of one of them while another group later supports the girl— might be thought to have moments of reflection and weighing within the process, particularly among the second group of later supporters, who presumably weighed the arguments of the first group in their accounts, if only minimally. But, as a whole, this interaction would not be considered deliberative, because it seems to include little reflection or weighing.

In short, a communicative process that includes little or no reflective interactive weighing is not by itself deliberation. Such a process may nevertheless play an important role in a larger deliberative system. A systemic approach to deliberation considers the quality of deliberation in a deliberative system as a whole. It directs attention to the different ways that smaller unreflective and nondeliberative acts can figure crucially in the weighing and reflecting functions of a larger deliberative interaction. Such acts may, for example, bring out considerations that otherwise would have never been heard, which can then be weighed elsewhere in the deliberative system. When different parts of a system perform complementary functions, the larger system may approach deliberative standards more closely than any of the parts. When one part in a system displaces another, that displacement may undermine the deliberative quality of the system as a whole.

Defining deliberation

The word *deliberation* has distinct normative connotations. In its very character, the word is thus "evaluative-descriptive."[1] The term itself derives from the Latin root *liber* (scale) and thus connotes some weighing of pros and cons. Thomas Hobbes wrote that "deliberation is simply weighing up the advantages and disadvantages of the action we are addressing (as if on a pair of scales)" (1998 [1642], 152). The word also has the connotation of a deliberate—that is, well-considered and not hasty—process.

The broad definition of deliberation in the public sphere that I suggest—mutual communication that involves weighing and reflecting on preferences, values, and interests regarding matters of common concern—captures some but not all of the traditional connotations in the way ordinary language speakers have used the word *deliberation*. Artificially, for purposes of conceptual clarity, it carves out one small set of connotations from the larger cluster of connotations the word ordinarily carries.

The first word in the definition—*mutual*—distinguishes deliberation between two (or more) people from deliberation solely in the mind of one individual (what Robert Goodin [2000] calls "deliberation within"). Although any mutual deliberation will include deliberation within the minds of the individuals involved, the word *mutual* requires some two-way communication. On a system level, deliberation can include one-way communication, but the system will be deliberative only if that communication is reciprocated somewhere in the system.

The second component of the definition—weighing and reflecting—captures some of the elements of care and thoughtful consideration central to the constellation of meanings that in ordinary language adhere to the term *deliberation*. These terms usually have normatively positive connotations, because stopping to reflect, to weigh options, and to act carefully usually improves outcomes.[2] Compared with many components of other definitions of deliberation, however, these terms are relatively neutral normatively.

The final component of the definition—specifying that the object of reflection be preferences, values, and interests on matters of common concern—distinguishes talk on matters that involve a collective from talk that is relevant only to individuals or dyads.

This somewhat neutral and minimalist definition of deliberation and a deliberative system allows users of these terms to specify the conditions of "good" and "bad" deliberation without having those standards built into the word *deliberation* itself. In order to facilitate this specification, the definition itself does not include, as many earlier definitions do, any reference to giving reasons, creating arguments that others have good reason to accept, affording mutual respect and equal voice, relating to the common will, or including conditions of noncoercion. These conditions become instead standards for good deliberation.

In ordinary speech, the word *deliberation* is often used to mean "good deliberation," as in the comment, "That's not real deliberation." In daily life the fact that this usage packs the standards for good deliberation into the term itself poses no problems. For analytic clarity, however, it helps to separate out the standards from the definition. The separation is intended to promote specificity in analysis and facilitate controversy over the appropriate standards.

I suggest this relatively neutral and minimalist definition for analytic convenience, not to make a philosophical point. It seems unfruitful to spend much time in a controversy over how to define *deliberation*. I have myself at times included several normative considerations as part of the definition of deliberation. In one article, eight co-authors and I stated that mutual respect "is *intrinsically* a part of deliberation. To deliberate with another is to understand the other as a self-authoring source of reasons and claims" (Mansbridge and others 2012). One could also consider noncoercion intrinsically part of deliberation, because persuasion is essentially noncoercive. The search for epistemic value, or better knowledge, might also be intrinsic to the concept, because the point of weighing and reflecting is to improve one's understanding. Equality and inclusion are intrinsic to *democratic* deliberation. All of these concepts, which I present later in this chapter as standards for good democratic deliberation, could be considered part of the definition itself. In offering a stripped-down, minimalist definition, I do not want to provoke quarrels over whether this definition is or is not right or about the degree to which one or another standard for good deliberation should be considered intrinsic to deliberation or not. Rather, I seek to redirect analytic attention, including the attention of practitioners, to the more important question of what constitutes good deliberation.

Does deliberation require a binding decision?

Before turning to the question of standards, I examine the controversial issue of whether or not deliberation requires a binding decision. I do not include the requirement of a binding decision in my minimalist definition of deliberation. I do not even list this requirement among the standards of good deliberation. Yet I agree with the following propositions, often stressed by scholars who include in the definition of deliberation the requirement that a decision be binding:

1. A decision—or at least action—is implied in some of the ordinary connotations of the term.
2. The state per se plays a crucial role in any deliberative system through its legitimate monopoly of the means of violence.
3. Anyone concerned with the legitimacy of the state must be concerned with the legitimacy of the deliberation leading to its binding decisions.
4. The degree to which any given forum or node in the deliberative system is empowered to make a binding decision or is merely consultative is a critical dimension of that forum's importance in the deliberative system.

Working through each of these points takes several pages; readers not concerned with the issue of binding decisions can skip to the next section.

By not requiring that deliberation end in a decision, the definition advanced here differs from the definitions given by various other theorists. Theorists who are particularly concerned with political legitimacy have emphatically and explicitly defined deliberation as aiming only at a binding decision. Joshua Cohen, who wrote the first major analytic article on democratic deliberation in 1989, clarified later that he intends deliberation only in this decision-oriented way. As he put it, "Deliberation, generically understood, is about weighing the reasons relevant to a decision *with a view to making a decision* on the basis of that weighing" (Cohen 2007, 219, my emphasis). Dennis Thompson, the coauthor of an important early book on deliberation (Guttman and Thompson 1996), also uses *deliberation* to mean only "decision-oriented discussion" that "leads *directly* to *binding* decisions" (2008, 503–04, my emphasis). He explicitly distinguishes deliberation so defined from "pure discussion." In Thompson's view, randomly selected citizens coming together for a weekend to discuss a public policy in Deliberative Polls (the randomly selected "mini-publics" that follow James Fishkin's [2009] design) are not strictly speaking engaged in deliberation because their discussions do not lead directly to binding decisions. For Thompson, the "pure discussion" in Deliberative Polls is relevant to deliberation but not deliberation per se.[3]

Cohen's and Thompson's emphasis on binding decision is understandable for two main reasons. First, the notion of binding is implicit in traditional usage, although that usage may now be changing. The 1989 *Oxford English Dictionary* defined *deliberation* as "weighing a thing in the mind; careful consideration with a view to decision." It defined *deliberateness* as "showing careful consideration; absence of haste in decision." Both definitions explicitly mention "decision." Thirteen years later the American *Webster's Third New International Dictionary* defined *deliberation* as "weighing and examining the reasons for and against a choice or measure; careful consideration; mature reflection." It defined *deliberateness* as "calm well-poised slowness (as of thought, speech, or bodily movement)." Neither definition included the word *decision*. In the first definition in *Webster's*, *choice* and *measure* may not differ greatly from *decision*, but in the second definition even *choice* and *measure* have been dropped. A few years later still, and explicitly reflecting usage on the American side of the Atlantic, the 2005 *New Oxford American Dictionary* defined deliberation as "long and careful consideration or discussion," with no mention of decision or even choice. (This dictionary did not define *deliberateness*.) These different definitions may indicate an evolution in usage, particularly in the United States. Despite this possible evolution in usage, however, the hint of decision cannot be eliminated from the ordinary connotations of the word. There would be little point to careful weighing if no "action" (in Hobbes' terms), no eventual choice, including the choice not to act, were to follow.

Second, many political theorists have discussed deliberation in the context of the legitimacy of state decisions. The state in modern societies has in some sense the ultimate say in matters of public concern, even when a constitution explicitly or implicitly cordons off some areas of life from state intervention, because constitutional amendments can potentially open even those arenas to state intervention. In addition to this potential power, modern states make numerous decisions that dramatically affect the lives of their citizens. For democratic theorists, these decisions are more or less normatively legitimate (meaning "rightly" made, their procedures being what they "ought" to be), depending on how well their processes meet established standards for making democratic decisions. Those standards, in turn, derive from the considerations that human beings, thinking about and discussing these issues with one another, have developed from their experiences and thought. In order to ask how normatively legitimate any government's laws might be, one must consider, and develop standards for considering, what features go into the creation of normative legitimacy.

Scholars who are not normative theorists may find it useful to understand that in the academic division of labor, normative theorists addressing politics have the task of trying to think through as thoroughly and systematically as possible what the public's standards for judging actions and institutions ought to be. They aim to sharpen intuitions, pinpoint contradictions, and suggest logical extensions, as part of a process that John Rawls (1971) calls "reflective equilibrium." Normative theorists do not ask the descriptive or sociological question of when citizens believe a government or a government's decision to be legitimate (the question of perceived legitimacy); instead, they ask what standards citizens ought to use to judge a government or government decision legitimate (the question of normative legitimacy). The efforts of normative theorists are based on the premise that "ought" questions deserve more than passing thought.

Once formulated, the standards by which governments and individuals ought to act often take the form of "regulative" ideals. A regulative ideal is an ideal that is often unachievable in its full state but sets the goal that one should try to approach.[4] Being unachievable is thus not a definitive argument against an ideal. To take an extreme example from the Christian Bible, "Be perfect, therefore, as your heavenly father is perfect" (Matthew 5: 48) is a regulative ideal. The ideal is to be perfect, but because no one can be like God, the fact that human beings will never achieve this ideal is built into the concept. A regulative ideal may be unachievable in its full state for practical reasons (for example, in deliberation neither the ideal of the absence of coercive power nor the ideal of completely equal power can be achieved in practice). A regulative ideal may also be unachievable in some instances because it conflicts with other ideals (for example, when the ideal of equality conflicts with the ideal of liberty). Regulative ideals often conflict.

In the second half of the 20th century, one significant task for democratic theorists was thinking through the standards, or regulative ideals, that make an electoral democracy relatively legitimate. This electorally oriented task primarily addressed the issues raised by aggregation, or the processes of adding up preferences. The aggregative standards developed include various criteria for free, fair, and inclusive elections (see the criteria in Dahl 1989).

Recently, theorists have taken on the task of thinking through the standards for deliberation to reach a relatively legitimate decision. These standards are the subject of the next section. Here it suffices to point out that a legitimacy rationale for thinking about deliberative standards automatically focuses on binding decisions, because the state's laws, which are judged as more or less legitimate, derive from such decisions.

Outside the profession of normative political theory, however, the discussion of deliberation has jumped these narrow tracks. Not only has the common usage of the word broadened (if the evolution in the three dictionaries cited above can be trusted); the concept itself has taken on new life beyond the confines of academic discourse.

Google's Ngram tool allows users to search the incidence of words and phrases in a sample of Google's collection of books in English. Doing so shows that as a percentage of all the words in such books, the use of the word *deliberation* peaked around 1790, about the time of the framing of the U.S. constitution and the U.S. and French bills of rights, then declined dramatically in the next two centuries. It began to rebound around 1980. By 2008 it had reached the same level it had achieved in 1928, although it never again reached anywhere near the heights of the revolutionary period.[5] Use of the compound term *deliberative democracy*, introduced definitively in 1980, rose dramatically between 1988 and 2000, leveling off around 2003.[6]

Communities concerned with the quality of citizen participation seem to find deliberation an increasingly helpful concept in contexts unconnected with binding decisions. Practitioners in such communities often use the word *deliberation* without reference to any decision. The relatively neutral and minimal definition I suggest here encompasses this common usage not connected to a binding decision.

A relatively neutral definition that does not include the quality of being binding not only captures possibly evolving usage; it also facilitates the use of adjectives to modify the forms of deliberation. The adjective *binding* can specify deliberation in forums that are empowered to make binding decisions.[7]

The distinction between binding (or empowered) and consultative deliberation is crucial in both theory and practice. Authoritarian governments are often enthusiastic about consultative deliberation because, unlike many forms of citizen input, it can be designed to provide little opportunity for political organizing. Consultative deliberation with a randomly selected group of citizens can allow a government to find out what citizens want and promote belief in the legitimacy of the government but at the same time avoid public hearings, which both encourage political mobilization and are often unrepresentative, dominated by people with intense views or concentrated interests (such as business interests in China). If the design of such a deliberative forum is perceived as fair—based on the combination of an observable random selection that treats everyone equally, an unbiased, balanced, and transparent set of materials giving reasons for and against the different alternatives, and a process that in other ways does not obviously tilt toward one alternative or the other—the citizens affected by the ensuing decision are likely to believe that the results are legitimate and therefore be more likely to obey the laws that derive from them. Using the results of such processes to make decisions also helps prevent the common form of corruption in which local cadres choose and implement public works projects that primarily benefit their extended families. In China, for example, central state actors benefit from curbing local corruption because it undermines overall state legitimacy without benefiting the central state.[8]

The degree of empowerment of any particular forum may evolve in ways that are not fully under the authorities' control. A forum designed to be purely consultative may slowly become empowered through the dynamics of sociological legitimacy on the ground. In 2005, for example, Communist Party Secretary Jiang Zaohua of Zeguo Township in Wenling City commissioned a Deliberative Poll of randomly selected citizens to suggest infrastructure priorities for the town. The local People's Congress then implemented the citizens' suggestions. The next year Jiang commissioned another Deliberative Poll of randomly selected citizens, and the local People's Congress followed those recommendations as well. Two years later a Deliberative Poll considered priorities for the entire town budget, an event observed by most of the deputies to the local People's Congress, who then adjusted the town's budget in light of what they learned. After three iterations, the Deliberative Polls began to acquire a de facto legitimacy that could have created costs for an administrator who decided not to implement the decisions that citizens had made in those forums (He and Warren 2011). Consultative forums may thus slowly morph into more empowered forums, even while formal power and the state's legitimate monopoly on violence remain in the hands of state administrators.

A relatively neutral definition of deliberation unconnected to the presence or absence of a binding decision allows an analyst to describe a consultative forum as deliberative and at the same time ask what binding and/or regime-preserving features it may have. A relatively neutral description can also facilitate investigation into and controversy over the standards for good deliberation. The next section discusses those standards.

Evolving standards for deliberation

Under scrutiny by normative theorists, the standards for good deliberation have evolved over the past 20 years. In many ways they have moved away from the "classic" standards enunciated by major late 20th century thinkers, including Jürgen Habermas, Joshua Cohen, and Amy Gutmann and Dennis Thompson. As recently as 2005, Robert Goodin could write, "As regards standards for what counts as 'good' discourse and deliberation, there seems to be an impressively broad scholarly consensus" (2005, 183). He summarized those consensual standards as open participation, justification of assertions and validity claims, consideration of the common good, respect, aim at a rationally motivated consensus, and authenticity (2005). Earlier, Gutmann and Thompson (1996) had enunciated three cardinal deliberative principles for legislatures and other public forums: reciprocity, publicity, and accountability. Jurg Steiner and his colleagues (2004) derived from Habermas five standards for good deliberation—justification rationality, common good orientation, respect, constructive politics, and equal participation—which they combined into a Discourse Quality Index to measure the quality of legislative deliberation. Andre Bächtiger and his coauthors refer to these standards as the standards of "Type I" deliberation (Bächtiger and others 2010). They can also be called (as I do here) "classic" standards (Mansbridge and others 2010).

As the field of deliberation and deliberative democracy has evolved, only two standards—respect and the absence of power—have remained unchallenged and unchanged. The other classic standards have been refined or revised. At the same time, a new standard of epistemic value has been formulated and added (table 2.1). These standards are contestable. They may conflict with one another. They should also be interpreted as regulative ideals (ideals that are usually not possible to fully achieve in practice).

Respect and power

The standard of respect is perhaps the deepest democratic value. Not yet challenged or revised as a standard for good deliberation, it involves respecting the fundamental worth and dignity of others. In deliberation it involves, among other things, listening to what the other says and offering justifications that the other might accept. To measure respect, coders of legislative interactions have looked to see whether legislators recognized the arguments of others in their responses and responded to those arguments specifically (Steiner and others 2004). Respect is also evinced in tone of voice, attention, and consideration. A deliberation cannot be considered good without high levels of mutual respect.

TABLE 2.1 Standards for good deliberation

Classic	Evolved	New
Respect	Unchallenged, unrevised	
Absence of power	Unchallenged, unrevised	
Reasons	Rational and emotional considerations	
Aim at consensus	Aim at consensus and at clarifying interests when interests conflict	
Common good orientation	Orientation to common good and to self-interest when constrained by fairness	
Equal participation/power	Equal opportunity of access to political influence	
Inclusion of all with legal rights	Inclusion of all affected individuals (this standard is highly contested)	
Accountability to constituents	Accountability to constituents when elected and to other participants and citizens when not elected	
Publicity/transparency	Publicity/transparency in public forums and nontransparency in certain other conditions (for example, in negotiations when a principal can trust the agent)	
Sincerity	Sincerity in matters of importance along with insincerity in certain greetings, compliments, and other gestures intended to increase sociality	
		Epistemic value Substantive balance

The absence of power (where power is defined as coercive power, namely the threat of sanction or the use of force) has also not yet been challenged or revised as a standard for good deliberation. Of all the standards, however, the absence of coercive power is perhaps most clearly only a regulative ideal, serving as a goal, because no human interactions are free of any form of force or threat of sanction. To illustrate the differences between the two types of coercive power and persuasion, consider that I can get you to leave a room in at least three ways. I can correctly draw your attention to the fire in the corner of the room and point out that it is in your interest to leave (persuasion). I can put a gun to your head and tell you that if you do not leave I will shoot you (threat of sanction). Or I can pick you up and carry you out of the room kicking and screaming (force). When I threaten sanctions, you have the option of saying, "Shoot me," in which case I will have a dead body on the floor, not you out of the room. Your will is at least minimally involved. When I use force, your will is not involved. Of these three, only persuasion, or as Habermas once put it, "the unforced force of the better argument," is, in the ideal, normatively allowed in deliberation.[10]

Force and the threat of sanction, however, are involved in all communication. Deliberations take place through language. Everyone is forced to use the language he or she speaks, often unaware of the way that language itself shapes thoughts. In some languages, when a woman speaks, her own language requires locutions, such as universal pronouns gendered as male, that subtly undermine her claim to equality. Whenever we attempt to communicate, perhaps using a hegemonic language that is not our native tongue, we are always threatened with the potential sanction of another's misunderstanding. A complete absence of power in deliberation is therefore unachievable. Yet there is a big difference between situations such as Habermas's coffeehouses or a discussion among friends, where power is relatively absent, and situations in which power massively structures the deliberative field in ways inimical to some of the parties' interests. The closer one can get to an absence of power, the better the deliberation is on normative grounds.

As theorists have thought through the standards for deliberation other than respect and the absence of power, they have suggested several revisions in the classic formulations. Reason, consensus, and the common good are discussed in some detail below. Equal participation and equal power (itself a default standard, because power cannot be eliminated) have been recast as the equal opportunity of access to political influence. Inclusion, once seen to require only admitting to the deliberation over a decision anyone legally bound by that decision (e.g., citizens), is now sometimes thought to require admitting all those affected by a decision. Theorists are currently debating whether the "all affected principle" is the right standard for inclusion, or whether it should apply in proportion to the degree affected, and how it might be pursued in practice. Accountability is now seen to apply most directly to elected legislatures and perhaps other representative bodies rather than having full force across the whole deliberative system. Publicity in the form of transparency is now viewed as inappropriate for all parts of the deliberative system, because many sensitive matters require closed doors for open and fruitful discussion. Complete sincerity in the sense of full revelation is now thought to undermine good deliberation in some circumstances, although sincerity on essentials is still required to undergird respect and epistemic value.[11] The role of reason in deliberation and the goals of consensus and orientation to the common good require more discussion here, as does the recently added standard of epistemic value.

The role of reason

Writers in the tradition of Habermas (1986 [1981]) and those in the tradition of Rawls (1971), such as Cohen (1989), have made "reason" and "reasoning" central to their definitions of deliberation. Cohen states that "discursive participation. . . is not the same as deliberation" because "deliberation is about reasoning, not simply discussing" (2007, 222–23). He makes a clear distinction between deliberation and discussion, contrasting "mere discussion" with "reasoning of the right kind" and the "defense of positions with reasons."

The requirement that deliberation involve "reason" has met considerable opposition for several reasons. First, reason is often contrasted with emotion, but human beings cannot reason without emotion. Arguments based on emotions also often serve as what most people consider reasons—that is, explanations for why one ought to act in one way or another.[12] For this reason, many theorists now use the word *considerations* to express the content that the parties to a deliberation advance to one another (see, for example, Warren and others 2014).

Differences by social class (and perhaps other group characteristics) may also affect the explicit use of reasons. When speaking together about collectively important issues, the less educated may be more likely than the more educated to use stories rather than a list of reasons to explain what they have on their minds.[13] In addition, for everyone stories can establish credibility, create empathy, and trigger a sense of injustice. Building "reason" or "reasons" into the definition of deliberation excludes a great deal of mutual thought and communication on public issues couched in practices such as storytelling. The term *considerations* accommodates narratives and other emotionally based and expressed explanations and justifications.

The goals of consensus and the common good

Standards regarding the goal of deliberation have also evolved. The classic ideal of deliberation to consensus on the common good implied a relatively unitary conception of the common good, contested but discoverable through reason. A few early theorists and many later ones have pointed out, however, that even ideally the giving of good reasons and other considerations in a setting characterized by mutual respect, freedom, equality, and the relative absence of power will not always lead to a consensual result. When interests or values conflict irreconcilably, deliberation ideally ends not in consensus but in a clarification of conflict and a structuring of disagreement, which sets the stage for a decision by nondeliberative methods, such as aggregation through the vote. Homogeneity is not automatically better than pluralism, and with pluralism comes conflicting interests. Particularly when more powerful actors have exercised intellectual hegemony to get everyone to accept as the common interest a situation that disadvantages some, good deliberation ought to make less powerful actors more aware of their own interests and, when those interests conflict with others' interests, clarify the nature of the conflict. In such instances, clarification, not consensus, is the goal.

Although classic deliberative democrats such as Habermas place a high value on the contestation of opinions, they believe the deliberative focus should be solely on the common good. For such theorists, it was not conflict per se but the conflict of self-interests that contaminated the process. More recent theorists (and Barber 1984 among earlier theorists) have argued that the ideal of deliberative democracy must include self-interest—and conflicts among those interests—in order to recognize and celebrate within the democratic ideal the diversity of free and equal human beings. From this perspective, bringing one's self-interests and group interests to the table when those interests are relevant to the decision is not only consonant with but required by the standards for good deliberation. Without doing so, it is not possible to forge a common interest out of what were previously seen as conflicting interests or to work out fair ways of handling irreconcilable conflicts of interest. From this perspective, relevant self-interests should not be condemned but incorporated in deliberation and decision under the constraints of fairness.[14]

Epistemic goals

In a significant evolution in democratic theory over the past two decades, the epistemic, or knowledge-based, goals of deliberation have come to the fore (see Estlund 1993, 2008; Landemore 2013). As people talk with one another to reach greater understanding or solve problems, their understanding can be better or worse and their solutions relatively effective or ineffective, deriving from differential access to relevant facts and insights. Josiah Ober (2008) argues that Cliesthanes's reforms in ancient Athens, which created ten artificial tribes, each one drawing members from a coastal, an inland, and an urban part of the larger Athenian territory, had the functions not only of unifying Athens but also facilitating effective deliberation. The Athenian Council of 500, drawn from those ten tribes by lot, had access to a diversity of information that helped it make good decisions.

In *The Politics*, Aristotle noted that although "each individual is but an ordinary person," when many ordinary people meet together, they "may very likely be better than the few good, if regarded not individually but collectively, just as a feast to which many contribute is better than a dinner provided out of a single purse" (2000, 1281b). Many theorists have read this passage to mean that different citizens bring different insights and information to the table the way they might bring different dishes to a potluck. Such a reading probably misinterprets Aristotle, but even if the passage means only that more individuals will bring more information, the goal is still one of improving collective knowledge.[15]

Although the goal of generating better collective insight from the wisdom of the multitude is only prudential and pragmatic, it nevertheless creates an important standard for deliberation. A deliberation of high quality will bring out and process well the important facts and perspectives needed for greater mutual understanding or a good decision. Evolutionarily, systems of deliberation are not likely to survive unless they produce tolerably good decisions. For this reason, one standard for an individual instance of deliberation or a larger deliberative system is how well it achieves the epistemic goal.

Another recently suggested new standard is that of substantive balance in the weighing of considerations. To the degree possible, good deliberation should take account of considerations on all sides of the relevant issues (Fishkin 2009).

In short, the standards of good deliberation have evolved over time. Whether classic, evolved, or newly enunciated, these standards are not all necessarily congruent. Although in some situations it may be possible to achieve all at the same time, in others tradeoffs may be necessary— between, for example, equal opportunity of access to influence and epistemic clarity in the discussion. Nor are the standards set in stone. Normative theorists continue to deliberate about them, sharpening the definitions, examining possible implications and contradictions, and trying out tentative new formulations. They can use help from practitioners in regard to the possible congruence and conflicts between standards, possible challenges to these standards, and the surfacing of new standards that for one reason or another have not been articulated for the current list.

The concept of a deliberative system[16]

A deliberative system includes many nodes, forums, and processes. When a particular deliberative interchange falls short on one or more standards, one may judge that interchange not only on its own but as part of a larger process or a larger deliberative system. The boundaries of a particular political process are often those of a single forum or a set of meetings designed to work as a whole. The boundaries of a deliberative system are often set by the formal boundaries of an institution or institutions or by the contours of an issue that will be decided by a particular state or society.

A "system" in this context means "a set of distinguishable, differentiated but to some degree interdependent parts, often with distributed functions and a division of labor, connected to form a complex whole" (Mansbridge and others 2012, 4). The concept is not intended to be mechanistic. It does not require that every component have a function; nor that every component be interdependent with every other, such that changes in one will automatically bring about changes in all others; nor that the system be static rather than fluid. It does require differentiation among the parts. It also requires "some functional division of labor, so that some parts do work that others cannot do as well. And it requires some relational interdependence, so that a change in one component will bring about changes in some others. . . . Normatively, a systemic approach means that the system should be judged as a whole in addition to the parts being judged independently" (Mansbridge and others 2012, 5). In a dynamic of deliberative complementarity, when one instance within a process or one forum within a system is low in deliberative quality, it may nevertheless contribute to the overall quality of the process or the system as a whole. In a dynamic of deliberative displacement, introducing a forum of relatively high deliberative quality into a deliberative system or an interchange of relatively high deliberative quality into a particular deliberative process may undermine or destroy interchanges of lower deliberative quality that nevertheless made irreplaceable contributions to that system or process.

In the dynamic of complementarity, two wrongs may make a right. In observing the peace process in Northern Ireland, John Dryzek (2010, 83) wrote, "Only when the extremists on both sides (Sinn Fein and the Democratic Unionist Party) had disposed of their more moderate opponents. . . could dialogue across the two sides be effective, and eventually a power-sharing government formed. For neither leadership then had to look over its shoulder at anyone more extreme on their own side." The standards for good deliberation prescribe inclusion and respect for all affected parties—standards on which both Sinn Fein and the Democratic Unionist Party were abysmally low. But their very acts of exclusion helped them deliberate toward an agreement to which, in large part, the excluded parties themselves would have agreed. In the same way, on a process level, bursts of anger and the refusal to listen to others—themselves undeliberative acts because they reject the activity of reflective weighing—can contribute to a more deliberative overall process by bringing out information and including perspectives that would otherwise be excluded or marginalized.

On the level of the larger deliberative system, an example of complementarity comes from the interaction of activist variation and everyday selection. In the United States in the late 1960s, many of the most innovative ideas of the "second wave" of the women's movement came from enclaves of organized activists. These enclaves—consisting of movement organizations, women's studies departments at universities, sympathetic churches, friendship networks, and a plethora of cultural venues, such as coffeehouses and bookstores—were to some degree protected against mainstream ideology through their practices of talking only to one another and their disdain for mainstream ideas. This ideological protection combined with intense interaction to produce an explosion of new concepts and ideas—some fantastic and unrealizable, some more assimilable to everyday life. From that enclave-produced variation, in a separate, everyday process of selection, other women in homes and workplaces chose ideas they could use in their more vulnerable positions.[17] Neither the process of enclave variation nor that of everyday selection came close to approaching the standards for good deliberation; both often failed to include respect, an aim at either consensus or clarifying interests, or a level of reflection appropriate to increasing epistemic value. Yet over time and in conjunction with often equally perfunctory oppositional responses, the enclave and everyday processes worked together to create a larger deliberative system in which the normative challengers and the opposition to the challengers produced arguments that caused many citizens to listen to one another, reflect on the considerations advanced by each side, and weigh those considerations in the light of both clarifying interests and the crafting of a new conception of the common good. The overall deliberative system may not have reached the highest standards of deliberative quality, but the system as a whole had a higher deliberative quality than its parts.

Along with complementarity, the idea of displacement is also central to the concept of a deliberative system. The introduction of any new element into a deliberative system may displace or change the function of earlier elements, for better or for worse. When a constitutional court evolves to be the primary deliberative forum in a governmental system, for example, the legislature is less likely to take its deliberative responsibilities seriously (Gutmann and Thompson 1996; see also Dryzek 2010). The British government's introduction of citizens' juries, a form of randomized deliberative forum, into the health service debate undermined the legitimacy and political influence of existing advocacy groups, which had had a significant mobilizing and epistemic function (Parkinson 2006). Any introduction of a new deliberative entity into an existing deliberative system has the potential to undermine an existing equilibrium by creating new citizen "experts" and trusted proxies and thus disadvantage political parties and advocacy groups that had previously invested considerable political and social capital in creating deliberative trust. Sometimes this disruption and displacement is exactly what the system as a whole needs; sometimes it can undermine the epistemic, ethical, and inclusive functions of the whole.

The concept of a deliberative system allows one to gauge the contributions to the larger system of acts that lay the groundwork for other acts, as in the "deliberative chains" of performative work described by Appadurai in chapter 4 of this volume. In his analysis, because of their mobilizing effects, even acts that fail in their intended goals in their original context have the potential to change the frames or context for later acts.

The functions of a deliberative system

The standards for a good deliberation or a good deliberative system can be understood best in the light of three overarching functions of democratic deliberation: the epistemic, ethical, and political functions.

The epistemic function of deliberation, and thus of a deliberative system, is to generate opinions, preferences, and decisions that are appropriately informed by facts and logic and derive from substantive and meaningful consideration of relevant reasons. In a healthy deliberative system, relevant considerations are brought forth from all corners, aired, discussed, and appropriately weighed. The deliberations may not always be public, although the absence of publicity often limits deliberative capacity. Because the topics of these deliberations are by definition issues of common concern, an epistemically well-functioning deliberative system will evoke, be informed by, and take into consideration the preferences and opinions of those affected by the decision.

The primary ethical function of deliberation and a deliberative system is to promote mutual respect among citizens. Prudentially, mutual respect helps keep the deliberative system running. It serves as the lubricant of effective communication. Ethically, mutual respect is a good in itself and a normative requirement of democracies; citizens should be treated "not merely as objects of legislation, as passive subjects to be ruled, but as autonomous agents who take part in the governance of their society, directly or through their representatives" (Gutmann and Thompson 2004, 3). Although this moral basis is not controversial, how mutual respect should be interpreted in practice may be. Mutual respect is more contestable than the epistemic function of simply learning about others' preferences, opinions, and decisions. It does, however, imply listening attentively. Although in the context of aggregation equal respect implies counting inputs on the basis of equal power, in the context of deliberation it implies the absence of coercive power. Getting people to do something on the basis of coercive power (the threat of sanction or the use of force) is directly opposed to getting them to do something via deliberation on the basis of genuine persuasion on the merits.

A final function of democratic deliberation and a democratic deliberative system is to promote an inclusive and egalitarian political process. A deliberative system becomes democratic by including multiple and plural voices, interests, concerns, and claims on the basis of feasible equality. The inclusion and equality of the process affect both its epistemic content and its legitimacy. A well-functioning democratic deliberative system must not systematically exclude any citizens from the process without strong justification that might be reasonably accepted by all citizens, including the excluded themselves. On the positive side, it also ought to actively promote and facilitate inclusion and the equal opportunities to participate in the system.

Successfully realizing all three functions promotes the democratic legitimacy of decisions by ensuring reasonably sound decisions based on mutual respect among citizens and an inclusive process of collective choice. This legitimacy, in turn, maximizes the chances that people who share a common fate and common problems will willingly agree to the terms of their common cooperation.

Conclusion

Why has deliberation become so popular in recent years? The shallow explanation is that in the world of practice, the term provides a more up-to-date stand-in for what was once called participation. Practitioners constantly face dashed hopes in confronting a recalcitrant reality. They also face donor fatigue. Accordingly, when one initiative designed to give more power to the poor does not pan out, it helps to relabel it and start again.

A deeper explanation is that many activists, planners, and community organizers, along with democratic theorists, have noticed that people of all classes, including poor people, need to think through their needs and wants in interaction with others. When they have access to deliberative processes in which they can reflect on what they really want and weigh the options, citizens learn, try out their ideas on people who may think differently, listen to people whose views and interests conflict with their own, and get people who in other circumstances might be deaf to their voices to listen to what they have to say. Deliberative forums can also provide venues for negotiation and compromise, inspiration and creativity, and internal transformations that bind the deliberators to a shared vision of the common good. Recognizing that people in many cultures act in this way, organizations promoting development have become interested in deliberative processes, in addition to electoral aggregative processes, as channels for making it more likely that development actually serves the needs of the less powerful.

The minimalist and relatively neutral definition of deliberation proposed in this chapter allows for an evolution of standards and considerable pluralism among discursive spaces with a deliberative system. It invites practitioners to contribute to the continuing evolution of thought on this subject in both its practice and its theory. Practitioners can help identify and develop practices that in different contexts promote the epistemic, ethical, and egalitarian-inclusive functions of deliberation. They can also help refine, expand, and criticize the standards for good deliberation that have been developed up to this point. From a deliberative perspective, theory belongs to the people.

Notes

1. The term is from Neblo (2007), who adopted it from Skinner (1974). See Neblo (2007) for a careful and less minimalist analysis of these definitional issues.

2. In some circumstances, however, more impulsive decisions produce better outcomes. For a popular treatment, see Gladwell (2005).

3. Thompson writes, "The criterion specifying that deliberation should be decision-oriented does not imply that studies of groups that only discuss politics, such as Fishkin's Deliberative Polls, are not *relevant* to the study of deliberative democracy. . . . Although participants in discussions of this kind may not *make* collective decisions, they may be seen as taking part in an early phase of a process that *leads to* a deliberative decision. Like subjects in some other studies of pure discussion, Fishkin's subjects are *preparing for* (or can be seen as modeling citizens who are preparing for) the making of political decisions for the collectivity" (2008, 503, my emphasis).

4. On regulative ideals, see Kant (1998 [1781]) and Mansbridge and others (2010). For reasons of the second best, in some instances it may be right to act contrary to a regulative ideal (see Mansbridge and others 2010 and works cited therein).

5. The number of books in English in the 1700s is much smaller than the number in later centuries, but because the pattern of rise and fall is consistent from 1700 to 1900, it is almost certainly not caused by chance. See Michel and others (2011) for technical details on the Ngram database.

6. For the phrase *deliberative democracy*, Ngram indicates only a few usages before 1988. Alexander Bickel, a distinguished analyst of the Supreme Court, and Arnold Kaufman, who invented the term *participatory democracy*, each separately coined the phrase *deliberative democracy* in 1968, but readers seem not to have taken it up. In 1980 Joseph Bessette independently coined the term again. In 1989 Joshua Cohen wrote the seminal philosophical article on the topic. Reporting at three-year intervals, Google Books (which, in contrast to Ngram, gives absolute numbers, not percentages) reports 7 mentions of *deliberative democracy* in 1979–81 and 16,500 in 2006–08.

7. One possibility involves using the term *deliberative democracy,* in contrast to *democratic deliberation,* to describe instances of deliberation that result in a binding decision. Both Simone Chambers (2009) and I (Mansbridge 2008) made this distinction independently, but each chose a somewhat different—and to some degree opposing—set of definitions. This experience has taught me that because there is no agreed upon usage in either the scholarly field or ordinary language and because the two phrases sound so much alike, this terminological contrast does not greatly advance analytic clarity.

8. For descriptions of China and the use of deliberative forums in authoritarian regimes, see Fishkin and others (2010) and He and Warren (2011).

9. The persuasive effect of Foucault's formulation that power is everywhere derives in part from his conflating power as capacity with power as the threat of sanction or the use of force. Nevertheless, in no interaction is force or the threat of sanction entirely absent. For more on power in deliberation, see Mansbridge and others (2010).

10. A fourth method is inducement: I may get you to do something you might otherwise not do by offering to better your situation from the status quo. Inducements pose an analytic problem. On the one hand, analytically they seem to be no more than the flip side of (negative) sanctions. One may speak of "positive" and "negative" sanctions, meaning inducements and punishments, using the same metric for both. On the other hand, the status quo seems to have a privileged normative status, so that negative movements from this position differ qualitatively from positive movements. The difference is normative, not simply the quantitative descriptive difference that Bentham (2007 [1789]) noticed, deriving from the fact that human beings experience losses more deeply than gains. For more on positive incentives, see Barry (1991). For the unforced force, see Habermas (1975).

11. On the evolution of the standard of equal participation and power, see Knight and Johnson (1997); on equal authority, see Karpowitz and Mendelberg (2014); on the debate over the "all affected" principle of inclusion, see Goodin (2007), Nasstrom (2010), Song (2012), and Owen (2012); on the evolution of the standard of publicity, see Chambers (2004), Mansbridge (2005), and Mansbridge and others (2012); on the evolution of the standard of sincerity, see Warren (2006), Neblo (2007), Thompson (2008), and Bächtiger and others (2010).

12. On the interaction of emotion and reason, see Damasio (1994), Rorty (1985), Nussbaum (2003), Hall (2007), Krause (2008), and Morrell (2010). Neblo (2007) considers the inclusion of emotion to be a "manageable" addition to an understanding of deliberation on which theorists can coordinate. He suggests twelve distinct roles that the emotions play in deliberation (Neblo 2003).

13. On the possible class basis of "reasoned" deliberation, see the linguist Basil Bernstein (1971) on reporting the "restricted" codes of the working class compared with the "elaborated" codes of the better educated. For theories relating class and storytelling, see Lynn Sanders (1997) and Iris Marion Young (1996). In a study of the self-selected group that participated in an on-line deliberative forum on the design of the new World Trade Center in New York, however, Francesca Polletta and John Lee (2006) found a relation between storytelling and gender but not income, education, or race.

14. For more on the evolution of consensual aim and common good orientation to a new standard that includes clarifying conflict and the inclusion of self-interest, see Mansbridge and others (2010).

15. Waldron (1995) summarizes the conventional interpretation of this passage from Aristotle's *Politics* on "the wisdom of the multitude." Cammack (2013) argues to the contrary that because Athenian feasts were never potlucks in which different citizens brought different dishes, but instead occasions on which large amounts of meat were cooked, one should interpret this passage as saying that many citizens can bring more information, not diverse pieces of information, to the table. For empirical evidence suggesting that diversity rather than quantity in deliberation produces better answers, see Page (2007). On epistemic arguments for democracy, see Estlund (2008) and Landemore (2013).

16. The two subsequent sections on deliberative systems rely on the collective thought reported in Mansbridge and others (2012).

17. For the role of everyday talk in the deliberative system and for enclaves, see Mansbridge (1996, 1999). For the process of enclave variation and everyday selection, see Mansbridge and Flaster (2007) and Mansbridge (2013).

References

Aristotle. 2000. *Politics*. Toronto: Dover.

Bächtiger, André, Simon Niemeyer, Michael Neblo, Marco R. Steenbergen, and Jürg Steiner. 2010. "Disentangling Diversity in Deliberative Democracy:

Competing Theories, Their Blind Spots and Complementarities." *Journal of Political Philosophy* 18 (1): 32–63.

Barry, Brian. 1991. "Power: An Economic Analysis." In *Democracy and Power: Essays in Political Theory I.* Oxford: Oxford University Press.

Bentham, Jeremy. 2007 (1789). *Introduction to the Principles of Morals and Legislation.* Mineola, NY: Dover Publications.

Bernstein, Basil. 1971. *Class, Codes, and Control: Theoretical Studies towards a Sociology of Language.* London: Routledge and Kegan Paul.

Cammack, Daniela. 2013. "Aristotle on the Virtue of the Multitude." *Political Theory* 41 (2) 175–202.

Chambers, Simone. 2004. "Behind Closed Doors: Publicity, Secrecy, and the Quality of Deliberation." *Journal of Political Philosophy* 12 (4): 389–410.

———. 2009. "Rhetoric and the Public Sphere: Has Deliberative Democracy Abandoned Mass Democracy?" *Political Theory* 37 (3): 323–50.

Cohen, Joshua. 1989. "Deliberation and Democratic Legitimacy." In *The Good Polity: Normative Analysis of the State*, ed. A. Hamlin and P. Pettit, 17–34. Oxford: Blackwell.

———. 2007. "Deliberative Democracy." In *Deliberation, Participation, and Democracy: Can the People Govern?* ed. S. W. Rosenberg, 219–36. New York: Palgrave Macmillan.

Dahl, Robert A. 1989. *Democracy and Its Critics.* New Haven, CT: Yale University Press.

Damasio, Antonio R. 1994. *Descartes' Error: Emotion, Reason, and the Human Brain.* London: Putnam.

Dryzek, John. 2000. *Deliberative Democracy and Beyond: Liberals, Critics, Contestations.* Oxford: Oxford University Press.

———. 2010. *Foundations and Frontiers of Deliberative Governance.* Oxford: Oxford University Press.

Estlund, David. 1993. "Making Truth Safe for Democracy." In *The Idea of Democracy*, ed. D. Copp, J. Hampton, and J. E. Roemer, 71–100. New York: Cambridge University Press.

———. 2008. *Democratic Authority: A Philosophical Framework.* Princeton, NJ: Princeton University Press.

Fishkin, James S. 2009. *When the People Speak: Deliberative Democracy and Public Consultation.* New York: Oxford University Press.

Fishkin, James S., Baogang He, Robert C. Luskin, and Alice Siu. 2010. "Deliberative Democracy in an Unlikely Place: Deliberative Polling in China." *British Journal of Political Science* 40 (2): 435–48.

Gladwell, Malcolm. 2005. *Blink: The Power of Thinking without Thinking.* New York: Little, Brown.

Goodin, Robert E. 2000. "Democratic Deliberation Within." *Philosophy & Public Affairs* 29 (1): 81–109.

———. 2005. "Sequencing Deliberative Moments." *Acta Politica* 40: 182–96.

————. 2007. "Enfranchising All Affected Interests, and Its Alternatives." *Philosophy and Public Affairs* 35 (1): 40–68.

Gutmann, Amy, and Dennis Thompson. 1996. *Democracy and Disagreement.* Cambridge, MA: Belknap Press of Harvard University Press.

————. 2004. *Why Deliberative Democracy?* Princeton, NJ: Princeton University Press.

Habermas, Jürgen. 1975. *Legitimation Crisis.* Boston: Beacon Press.

————. 1986 (1981). *The Theory of Communicative Action. Vol. I: Reason and the Rationalization of Society.* Boston: Beacon Press.

Hall, Cheryl. 2007. "Recognizing the Passion in Deliberation: Toward a More Democratic Theory of Deliberative Democracy." *Hypatia* 22 (4): 81–95.

He, Baogang, and Mark E. Warren. 2011. "Authoritarian Deliberation: The Deliberative Turn in Chinese Political Development." *Perspectives on Politics* 9 (2): 269–89.

Hobbes, Thomas. 1998 (1642). *On the Citizen,* ed. Richard Tuck and Michael Silverthorne. Cambridge: Cambridge University Press.

Kant, Immanuel. 1998 (1781). *Critique of Pure Reason,* ed. P. Guyer and A. Wood. New York: Cambridge University Press.

Karpowitz, Christopher F. and Tali Mendelberg. 2014. *The Silent Sex: Gender, Deliberation, and Institutions.* Princeton, NJ: Princeton University Press.

Knight, Jack, and James Johnson. 1997. "What Sort of Political Equality Does Democratic Deliberation Require?" In *Deliberative Democracy,* ed. J. Bohman and W. Rehg. Cambridge, MA: MIT Press.

Krause, Sharon R. 2008. *Civil Passions: Moral Sentiment and Democratic Deliberation.* Princeton, NJ: Princeton University Press.

Landemore, Helene. 2013. *Democratic Reason: Politics, Collective Intelligence, and the Rule of the Many.* Princeton, NJ: Princeton University Press.

Mansbridge, Jane. 1996. "Using Power/Fighting Power: The Polity." In *Democracy and Difference,* ed. Seyla Benhabib, 46–56. Princeton, NJ: Princeton University Press.

————. 1999. "Everyday Talk in the Deliberative System." In *Deliberative Politics: Essays on 'Democracy and Disagreement',* ed. S. Macedo, 211–39. New York: Oxford University Press.

————. 2005. "The Fallacy of Tightening the Reins." *Österreichische Zeitschrift für Politikwissenschaft* 34 (3): 233–47.

————. 2008. "Deliberative Democracy or Democratic Deliberation?" In *Deliberation, Participation, and Democracy: Can the People Govern?* ed. Shawn W. Rosenberg, 251–71. New York: Palgrave Macmillan.

————. 2013. "Everyday Activism." In *The Wiley-Blackwell Encyclopedia of Political and Social Movements,* ed. David Snow, Donatella della Porte, Bert Klandermans, and Doug McAdams. Oxford: Blackwell.

Mansbridge, Jane, and Katherine Flaster. 2007. "The Cultural Politics of Everyday Discourse: The Case of 'Male Chauvinist.'" *Critical Sociology* 33 (4): 627–60.

Mansbridge, Jane, James Bohman, Simone Chambers, Thomas Christiano, Archon Fung, John Parkinson, Dennis Thompson, and Mark E. Warren. 2012. "The Deliberative System." In *The Deliberative System*, ed. John Parkinson and Jane Mansbridge. Cambridge: Cambridge University Press.

Mansbridge, Jane, James Bohman, Simone Chambers, David Estlund, Andreas Føllesdal, Archon Fung, Cristina Lafont, Bernard Manin, and José Luis Martí. 2010. "The Place of Self-Interest and the Role of Power in Deliberative Democracy." *Journal of Political Philosophy* 18 (1): 64–100.

Michel, Jean-Baptiste, Yuan Kui Shen, Aviva Presser Aiden, Adrian Veres, Matthew K. Gray, William Brockman, The Google Books Team, Joseph P. Pickett, Dale Hoiberg, Dan Clancy, Peter Norvig, Jon Orwant, Steven Pinker, Martin A. Nowak, and Erez Lieberman Aiden. 2011. "Quantitative Analysis of Culture Using Millions of Digitized Books." *Science* 331 (6014): 178–82.

Morrell, Michael E. 2010. *Empathy and Democracy: Feeling, Thinking, and Deliberation*. University Park, PA: Penn State University Press.

Näsström, Sofia. 2011. "The Challenge of the All-Affected Principle." *Political Studies* 59 (1): 116–34.

Neblo, Michael A. 2003. "Impassioned Democracy: The Role of Emotion in Deliberative Theory." Paper presented at the Democracy Collaborative Affiliates Conference, Washington, DC.

———. 2007. "Family Disputes: Diversity in Defining and Measuring Deliberation." *Swiss Political Science Review* 13 (4): 527–57.

Nussbaum, Martha C. 2003. *Upheavals of Thought: The Intelligence of Emotions*. Cambridge: Cambridge University Press.

Ober, Josiah. 2008. *Democracy and Knowledge: Innovation and Learning in Classical Athens*. Princeton, NJ: Princeton University Press.

Owen, David. 2012. "Constituting the Polity, Constituting the Demos: On the Place of the All Affected Interests Principle in Democratic Theory and in Resolving the Democratic Boundary Problem." *Ethics and Global Politics* 5 (3): 129–52.

Page, Scott E. 2007. *The Difference: How the Power of Diversity Creates Better Groups, Firms, Schools, and Societies*. Princeton, NJ: Princeton University Press.

Parkinson, John. 2006. *Deliberating in the Real World: Problems of Legitimacy in Deliberative Democracy*. Oxford: Oxford University Press.

Polletta, Francesca, and John Lee. 2006. "Is Telling Stories Good for Democracy? Rhetoric in Public Deliberation after 9/11." *American Sociological Review* 71 (5): 699–723.

Rawls, John. 1971. *A Theory of Justice*. New York: Oxford University Press.

Rorty, Amélie Oksenberg. 1985. "Varieties of Rationality, Varieties of Emotion." *Social Science Information* 24: 343–53.

Sanders, Lynn. 1997. "Against Deliberation." *Political Theory* 25 (3): 347–76.

Skinner, Quentin. 1974. "Some Problems in the Analysis of Political Thought and Action." *Political Theory* 2 (3): 277–303.

Song, Sarah. 2012. "The Boundary Problem in Democratic Theory: Why the Demos Should be Bounded by the State." *International Theory* 4 (1): 39–68.

Steiner, Jürg, André Bächtiger, Markus Spörndli, and Marco Steenbergen. 2004. *Deliberative Politics in Action: Analysing Parliamentary Discourse.* Cambridge: Cambridge University Press.

Thompson, Dennis. 2008. "Deliberative Democratic Theory and Empirical Political Science." *Annual Review of Political Science* 11: 497–520.

Waldron, Jeremy. 1995. "The Wisdom of the Multitude: Some Reflections on Book 3, Chapter 11 of Aristotle's Politics." *Political Theory* 23 (4): 563–84.

Warren, Mark E. 2006. "What Should and Should Not Be Said: Deliberating Sensitive Issues." *Journal of Social Philosophy* 37 (2): 163–81.

Warren, Mark E., and Jane Mansbridge, with André Bächtiger, Maxwell A. Cameron, Simone Chambers, John Ferejohn, Alan Jacobs, Jack Knight, Daniel Naurin, Melissa Schwartzberg, Yael Tamir, Dennis Thompson, and Melissa Williams. 2014. "Deliberative Negotiation." In *Negotiating Agreement in Politics*, ed. Jane Mansbridge and Cathie Jo Martin, 86–120. Washington, DC: American Political Science Association.

Young, Iris Marion. 1996. "Communication and the Other: Beyond Deliberative Democracy." In *Democracy and Difference*, ed. Seyla Benhabib, 120–35. Princeton, NJ: Princeton University Press.

CHAPTER 3

Bringing Deliberation into the Developmental State

Peter Evans

Stereotypical visions of the state depict it as the antithesis of a deliberative space. States use bureaucratic hierarchies and command and control, not deliberation, to pursue their ends. Weber, not Habermas or Sen, is the relevant theorist.

Although these stereotypes capture an essential feature of the state, they are also deeply misleading. Effective state structures have always depended on deliberative spaces that include both key actors within the state apparatus and powerful private interlocutors. In the 21st century, deliberation has become even more crucial, because the state faces a set of tasks that require bringing in deliberation in a way that goes well beyond established traditions.

The success of early capitalist states was based on having deliberative systems as the core of the state. The interactions of the Doge's Council and Venetian merchants when the Venetian city-state was at its peak are a good example. Like Venice, the Dutch hegemony exemplified Marx's vision of the state as "the executive committee of the bourgeoisie" (Arrighi 1990). The ability of these states to effectively carry out a project of capitalist development depended on the deliberative processing of a full range of relevant information and decision making that reflected the shifting collective needs and interests of the capitalist class.

Deliberation played a role in the practices of the 20th century "developmental state" consistent with these earlier models. In Tokyo, Seoul, and Taipei, as in Venice and Amsterdam, successful state action depended on deliberative interchange with key capitalist elites. In the 20th century developmental state, the project was industrialization rather than commercial expansion, and the key interlocutors were industrialists.

Deliberation was crucial to the success of the 20th century developmental state in several ways. Discussions with industrialists were more effective than bureaucratic channels as a way of getting accurate information on what sort of industrial projects private capital was willing and able to support. Deliberative interactions were also an important part of securing private sector "buy-in." The result was not just the reinforcement of networks connecting the state and capital; deliberative interactions also contributed to the emergence of a more cohesive capitalist class with a sense of a shared national project. By bringing competitors together to discuss various projects of industrialization, the state facilitated communication among capitalists as well as its own communication with them. In contrast to predatory states, whose actions disorganized all classes, development states helped build a more cohesive capitalist class, in part through the deliberative arenas they fostered (Evans 1995).

If successful capitalist states have always depended on deliberative spaces connecting state managers with key actors from the fractions of capital most crucial to projects of accumulation, what does it mean to argue that bringing deliberation into the 21st century developmental state constitutes a new institutional challenge? To begin with, the deliberative processes that connect state actors and privileged sectors of the capitalist elite are too exclusionary to provide legitimacy in the contemporary world. The almost instantaneous delegitimization of the East Asian states after the 1997–98 financial crisis as cesspools of "crony capitalism" provided an excellent illustration of the vulnerability of these forms of legitimacy. Even more important is the inability of earlier exclusionary forms of deliberation to serve as effective instruments of the contemporary development agenda.

States whose aim is to promote the broader conception of development that Heller and Rao reference in chapter 1 need correspondingly broader forms of deliberative connections to society. Traditional forms of deliberation will no longer serve developmental states, for at least two interconnected reasons. First, contemporary conceptions of the goals have changed. As Heller and Rao (invoking Sen) put it in chapter 1, "the very understanding of development has dramatically shifted, from a narrow focus on economic transformation (summarized by either growth rates or industrialization) to a more holistic view." Second, and equally important, the processes that produce "development" in the old-fashioned sense of robust secular increases in productivity defined in conventional terms have come to be understood as depending much more on human capabilities than on the physical accumulation of capital. Expanding human capabilities requires a broader set of state society connections and therefore a very different model of deliberation.

In the brief comments that follow, I focus on two issues relating to the contemporary relation between deliberation and the state's efficacy as an agent of development. First, I explain why more deliberative state-society connections are essential to the developmental efficacy of the state (arguments I made in Evans 2010, 2014). Second, I review the challenges that states confront in realizing an expanded system of deliberation, considering both reasons why meeting these challenges is likely to be difficult and strategies for overcoming at least some of the obstacles.

Underlying both of these discussions is a simple basic proposition: just as the state must inevitably be part of any "deliberative system," states need to develop a special subset of the "nodes, forums, and processes" that constitute a deliberative system if they are to be effective.[1] Indeed, one could argue that this project constitutes one of the most central tasks of the modern developmental state. "Deliberative development" (Evans 2004) has become the foundation of effective public policy and efficient economic strategy; "bringing deliberation into the state" is crucial to the construction of a successful developmental state.

Recognizing the centrality of transforming the deliberative systems of the state also forces one to confront a sobering negative thesis. If an expanded deliberative system is essential but lies outside the politically feasible boundaries of institution building, then focusing on deliberation requires recognizing the likelihood that the project of the 21st century developmental state will fail. Providing a clear-headed assessment of this prospect without succumbing to uncompromising pessimism is the goal of the discussion that follows.

Why is deliberation essential to the 21st century developmental state?

At the most abstract level, any developmental state must perform at least three general roles:

- Be a vehicle for making social choices and defining developmental goals. Effectively implementing goals that are not what society wants is no better than being ineffectual.
- Foster the institutional capacity for collective action that maximizes the possibility of implementing the goals.
- Support a distribution of basic rights that gives individuals incentives to invest in their own capabilities and support such rights with "a program of skillful social support for health care, education and other relevant social arrangements" (Sen 1999, 46). Implementing such a program of social support also turns out to require deliberative systems.

For a developmental state focused on expanding its capabilities, the need for information and engagement from the broadest possible set of societal partners creates informational requisites vastly greater than those of a state seeking only to respond to and channel the interests of capital. Whether a particular state initiative is worthwhile depends not on some simple technocratic measure, such as rate of return on investment or projected market share, but on how well its results correspond to the collective preferences of the communities being served.

The collective preferences whose fulfillment is the measure of success do not exist a priori. As Sen insists, they can be discovered only in a process of public interchange. They emerge and evolve in the context of deliberative processes. Without deliberation, the state has no way of ensuring that it will not misdirect public investments and its own energies, undermining the impact of its developmental efforts. In their introduction to this volume (chapter 1), Heller and Rao propose that deliberation is a necessary condition for deepening democracy. It is equally reasonable to propose that deliberation is a necessary condition for effective developmental states.

The centrality of deliberation to effective state action goes beyond figuring out what kinds of public investments and programs correspond to collective preferences. Effective implementation depends on buy-in by citizens. Even programs that seem a priori to be of value for individual citizens are often woefully underutilized, even in developed countries.[2] In the case of capability-expanding services, effective engagement goes beyond simply accessing services. As Ostrom (1996) emphasizes, capability-enhancing services are always co-produced by their "recipients." The state needs their active engagement in the delivery of those services in order to ensure that they achieve their goals.

None of this is to argue that deliberation substitutes for coherent, well-managed bureaucratic apparatuses. Baiocchi, Heller, and Silva (2011) observe that in the case of participatory budgeting at the municipal level, once deliberation has produced a set of priorities for infrastructure spending (the execution of which does not require co-production), the biggest challenge to the legitimacy of the deliberative process is making sure that deliberative decisions get translated into actual infrastructure on the ground. Thus, just as deliberative processes are key to legitimating the bureaucratic apparatus of the state, effective bureaucracies play a key role in legitimating deliberative processes. Marrying the two is one of the principal challenges to building a deliberative system into the developmental state.

Obstacles to building developmental deliberative systems

Before examining the difficulties involved in marrying deliberative institutions with the hierarchical apparatuses that must continue to play a central role in state action, it is worth underlining the intrinsic difficulties involved in building deliberative systems. These institutions are simply very hard to build. In the absence of sustained commitment and politically astute strategizing, they will not emerge, even in the absence of concerted resistance—and resistance from within the state apparatus is likely. The problem is not simple one of "clashing cultures." It also reflects the fact that, by definition, deliberative systems reduce the power of state officials.

Having explored the "marriage problem," I turn to what is perhaps the most daunting obstacle to bringing deliberation into the state: resistance from the capitalist elites who were the principal beneficiaries of the traditional deliberative forms. These private elites are likely to resist the expansion of deliberative participation, and they have the power to do so effectively. The same political dynamics that are implicated in the "hollowing out" of representative democratic institutions (Evans 2004) also stand in the way of the expansion of deliberative forms.

Institution building is always onerous, but the construction of deliberative systems is a particularly demanding kind of institutional construction. Mackie's discussion (in chapter 5 of this volume) of the process through which the nongovernmental organization (NGO) Totsan went about constructing a deliberative system to support the abandonment of female genital cutting in Senegal is a perfect example. Institution building was unexpectedly successful around an issue that most people would have considered so deeply embedded in culture and history as to generate implacable popular resistance to change. Almost 5,000 villages embraced abandonment, and the government adopted a coordinated abandonment strategy that is projected to culminate in a national declaration of abandonment.

This success in expanding Senegal's deliberative system is heartening. Yet at the same time, the case underlines how arduous institution building is. Mackie notes that it took the most effective female genital cutting abandonment programs 1.5–3 years to facilitate deliberations about values among small core groups (as little as 1 percent of the population) (see chapter 5). These core groups actively diffuse those deliberations through the community, and three to five years after the program begins, remarkable community changes result. State officials looking for "results" would, in all likelihood, have given up on the project, given its tortoise-paced progress during the first three years or attempted to force the outcome, destroying the deliberative foundations that had been built and creating popular backlash. In short, this success makes it easy to understand why similar efforts may fail. The long-game

Resistance to the expansion of deliberative systems from within the state is easy to understand. Traditional state deliberative systems operated primarily at the pinnacles of state power, where, as Weber notes, politics dominates bureaucratic rules. An expanded deliberative system does not have this luxury. It must engage the middle and lower levels of the state apparatus and be supported by elite state managers. The hierarchical command and control moment of the state powerfully shapes the practices and consciousness of ordinary state officials. Asking them to embrace a different mode of decision making is asking them to give up the power, status, and privileges of being the official "deciders."

Relinquishing the power to direct state efforts and allocate resources has a variety of costs from the point of view of state managers. For some, the lost potential for diverting resources to their own ends may be primary. But even "clean," dedicated bureaucrats may find it difficult to give precedence to deliberative decisions. Elevating deliberative outcomes inevitably diminishes the value attributed to the training and expertise of bureaucrats. It is not simply a matter of threatened pride. The "wisdom of the crowd" is fallible. Community members may well make collective decisions that do not serve their own long-term interests. Expert state managers may be able to see the impending pitfalls without being able to persuade communities that their decisions will not bring them collectively closer to lives they have reason to value. To make matters worse, state incumbents are likely to be held accountable for outcomes even if decisions are made deliberatively. Trying to avoid this painful prospect could lead even the most well-meaning and sympathetic bureaucrat to resist the imposition of deliberative institutions.

The resistance of private elites is likely to be even more obdurate. The institutions of representative democracy have arguably been effective in providing capital with predictable rules and the core set of reliable institutions it needs. Nonetheless, Lenin's dictum that "a democratic republic is the best possible political shell for capitalism" needs some specification. Democratic politics is acceptable to capital insofar as it facilitates the productive adjudication of disputes among the most powerful private elites. Combining democratic forms with traditional exclusionary deliberative institutions is an attractive political amalgam for capital. If democratic forms become responsive to popular demands that are perceived to threaten elite interests, that attractiveness disappears.

Some observers would argue that the contemporary "hollowing out" of democratic institutions represents a deliberate and successful effort by capital to reshape representative democracy into a form more innocuous to its interests. Wolfgang Streeck (2011, 29), for example, laments "the drama of democratic states being turned into debt-collecting agencies on behalf of a global oligarchy of investors." Heller (2011, 2) does not directly finger the role of capital but has an equally critical analysis of the evolution of representative institutions, noting that "at an institutional level, the consolidation of formal representative institutions and the introduction of universal suffrage has failed to make the state and the process of making and implementing policies responsive to popular sovereignty."

If capital has an interest in subverting the institutions of representative democracy as instruments of popular sovereignty and a demonstrated capacity to do so, the prospects of constructing the kind of deliberative system that the 21st century state needs to succeed are reduced. One can imagine state managers eventually being convinced that deliberative institutions will enable them to do their jobs more effectively, but it is hard to imagine persuading capital of the same proposition.

In addition to confronting the intrinsic difficulties of building deliberative institutions—the "marriage problem" and the "capital problem"—any strategy for expanding deliberative institutions must also deal with "political society." Expansion of deliberation is not just about reconfiguring the relation between the state and "civil society." The formulation of collective preferences and their implementation must not only marry deliberative forms with the hierarchical aspects of the state apparatus and overcome the resistance of private elites; it must also marry the hard instrumental logic of political contestation to Senian deliberation and the Habermasian public sphere. Like it or not, "political society," with its self-interested political actors and the organizational vehicles and ideological projects they build to secure their ends, cannot be excluded from dynamics that connect the state to society.

It would be easy to conclude that the cumulative effect of these obstacles makes the construction of the deliberative system that the state needs to realize a 21st century developmental agenda a mission impossible. But this gloomy assessment is at odds with the recent spread of deliberative experiments. What accounts for the proliferation of deliberative innovations at the turn of the millennium?

The momentum of deliberative systems

If resistance by capital is the most powerful obstacle to constructing a deliberative system that will work for the developmental state, the powerful attraction of deliberative processes for ordinary citizens is the most obvious source of momentum. Deliberative systems are also attractive for a range of actors in political society.

In contrast to the limited degree to which it has been possible to translate deliberative decision making into concrete results, deliberative procedures have been remarkably successful in capturing the loyalties of participants. Just as the charisma of electoral democracy persists around the world despite the shallowness of its institutional instantiations, deliberative political forms have shown a surprising capacity to spread and gain adherents despite the paucity of their effects on resource allocation. Deliberative forms have shown an extraordinary ability to spread.

The rapid diffusion of participatory budgeting (see chapter 6 of this volume, by Gianpaolo Baiocchi) offers a dramatic illustration of the attractiveness of the promise of being able to allocate public resources through deliberative mechanisms. In the short space of 25 years, participatory budgeting has "been implemented in hundreds of cities on seven continents," according to Baiocchi. Clearly, like its ideological predecessor (democracy), the idea of deliberation has impressive political "legs." Complaints that in order to achieve worldwide success this particular deliberative form had to be instantiated in a form that made it unthreatening to private elites and state apparatuses are unquestionably true. But this fact does not negate the attractiveness of deliberation as a popular goal.

One of the best illustrations of the popularity of expanding these delibera-tive institutions is Hetland's (2014) ethnographic analysis of participatory budgeting in two Venezuelan cities during the Chavista period. He details how official (though highly ambivalent) support of the ruling party for participatory budgeting at the municipal level provided a natural experi-ment testing popular responses in the absence of real elite buy-in. The sub-sequent political trajectory showed the ability of participatory budgeting to generate a following among the local citizenry even when not imple-mented effectively. In the more progressive of the two cities, backlash caused by half-hearted implementation led to the replacement of the mayor with one more committed to participatory budgeting. In the more conser-vative municipality, the right of center mayor, who had no natural ideo-logical affinity for deliberative forms, embraced participatory budgeting as a means of increasing political support.

An optimistic reading of Hetland's Venezuelan cases would suggest that deliberative institutions carry a momentum of their own.[3] At least for some period of time, this momentum is relatively independent of the ability of these institutional innovations to deliver concrete payoffs. And discontent over the outcomes produced by deliberative forms is as likely to result in mobilization that deepens and strengthens deliberative forms as it is to lead to their abandonment.

The implication of these examples is that the intrinsic appeal of delib-erative systems is likely to make their expansion an attractive strategy, not just for ordinary citizens with a thirst for more control over their public institutions but also for the people who command political society. This attractiveness is the other face of the lack of threat to the status quo that incenses critics of the "sanitized" forms of participatory budgeting. It pro-vides a springboard for practical strategies to strengthen the deliberative moment.

Strategies for strengthening the deliberative moment

Three examples illustrate some of the strategic possibilities for expanding the deliberative system in ways that strengthen the state's developmental capacity. The first two are variations on the theme of political society serv-ing as the vehicle for the expansion of the deliberative system.

In the first variation (Kerala, India), the mobilizing democratic party state is the central actor, facilitating and benefiting from the emergence of civil society allies. The second variation (Brazil) is "a project civil society" in which "a wide range of associational forms and movements have devel-oped autonomous organizational capacity" (Heller 2011, 3). Alliances between political society (most obviously the Workers' Party) and civil society are central, but civil society also manages to project itself into the state apparatus. Both of these models depend on the commitment of political society (essentially political parties) and the state apparatus itself, in alliance with civil society groups, for the expansion of deliberation.

The third example is somewhat different. Dubbed by Fox (1994) the "sandwich" model, it relies on higher officials within the state apparatus who see political changes as necessary to realizing their agendas seizing on deliberative strategies as a way of finding a way around lower-level elites intent on blocking change. The World Bank–sponsored Kecamatan Development Project (KDP), in Indonesia, is an unusual but heuristically interesting example of the sandwich strategy (for details on KDP, see Guggenheim 2006; Guggenheim and others 2006; Gibson and Woolcock 2008; Barron, Diprose, and Woolcock 2011).

The Kerala model is well known. Communist Party organizers needed energized mass mobilization to displace traditional elites. Their mobilizational success translated into traditional electoral success and a (discontinuous) share of state power. But the fraction of the party that retained a transformative agenda found that participatory deliberative institutions were an essential vehicle for preserving this agenda (Heller 2005; Heller and Isaac 2005).

This symbiotic relation between the goals of people in the party and the state and the agenda of expanded participatory deliberation was repeated in a different form in Brazil. Like the Communist Party in Kerala, the Workers' Party in Brazil, in its phase as a mobilizing minority party, found participatory institutions a valuable vehicle for building oppositional strength. At the same time, the success of a broad, antiauthoritarian, cross-class alliance of civil society currents in an overall project of democratization led to a variety of civil society actors being incorporated directly into decision-making positions in the state apparatus, giving participatory projects launched from civil society the leverage they needed to succeed in a variety of policy projects. "It was social movements and a vibrant sector of activist NGOs that drew the state in by demanding participatory institutions of engagement and then projecting themselves into the state" (Evans and Heller 2015, 18). Effective state-society relations involved the transformation of the state itself, in terms of both adding state organizations such as sectoral policy councils and participatory budgeting councils, which institutionalize the participation of civil society within the state, and incorporating actors who identify themselves as agents of civil society into more traditional state agencies and bureaus.[4]

In both Kerala and Brazil, it was not so much that some unusual aspect of local deliberative traditions led to success. Rather, it was the fact that actors in political society and within the state itself shared an agenda with deliberative civil society institutions and saw those institutions supporting their own political agendas. In both cases, expansion of the deliberative system was associated with an increased capacity to deliver broad-based developmental benefits. Kerala's success at social development is iconic (though hotly contested by critics of the "Kerala model"). In the first decades of the 21st century, Brazil finally relinquished its status as the world champion of inequality, as state policies expanded the income of the poor and the delivery of basic services such as health and education gradually began to expand and improve.

Both cases are also useful in underlining that the persistence of the momentum of the expansion of deliberative space cannot be taken for granted. The coalitions that enable the expansion of the deliberative system and the related improvements in state capacity are always vulnerable.

There are always people within parties, states, and civil society organizations whose vested interests deliberative practices threaten. In addition, any strategy of expanding deliberative space that centers on political society requires that the party and its allies convince a substantial portion of the rest of society that their agenda represents a worthy national project. In Kerala electoral defeats are always a prospect. In Brazil the apparent political hegemony of the Workers' Party seemed to evaporate in June 2013, as massive, politically ambiguous street demonstrations incorporated a strong anti-party thread (Alonso and Mische 2014).

The Kecamatan Development Project (KDP) is a different sort of case and yields additional lessons. It is a variation on the sandwich model in which the upper echelon agenda of change comes not from higher levels within the national state apparatus but from an external bureaucratic apparatus—in this case, the World Bank. Change-minded technocrats at the Bank bet that fostering new deliberative systems would facilitate the economic outcomes they wanted more effectively than the political status quo. At the time they designed the project, there was no point in trying to bring deliberation into the Indonesian state, which lacked even a commitment to representative democracy. But external funding made the projects attractive to the Indonesian state; if communities bought into deliberative/ participatory practices, the sandwich would neutralize resistance from local elites. As important as direct project outcomes would be changes in commonsense assumptions about how development projects should be organized.

The project ended up being more successful than its originators could have imagined. Serendipitously, a democratic transition at the national level soon after the project was initiated led to support for deliberative strategies by policy makers inside the state apparatus, and the Indonesian government ended up adopting the KDP model as the National Community Empowerment Program (PNPM), which was projected to reach the gamut of Indonesian villages (Barron, Diprose, and Woolcock 2011). The sandwich efforts of external technocrats ended up providing the template for a nationwide deliberative system.

Whether or not the KDP ended up achieving better outcomes than more conventional projects is open to debate. But the project did foster the construction of a novel set of local deliberative institutions. And even if one is skeptical about the project's enduring political effects, no one denies that it introduced a new deliberative system to tens of thousands of Indonesian villages, despite a political context that was initially thoroughly hostile to allowing decisions on resource allocation to escape the control of the traditional political and economic hierarchy.[5]

These trajectories suggest that political society can end up being a powerful ally in the expansion of deliberative systems. Precisely because of the popular appeal of deliberative institutions, explicit agendas for expanding them can be attractive to political actors with progressive agendas. New deliberative institutions are not just means for achieving substantive goals. They are also instruments for garnering political support in contests with competing political currents, whether they are other factions within a party or other parties in a politically competitive system. In the KDP, supporting deliberation gave technocrats who were officially barred from intervening in national or local politics a way of pursuing progressive political agendas.

The fact that deliberation can be attractive to political society as well as to communities and ordinary citizens obviously improves the prospects for expanding deliberative systems. The question remains, however: Are the kind of deliberative systems that are enabled the kind of deliberative systems that are necessary for the success of the developmental state? Critics like Li (2007) and Cook and Kothari (2001) suggest that the deliberative systems that are installed are feasible precisely because they cannot really enable the reallocation of resources or power. Are these critics right? If so, is the quest for deliberative systems that make a difference quixotic?

The trajectory of deliberation: prospects and limits   *Against the markets*

The antinomies of the trajectory of deliberation in recent decades are delicately balanced between encouraging and disheartening. On the one hand, arguments that the role of deliberative systems will continue to expand around the globe are plausible. On the other hand, it is hard to see how the current expansion of deliberative systems will breach the substantive limits set by the current political economy. The plausible political path for the expansion of deliberative systems relies primarily on the confluence of popular support and support from political society (and/or progressive technocrats). The question is whether this confluence is sufficient to induce change that might threaten the material and political interests of private elites. At first glance, a pessimistic assessment would seem in order.

Currently, the arenas in which deliberation and participation are instantiated are far from the central levers of state power. Local decision making, usually limited to the allocation of marginal public resources, is the prime site for deliberation. The contrast with the increasing insulation of the most

crucial arenas of state power from democratic inputs of any kind—
epitomized by the push toward "independent" central banks—is striking.
As Baiocchi points out in chapter 6, even when deliberation is restricted to
the allocation of marginal public resources, it is restricted to institutional
forms that minimize the extent to which it disrupts established political
practice.

Li's (2007) critique of the KDP illustrates the difficulty of determining
whether current limits undermine the value of trying to construct new
deliberative systems. She quotes the villagers Guggenheim (2006) describes
who rejected a government project because it had no procedures for taking
into account their deliberations: "From now on we only want projects that
involve us in decisions. If KDP can do it, other projects can do it too"
(2007, 254). Li then goes on to argue that the villagers were in fact only
acting "within the limits that experts had prescribed" and that the KDP
was "regime friendly" because it was unwilling to take up issues like land
distribution.

Underlying the fight between Li and Guggenheim are two different
theories of the consequences of deliberative practices. In Li's view, engagement in deliberative practices distracts attention and energy from more
contentious forms of mobilization.[6] Guggenheim's example implies that
the practical implantation of deliberative systems has robust effects on
community visions, normative expectations, and political practices—
effects that have the potential to spill over and spread.

The best test of which position is more telling is systematic observation
of what happens when a deliberative system hits the limits of what it can
deliver. Do the communities involved decide that the promise of enhanced
political efficacy is a chimera and therefore become disenchanted and
demobilized? Or does frustration lead to mobilization and fights to extend
the scope and power of deliberative institutions? Hetland's Venezuelan
example can be read to support the second possibility, but there are certainly examples of the first path. Continued experimentation in pushing the
limits of where deliberation is allowed to survive is certainly in order, but
the question of whether the developmental state can get the deliberative
systems it needs remains unresolved.

Can the developmental state get the deliberative system it needs?

This brief effort to highlight the centrality of debates on deliberation to
the analysis of the efficacy of 21st century developmental states started
with three basic propositions. To begin, I underlined the fact that capitalist
states have always had a deliberative moment that was an essential complement to their character as command and control apparatuses, relying
on deliberative interaction with those capitalists who were most crucial to
their project. Second, I outlined some of the reasons why the deliberative

moment has become much more essential for the modern developmental state. Third, I pointed out that the project of the 21st century developmental state requires a transformation of the old deliberative system into one that encompasses a broad cross-section of the population, especially the disprivileged, for whom state action is most central. This transformed deliberative system is much more demanding and harder to construct.

If a transformed deliberative system is both more central to success and more difficult to construct, its construction becomes a primary challenge to the modern developmental state. There are good reasons why meeting this challenge may be a mission impossible. Most of them derive from the ability of the elites, inside and outside the state, who dominated and benefited from earlier deliberative systems to subvert, undermine, or reverse efforts to construct a transformed deliberative system. At the same time, the expansion of deliberative systems has a logic and momentum that cannot be dismissed.

Strategies for expanding deliberative systems continue to evolve in intriguing and sometimes unexpected ways, but their limits to date cannot be ignored; whether they can develop the political muscle to make significant differences in the distribution of resources and power remains to be seen. If there is a tipping point at which political momentum turns into entropy, it has not been reached yet, and acceleration cannot be ruled out.

One thing is clear: deliberative theory and state theory must become intertwined if either sort of theorizing is to move forward. Theorists of the state, as well as state managers and policy makers, need to understand what analysts of deliberation have to tell them. Students of deliberation need to understand that the state is not just an external influence on deliberative systems, using its monopoly on violence to preserve space for deliberation or undermining the possibilities for deliberation by imposing outcomes that ignore the preferences arrived at through deliberation. The state itself, particularly at its interface with society, is one of the central testing grounds for the possibilities for deliberation. Whether it becomes an arena of success or failure may well determine the overall possibilities for a deliberative system.

Notes

1. I adopt the term *deliberative system* from Mansbridge (chapter 2 of this volume), as well as her argument that the state is inevitably implicated in deliberative systems.
2. Moynihan and Herd (2010) cite findings that only about a quarter of people eligible for Medicaid in the United States actually use their benefits.
3. Research by Hetland (2015) on Bolivian municipalities offers a counterpoint to his Venezuelan results that is consistent with the cautionary observation of Baiocchi, Heller, and Silva (2011). He finds that the difficulty of integrating

deliberative systems with the institutional apparatus required to deliver results undermined the expansion of these systems in Bolivia.
4. The Brazil case raises the obvious question of why a similar pattern of apparent symbiosis of party and civil society agendas and the incorporation of civil society actors into the state apparatus had such different results in South Africa. For a discussion, see Heller (2011).
5. Both the economic and political outcomes of the project are, not surprisingly, disputed. Li (2007), for example, is highly critical of claims that the program had positive political effects. For a general review of programs of this ilk, see Mansuri and Rao (2013).
6. Li (2007) gives an example of the fight of the farmers of the Dongi-Dongi valley to protect their land from being taken over by a national park.

References

Alonso, Angela, and Ann Mische. 2014. "Changing Repertoires and Partisan Ambivalence in the New Brazilian Protests." Paper presented at the conference on "Advances and Challenges in the Politics, Society, and Social Policies of Contemporary Brazil." Watson Institute, Brown University, Providence, RI, November 15.

Arrighi, Giovanni. 1990. "The Three Hegemonies of Historical Capitalism." *Review* 13 (3): 365–408.

Baiocchi, Gianpaolo, Patrick Heller, and Marcelo K. Silva. 2011. *Bootstrapping Democracy: Transforming Local Governance and Civil Society in Brazil.* Stanford, CA: Stanford University Press.

Barron, Patrick, Rachel Diprose, and Michael Woolcock. 2011. *Contesting Development: Participatory Projects and Local Conflict Dynamics in Indonesia.* New Haven, CT: Yale University Press.

Cooke, B., and U. Kothari, eds. 2001. *Participation: The New Tyranny?* London: Zed Books.

Evans, Peter. 1995. *Embedded Autonomy: States and Industrial Transformation.* Princeton, NJ: Princeton University Press.

———. 2004. "Development as Institutional Change: The Pitfalls of Monocropping and Potentials of Deliberation." *Studies in Comparative International Development* 38 (4): 30–53.

———. 2010. "Constructing the 21st Century Developmental State: Potentialities and Pitfalls." In *Constructing a Democratic Developmental State in South Africa Potentials and Challenges,* ed. Omano Edigheji, 37–58. Capetown: HSRC Press.

———. 2014. "The Developmental State: Divergent Responses to Modern Economic Theory and the 21st Century Economy." In *The End of the Developmental State?* ed. Michelle Williams, 220–40. New York: Routledge.

Evans, Peter B., and Patrick Heller. 2015. "Human Development, State Transformation and the Politics of the Developmental State." In *The Oxford*

Handbook of Transformations of the State, ed. Stephan Leibfried, Frank Nullmeier, Evelyne Huber, Matthew Lange, Jonah Levy, and John D. Stephens. Oxford: Oxford University Press.

Evans, Peter, Evelyne Huber, and John Stephens. 2015. "The Political Foundations of State Effectiveness." Watson Institute Working Paper 2015-24, Brown University, Providence, RI. http://ssrn.com/abstract=2563253.

Fox, Jonathan. 1994. "The Difficult Transition from Clientalism to Citizenship." *World Politics* 46 (2): 151–84.

Gibson, Christopher, and Michael Woolcock. 2008. "Empowerment, Deliberative Development, and Local-Level Politics in Indonesia: Participatory Projects as a Source of Countervailing Power." *Studies in Comparative International Development* 43: 151–80.

Guggenheim, Scott. 2006. "Crises and Contradictions: The Origins of a Community Development Project in Indonesia." In *The Search for Empowerment: Social Capital as Idea and Practice at the World Bank*, ed. Anthony Bebbington, Michael Woolcock, Scott Guggenheim, and Elizabeth Olson, 111–44. Bloomfield, CT: Kumarian Press.

Guggenheim, Scott, Tatag Wiranto, Yogana Prasta, and Susan Wong. 2006. *Indonesia's Kecamatan Development Program: A Large-Scale Use of Community Development to Reduce Poverty*. Washington, DC: World Bank.

Heller, Patrick. 2005. "Reinventing Public Power in the Age of Globalization: The Transformation of Movement Politics in Kerala." In *Social Movements in India: Poverty, Power and Politics*, ed. Raka Ray and Mary Katzenstein. New York: Rowman and Littlefield.

———. 2011. "Towards a Sociological Perspective on Democratization in the Global South: Lessons from Brazil, India and South Africa." Paper prepared for the Comparative Research Workshop, Yale University, New Haven, CT.

Heller, Patrick, and Thomas Isaac. 2005. "The Politics and Institutional Design of Participatory Democracy: Lessons from Kerala, India." In *Democratizing Democracy: Beyond the Liberal Democratic Canon*, ed. Boaventura de Sousa Santos, 405–46. London: Verso.

Hetland, Gabriel. 2014. "The Crooked Line: From Populist Mobilization to Participatory Democracy in Chávez-Era Venezuela." *Qualitative Sociology*, DOI: 10.1007/s11133-014-9285-9.

———. 2015. "The Missing Link: The Challenge of Institutionalizing Participation in Urban Bolivia." Department of Sociology, University of California, Berkeley.

Kerstenetzky, Celia Lessa. 2014. "The Brazilian Social Developmental State: A Progressive Agenda in a (Still) Conservative Political Society." In *The End of the Developmental State?* ed. Michelle Williams. New York: Routledge.

———. 2012. *O estado do bem estar social na idade da razão: a reinvenção do estado social no mundo contemporâneo*. Rio de Janeiro: Elsevier (Campus).

Li, Tania. 2007. *The Will to Improve: Governmentality, Development, and the Practice of Politics*. Durham, NC: Duke University Press.

Mansuri, G., and V. Rao. 2013. *Localizing Development: Does Participation Work?* Washington, DC: World Bank.

Moynihan, Donald, and Pamela Herd. 2010. "Red Tape and Democracy: How Rules Affect Citizenship Rights." *American Review of Public Administration.* doi:10.1177/0275074010366732.

Ostrom, Elinor. 1996. "Crossing the Great Divide: Coproduction, Synergy, and Development." *World Development* 24 (6): 1073–87.

Sen, Amartya. 1999. *Development as Freedom.* New York: Knopf.

Streeck, Wolfgang. 2011. "The Crises of Democratic Capitalism." *New Left Review* 71 (September–October): 5–29.

CHAPTER 4

Success and Failure in the Deliberative Economy

Arjun Appadurai

The evidence we have so far—and our general intuitions about the conditions of poverty worldwide—suggest that the efforts of the poor to change their conditions through processes of democratic deliberation have frequently failed. This seems to hold both for the history of pro-poor legislation in the last century and in the data on small-scale deliberative institutions in practice. There are two ways to understand these failures. One is to argue that deliberation is in principle the wrong place to invest hopes, because all deliberative processes are embedded in and defined and constrained by the macro-logic of power, law, and markets, which do not yield to deliberative interventions. The other is to argue that there is a way to redesign the conditions of deliberation so as to produce more successes than failures on a case by case basis, and to allow a gradual aggregation of successful outcomes for propoor policies, allocations, or preferences to emerge. Almost half a century of efforts of

I am grateful to Biju Rao and Patrick Heller for inviting me to a World Bank conference in 2011, for which I wrote an earlier draft of this chapter. Their critical comments on that draft significantly helped clarify and strengthen the argument. I am also grateful for the comments of the other participants at the conference, especially Anis Dani, Peter Evans, Jane Mansbridge, and Michael Woolcock. Biju Rao has been a long-term interlocutor on these issues. This chapter is a further testimony to our shared interests and conversations. Gabika Bockaj and Benjamin Lee offered close readings and excellent suggestions. I shared a recent version of this argument with an audience at the India Institute of King's College in London, where I received rich comments and criticisms. A slightly different version of this chapter appears in *Reclaiming Democracy*, edited by Albena Azmanova and Mihaela Mihai (Routledge 2015).

this type in many parts of the developing democratic world suggest that doing so is a Sisyphean effort.

This chapter proposes a modified version of the second strategy, which is to look at the nature of the failures themselves as a route to incremental success in changing the contextual conditions that currently militate against the voices of the poor. This strategy requires a detour into some technical regions of the philosophy of language, so a plea for the patience of the reader is in order. What follows amounts to an argument that one can learn from failure, because it is not always what it appears to be.

This chapter is my entry point into a study of the ecology of failure in contemporary societies which are differentially affected by globalization. My long-term aim is not to provide an objective, technocratic, or context-free account of failure in human social life. Instead, the chapter is, as befits an anthropologist, a study of the discourses, meanings, and narratives that surround failure.

Globalization involves, among other things, the global circulation of key terms, standards, and ideologies of failure (failed states, failed markets, failed technologies, failed diplomacy, failed social movements). Specific societies do not simply accept and apply such globally circulating standards, however; they bring their own understandings of the meanings, symptoms, and effects of failure. Actual discourses of failure are, in fact, complex negotiated crystallizations of global and local discourses of failure. By looking closely at failure in the context of a particular group of urban activists, I hope to open up this discursive dynamic to closer study.

In my previous work on this movement, I argued that the "capacity to aspire" is a navigational capacity whose maldistribution is both a symptom and a catalyst of redistributive failure (Appadurai 2004). In this chapter, I show how a better understanding of the gaps between understandings of failure among global and local players can help promote 'voice' among the poor and marginalized people of the world.

The problem of deliberation

There is a general consensus among theorists of Western democracy that deliberation is preferable to aggregation as a model for shaping group preferences in democratic practice (Elster 1998; Gutmann and Thompson 2004). It has also been observed that deliberation may alter individual preferences, thus providing some compatibility between the two modalities of participation. The paucity of detailed descriptions of sustained delibera-tion provides an opportunity to consider what might be gained by close examinations of deliberative failure and, particularly, what might be learned about the subaltern struggle for voice by doing so.[1]

There is considerable evidence that in large-scale democracies in which poverty remains massive, the public sphere, in the Habermasian sense, is very limited. In India, for example, the vast majority of the voting population does not share anything resembling substantive equality with the relatively small minority that controls major allocative decisions, both in the structure of government and in the market. Women, people from lower castes, and religious/cultural minorities constitute a disproportionately large share of people living below the poverty line. All of these groups have been shown to be silent, occluded, or excluded in most contexts of formal public deliberation.

Of course, subaltern populations in India have long been involved in a large variety of engaged forums. Shadow publics, counter-publics, partial publics, and aspirational publics are a major feature of India's story in the second half of the 20th century. The poor show a remarkable commitment to electoral politics (Banerjee 2011). They have lent their strengths to a wide variety of grassroots efforts to combat domestic abuse, alcoholism, environmental depredation, economic discrimination, financial exclusion, and many other inequities (Batliwala and Brown 2006). I myself have found evidence of remarkable forms of "deep democracy" among India's urban poor (Appadurai 2001), which I have taken to be part of the effort of marginal populations to develop their "capacity to aspire" (Appadurai 2004).

Nonetheless, I believe that the conditions for free, egalitarian, transparent, and consequential participation have been largely lacking for the poor in India and many other parts of the world. Many forms of agrarian resistance, protest, mobilization, and "voice" have characterized India's marginalized populations, not only in recent decades but also during and even before the colonial period. In this sense, the subaltern has always spoken. But the conditions in which voice, opinion, aspiration, and participation are extended to marginal groups have generally been adverse, unfair, and unfavorable. These conditions have produced many deliberative failures and disappointments. My interest is in studying these failures more closely, for they may yield clues regarding the conditions under which voice is gained by people who have been disfavored in its distribution.

In general, the factors that militate against the ability of the poor to effectively exercise voice in democratic decision-making processes are "elite capture," patronage politics, low literacy and lack of information, corruption, intimidation, and coercion. Against this discouraging picture, there is some evidence from India of the deep attachment of the poorest of the poor to electoral politics (Banerjee 2011), of the value of public performances in the political sphere to the development of the "capacity to aspire" (Appadurai 2004), of the benefits of progress, of the right to information for the rural poor, and of their lively engagement in debates about the right to employment.

Nonetheless, it is not self-evident that the promotion of deliberative opportunities for the poor is a goal that is worthy of endorsement, refinement, and further institutionalization. One therefore needs to build a prior case for why deliberation has the potential to make a difference in changing the terms of recognition for the poor in the context of development. This case needs to be normative as well as practical.

The problem of context

The primary obstacles to the realization of the normative ideals of the deliberative approach to democratic participation frequently lie in the context of relevant factors outside the deliberative frame. Such contextual factors include the nature of extra-deliberative politics, such as the dependence of participants in the "frame" of deliberation on more powerful players for resources in structures of inequality, power, and patronage outside the frame; the limited access of many poor people to vital facts that bear on matters outside the frame; the macro-structure of distribution, in which the actual exchange of views by participants is less relevant than the power of a single key player (frequently representing the state), who is the primary addressee of all arguments and claims; and the general unresponsiveness of factors outside the frame (such as caste, class, and gender in India) to the outcomes of deliberation within the frame.

These considerations overwhelmingly support the view that internal processes within most relevant deliberative frames (such as village *panchayat*s in India) are adversely context driven and rarely context-changing or context-shaping events. Before considering how to alter this state of affairs in the interests of more inclusive development, one needs to pay closer attention to the idea of context itself.

There has been some degree of self-conscious reflection among anthropologists and linguists in recent times about the idea of context (Dilley 1999; Duranti and Goodwin 1992; Coleman and Collins 2006; Kopytko 2003). Wittgenstein's writings on language-in-use and language games did much to detach the idea of linguistic meaning from its semantic field alone and launch a deep interest in language pragmatics (H. Paul Grice, John Langshaw Austin, John Searle, and others worked in the broadly Wittgensteinian tradition).

It may seem farfetched to look deeply into the idea of context in linguistic and philosophical discussions for help in analyzing deliberation and development. It is not. Context is a default concept in virtually all social science fields that are sensitive to the frame in which any action, cultural pattern, or institutional form is located. Most commentators attribute the concept of framing to the work of Erving Goffman, especially his 1974 book, *Frame Analysis: An Essay on the Organization of Experience*. Goffman used the idea of frames to label "schemata of interpretation" that allow individuals or groups "to locate, perceive, identify, and label" events and occurrences, thus rendering meaning, organizing experiences, and guiding actions.

The idea of context is part of the common sense of social science. Yet it is usually used uncritically. A more reflective and less commonsensical use of the idea of context is needed for a process such as deliberation, which, by definition, points to a space or site of discourse that is separated from the ordinary course of life. Context is even more relevant to the analysis of poverty, equality, and participation, in which poor people are frequently marginalized not by intraframe but by extraframe factors of the sort already discussed.

From the philosopher's point of view, Kopytko (2003) captures the frustration with the idea of context:

> The scope of interactional context is indefinite and infinite because each context is embedded in its own context that is embedded in its context and so on; in consequence, the situation of infinite contextual regress follows. Although for researchers this question remains a philosophical quandary, for language users it is much less so, because, after all, they are capable of communicating effectively most of the time.

Others have also expressed this frustration about context, the sense that it is an infinitely regressive Chinese box, with no limit (Culler 1981; Cicourel 1992). Jonathan Culler writes that "meaning is context-bound, but context is boundless" (1981, 23). He made the remark in a careful argument on behalf of Jacques Derrida, whom Searle attacked for his critique of Austin's famous discussion of how performatives are to be properly distinguished from constatives. This debate, which seems somewhat distant from the problems of deliberation, exclusion, and poverty, is in fact quite relevant, insofar as it refers to speech acts that are neither true nor false, produce effects by virtue of conforming to a set of conventions that surround them (in some sort of context) but cannot be read from the words themselves.

A famous Austinian example of a performative is the statement of the judge in the context of a marriage of the form "I now pronounce you man and wife," which takes effect and acquires illocutionary force from its contextual compliance with a series of conventions, such as the legal power of the judge to perform such an action, the serious intentions of the man and woman, the absence of prior unions by the two of them, and so forth. Austin's idea of illocutionary force has been the subject of much contention in the years since his original formulations, but it is invariably taken to refer to the force attaching to certain kinds of speech acts that cannot be reduced to their referential or truth value. Illocutionary force is what characterizes speech acts whose intention is to produce certain effects having to do not with the words that are used but with their conventional and contextual understanding by those who are in the relevant context or frame of the utterance.

Most deliberative contexts in which issues of development, equality, and voice are played out in the real world involve conventional ways of speaking that are intended to produce certain effects on the allocation of public resources, which are often in the hands of the (near or distant) developmental state. People who are marginal in the distribution of both material and symbolic resources in real world situations where deliberative procedures are part of the politics of resource allocation are almost always at a disadvantage in what one might call the "political economy of felicity" (in Austin's sense). By "felicity" Austin meant to indicate that set of contextual preconditions that make it possible for a speech act, such as a performative, to have illocutionary or perlocutionary force—in other words, for it to do something rather than simply say something.[2]

The Habermasian model of rational discourse, which is the normative condition for the exchange of views in the public sphere (his equivalent of the imagined space of deliberative discourse), presumes free actors who are in formally equal positions with respect to the matters at issue. This equality is both the formal prerequisite and the (deepened) substantive outcome of rational deliberation in the Habermasian public sphere. The problematic of global development is precisely the radical absence of these conditions, in regard to both the material disposition of resources among speakers and the prior disposition of the "terms of recognition" (Appadurai 2004).

In terms of the discursive and material conditions of radical inequality, the defining characteristic of the situations of most concern here, it can be argued that the problem of the political economy of felicity (namely, that feature of the conventions defining the probability that a particular speaker's performative argument about some change in the current disposition of resources will succeed as a performative) is that it will never favor the poor until the very context of conventions about felicity is changed. In short, how can one produce conditions that favor the possibility that the public arguments, claims, requests, and demands of the poor will have performative purchase? Creating such conditions amounts to increasing the probability that the poor will be able to change rather than merely comply with the context. Put yet another way, how can one pursue the objective of producing conditions in which the felicity of certain requests or demands consists not of their relative compliance with the conventions that define the relevant context but of their potential to change the conditions which define the context?

"Failed" performatives

The evidence presented so far on the speech forms deployed by the poor and the disadvantaged in contexts of public deliberation over resource allocations suggests that they are frequently in the form of requests, one of the important forms that performative speech acts can take. Statements contributed by women, marginal social groups, and the poor are often "failed performatives"—speech acts that fail to have the effects they seek on their addressees, whether one takes these addressees to be all members of the relevant forums or just the actors who make the final allocative decisions that are the subject of the request.

It is not my aim to contribute to the technical debates among linguists and philosophers about what can be learned from failed performatives. I would like to observe, however, that what is most interesting about the failure of requests by the poor to change the current disposition of resources through their requests in public deliberations is not that the requests fail in most instances (contingently, statistically, and post facto) but rather that they appear to be (generally) doomed to fail because of the political economy of the felicity conditions of these statements in their specific contexts.

Let me explain this important step in my argument. The idea of the failed performative is part of an important line of argument about Austin's ideas (Felman 1983; Butler 1990, 2004; Medina 2006) that seeks to uncover in the space of "failure" the logic of irony, subversion, resistance, and creativity. Judith Butler's work, perhaps the best known of these efforts, is based on a form of radical constructivism developed in the context of gender and queer theory and derived in part from the work of Jacques Lacan. This constructivism is used to make the argument that apparently biological forms, such as the gendered body, are in fact embodied constructions produced by the culturally normative repetitions of certain performative actions. As these performatives rely on established hetero-normative conventions, in Butler's argument, they produce installed, gendered bodies that are the product of preexisting scripts that have already been rehearsed.

Butler considers the possibility of failure in performatives, which she views as the "political promise of the performative" (1997, 161). She argues that because the performative needs its conventional power, convention itself has to be reiterated. In this reiteration, the performative can be expropriated by unauthorized usage and thus create new possible futures. "When Rosa Parks sat in the front of the bus," she explains, "she had no prior right to do so guaranteed by any . . . conventions of the South. And yet, in laying claim to the right for which she had no prior authorization, she endowed a certain authority on the act, and began the insurrectionary process of overthrowing those established codes of legitimacy" (Butler 1997, 147).

Shoshana Felman (2002, 45) takes up the question of the infelicitous utterance (the misfire) when she states that "infelicity, or failure, is not for Austin an accident of the performative, it is inherent in it, essential to it.

In other words . . . Austin conceives of failure not as external but as internal to the promise, as what actually constitutes it."

I would suggest that the approach to the "constitutive failure" at the heart of Austin's idea of the performative, which is shared by Felman and Butler, is the most fruitful in imagining the apparently hopeless efforts of the poor to gain voice in public deliberative forums. For Felman, the possibility of performative failure is inherent to all performatives; it is their structural Achilles' heel. Butler (1997) picks up on this idea. She notices that conventions need to be reiterated in order to retain their power as conventions but that this reiteration opens the door to "misfires," irony, subversion, and change. In her later work on queer politics (2004), she shows that reiteration is the route by which marginal or subaltern discourses uttered in semipublic (alternative) settings such as nightclubs and private homes can slowly inch their way into the public sphere, where they can (retrospectively) become the basis for the sort of identity declaration that constitutes "coming out" at the level of the queer individual and a transformation of the public sphere at the level of the category of queer people in a particular society or polity. In short, today's performative failure can be part of the basis for tomorrow's performative success, because all social conventions require iteration and repeat performance if they are to gain force and credibility.

It is important to make a few distinctions and qualifications. Not all performative failures are alike, and not all failures have the capacity to ignite a productive deliberative chain (a concept I discuss in the following section). Some performative contexts are structurally illegitimate. One example is forced or staged contexts, such as meetings between cynical outside commercial interests and community leaders in which the meeting is nothing but a charade. Another is when the state, in an effort to propitiate a donor, stages a local deliberative event, sparking hopes for state responsiveness after the project cycle is over. Failures in such contexts can reinforce cynicism, apathy, and even "exit" (in Albert Hirschman's sense of the term [1970]). Arguably, this sort of failure is more the rule than the exception in societies of deep structural inequality.

What is of greater interest is the fact that failures generate further efforts to create voice, producing something like an energy-producing performative chain. Unlike a nuclear reaction, however, this sort of performative chain can be gradual and discontinuous, spread out over months and years rather than seconds and minutes. Its social life is hard to predict, but it is possible to make some characterizations of this sort of event post facto.

It is this generative type of failed performative that has the greatest potential for increasing the voice of the poor in public deliberative forums in democratic societies. Taken by themselves, in single contexts, many statements by the poor have no positive effects and may be considered failures.

But as they are repeated, rehearsed, and reiterated, might their failure contain the seeds of performative success?

Evidence from the field

I present some vignettes from my fieldwork over the past 10 years with a global network of activist slum dwellers, spread across more than 30 countries, with a focus on India and South Africa. The purpose of this ethnographic exercise is to establish a preliminary method for identifying those performative actions, chains, and contexts that appear to change the context by generating fissile energies that other performative interventions by the poor fail to do.

The vignettes illustrate how failures in the sphere of public deliberation may open the space for success in conditions of extreme adversity, global demand to adjust and adapt, and unusual pressures to both react to crises and wait patiently for significant change in the material conditions of member communities. In Appadurai (2001, 2004) I describe my experiences with members of Slum/Shackdwellers International (SDI). This global network of activists, scholars, and urban slum dwellers works for secure tenure; economic rights; relocation and rehabilitation; and savings, credit, and sanitation initiatives on behalf of the poorest of the urban poor in more than 30 countries, mostly in Africa, India, and Southeast Asia. I worked with members of this network, primarily in India and in South Africa, for about a decade, to better understand, interpret, and represent to the scholarly and policy communities their vision, strategy, and politics, which evolved over almost two decades of learning, networking, and advocacy on behalf of the urban poor.

Between 2000 and 2007, I spent time with members of SDI at various levels and contexts, ranging from housing exhibitions, political negotiations, meetings, conferences, public rallies, and performances in Mumbai, Manila, Durban, Cape Town, Johannesburg, the Hague, London, New York, and Vancouver. These events included discussions with urban planners; strategic discussions with community members and leaders; consultations with funders, lenders, and scholars; and interventions with planners, politicians, and ministers concerned with housing in India, the Philippines, and South Africa.

A consistent feature of my encounters with the slum communities that are "federated" to form this global network is singing and dance as critical elements of their gatherings, both small and large. This contribution to the repertoire of SDI comes mostly from the poor women from various settlements in the poorest parts of South Africa, including Cape Town, Johannesburg, Durban, and many more remote communities.

When members of these communities visit India, they often build relations with Indian slum dwellers through song and dance. I witnessed one such encounter in 1998, in the apartment of a close friend, Sundar Burra, who first introduced me to SDI. The occasion was a learning-oriented visit to Mumbai by about a dozen poor female slum dwellers from Cape Town. It was the group's first visit to India. They were in the middle-class apartment of my friend, at that time in transition from a civil service career to full-time engagement with SDI. There were also about a dozen women from the core women's group that formed the base of the network in India, the Mahila Milan, about which I have written elsewhere (2001). Also present was a small group of shy young women from Nepal (mostly from Kathmandu) who belonged to a federation of the homeless.

The language gaps were considerable, with English a very loose contact language. The Mumbai women had come together for a meeting related to their savings activities and were relaxing after a business session. The Nepali women were exploring Mumbai for the first time. They were awed by the women from Cape Town. Before long, and without any alcohol, the conversations became raucous and the Cape Town women were on their feet, dancing and encouraging the Indian and Nepali women to dance and sing along with them.

Although some of the Indian women were former sex workers from one of Mumbai's roughest neighborhoods, their codes of public decorum, the relatively luxurious Mumbai apartment, and the presence of visitors and friends from overseas at first constrained their comportment. But their tendency toward the ribald and the raucous soon got the better of them, and they joined in, singing and dancing themselves. This moment was tricky, because for the Mumbai women from the Nagpada slums, dancing is associated with sex work (at least in its rosier images), and the presence of a few men in the room (several known to them) gave the scene some of the risqué ambience of the *mujra*.[3] The Nepali women, who were, on average, much younger than their Indian and South African counterparts, were shyest about joining in or contributing something from their own musical or dance repertoires. But they were clearly amused, shocked, intrigued, and delighted to be in this milieu of female solidarity and ribaldry. This was surely a Butlerian moment.

I witnessed many such occasions over the next 10 years or so and was able to see a process at work. In 2001, I participated in a major rally organized by the local African federation of SDI in Piesang River, a shack community on the outskirts of Durban. The rally was part of a major regional and national effort to convene and mobilize thousands of shack dwellers tied to the federation for a major public rally in Durban, which I also attended. The Piesang River gathering was on the home turf of some of the federation's most active leaders, several of whom lived there. The highlight was a visit to the community by the South African minister for housing.

How deliberative?

This description of the event comes from the website of a sister organization, the Asian Coalition for Housing Rights:

> Over 10,000 members of the South African Homeless Peoples'
> Federation and allied organizations descended on King's Park
> Sports Complex in Durban on Sunday, October 1st, for the Southern
> African launch of the UNCHS Campaign for Secure Tenure.
>
> Exceeding all expectations of the organizers, grassroots savings
> groups from all of South Africa's provinces traveled to the event in
> nearly 100 buses and dozens of minibus taxis. Joining them were
> delegations from urban poor Federations in Zimbabwe, Namibia,
> India, and the Philippines. The Filipino government also sent its
> housing minister. A. Jockin and Jesse Robredo, recipients of the
> prestigious 2000 Magsaysay Award, were also in attendance. Also
> represented were international development organizations such as
> the UNCHS [UN Habitat], the World Bank, and several bilateral
> development agencies.
>
> On hand to greet the visitors were politicians and officials from
> Durban, kwaZulu-Natal province, and the South African govern-
> ment. South African Housing Minister Sankie Mthembi-Mahanyele
> was the keynote speaker.
>
> Mthembi-Mahanyele captured the spirit of the carnival-like event
> by saying that South Africa's housing drive had been made pos-
> sible by "the partnership formed between the government and her
> people." She went on to say that "most of these [People's Housing
> Process] initiatives were led by women groups within the South
> African Homeless Peoples' Federation."
>
> An important goal of the UNCHS campaign is to gain concrete
> government support for secure tenure for the poor.
>
> Mthembi-Mahanyele took up the challenge: "On June of this year,
> the Agriculture and Land Affairs Minister announced in Parliament
> that government will transfer ownership of 15 million hectares of
> land in the next five years to the poor."
>
> Rose Molokoane, National Chairperson of the SAHPF [South
> African Homeless People's Federation], indicated that the Federation
> and allied groups would immediately begin work to prepare to par-
> ticipate in this programme. "Without land our people are dying a
> natural death. We have thousands of members all over South Africa
> who are willing and able to use secure tenure to build themselves
> and the country."

This description mentions the carnival-like spirit of the event. Indeed,
singing and dance were a major part of the celebrations. Young boys
performed Zulu dances in full martial attire, women and men sang the

national anthem, and the audience spontaneously broke into singing and dancing on several occasions. Later the minister paid a visit to the Piesang River community, where she was enveloped in a massive display of SDI community-based discourse, speeches, exhortations, promises, requests, and commands (a veritable feast of Austinian performatives) addressed to other members and to the visitors from India, the Philippines, Thailand, the United Kingdom, and the United States. Many of the speakers combined oratory in Zulu and English with exhortatory speeches and breaks into dance and playful ribaldry. The most important features of this extraordinary event was that the minister herself was drawn into the spirit of this carnivalesque feast of performatives and rendered both a subject and an object of the performative utterances about the importance of secure housing for the shack dwellers of her country.

The same year, members of SDI received permission to build a model house and a set of toilets in the main lobby of the United Nations (UN) headquarters in New York. When the Secretary-General, Kofi Anna, paid an unplanned visit to see the exhibits, SDI members engaged in a performative carnival. A delighted group of slum activists surrounded the Secretary-General and the Executive Director of the United Nations Human Settlements Programme (UN Habitat), Anna Tibaijuka, in a spontaneous scene of singing, dancing, and cheering, marking the aspirational presence of the poor in the hallowed lobby of the United Nations.

These events are just a few of the myriad occasions of gathering, speech making, mobilization, celebration, and public performance by members of the SDI network at numerous scales. A variety of outsiders—including bankers, scholars, consultants, donors, ministers, and ordinary passersby—witnessed these events, which took place in various venues, from homes to UN conferences; moods, from pessimism to hope; and milieus, from hospitable to hostile.

In isolation and confined to their most immediate context, these occasions could be considered failed performatives (or containing many failed performatives)—requests ignored, promises unkept, contracts broken—by a variety of powerful individuals and institutions. But in the decade or more that I have been observing these events, and noticing their performative qualities, I have noticed a certain logic of cumulation, context building, and altered subjectivity.[4] This logic needs to be precisely characterized.

I referred above to the political economy of felicity and to the important difference between context legibility (which is equivalent to felicity) and change in the effect of speech acts on their contexts. Too often the statements of the poor appear unable to change their contexts; as these contexts are already tailored so as to deny or diminish their voices, the process of context change is important to identify.

In the work of Felman and Butler, there is a sense that the possibility of failure is inherent in the nature of performatives (hence the term "constitutive failure") but that through reiteration, rehearsal, and repetition, certain apparent performative failures can lay the grounds (or incrementally "change the frame") for later speech acts, thus creating a terrain that can be retroactively mobilized to create a performative chain that yields success out of a string of apparent failures.[5]

The use of singing and dance in quasi-public or public performances can be seen as this sort of retroactive performative chain: the performances, in which various speech acts are embodied and embedded, are rehearsals of an ongoing strategy for binding the addressee to respect a claim, honor a request, or fulfill a promise. The public performance of a spontaneous dance in the lobby of the United Nations created a permanently recorded media moment in which Kofi Annan can be said to have legitimized and even "inaugurated" an exhibition of a model house and toilet complex in the belly of the UN headquarters. This act constituted a public promise by Kofi Annan that will never be subject to the full test of whether it was a success or a failure.

The United Nations' Millennium Development Goals (MDGs), the centerpiece of Annan's vision, were noteworthy for including an SDI leader, Sheela Patel, in deliberations in the early years of the millennium. SDI's spontaneous, ad hoc, and risky effort to beard the Secretary-General in his own den, by means of an adroitly staged public performance of speech, song, and dance, could not have occurred without a long and varied prior set of rehearsals in which other addressees, visitors, friends, and potential benefactors had been drawn into similar carnivalesque public promissory performances, any one of which might be designated in isolation as a "failed" performative. From this point of view, the predicament of people without voice in public forums, or people whom the rigidity of the adversarial context seems to doom to failed performatives, are obliged to cast many performative seeds on the ground, in order to "mark the territory" of their aspirations.[6] These markings, which are the traces of what appear to be failed performatives, constitute a bodily archive of actions, effects, memories, and desires that can be mobilized by the right emergent conjuncture of contextual conditions to yield a performative claim that may be harder to ignore.

What is important here is that from one performative context to another lies a chain of resemblances that might be called polythetic (Needham 1975), in which any two proximate events or experiments may resemble each other closely but commonalities are not found across the entire chain. Such polythetic classes (which also contain what Wittgenstein called "family resemblances") are generated by the active and steady production of failed performatives, which alter the context incrementally so that the political economy of felicity begins to shift in favor of the poor in forums of public deliberation. Insofar as these performative chains appear in deliberative contexts, one can regard them as producing deliberative chains.[7]

I use the term *deliberative chains* to refer to links between deliberative contexts that are not based on the similarity of successive contexts but on the similarity (polythetic and incremental) between failed performatives, each of which lays some of the ground for the next rehearsal but any one of which has the potential to have a frame-changing (or context-changing) effect because of the mobilized history of prior (apparent) failures. Not all performative failures produce deliberative chains; the SDI examples allow me to identify what distinguishes "true" failures from "apparent" failures—that is, failures that have the potential to create deliberative chains.

The situations in which generative failures occur appear to share three important characteristics:

1. Members of elite groups are brought into contexts controlled by the marginal or excluded population (community celebrations, political rallies, social gatherings, official ceremonies). In some cases, the context may be neutral or even hostile to the interests of the poor, but the poor are able to effect some sort of transformation (as in the lobby of the UN building) to render the space their own, even if temporarily. The poor host rather than appear as guests in the performative context.

2. The subaltern group controls the idiom of the performative context (song, dance, and other forms of community practice and discourse), to define the tone, affective state, and ethos of the event, within which bold performative events have the greatest chance of being felicitous and effective.

3. "Elite capture" exists, not in the standard negative sense of the term but in the sense that these events often involve surrounding targeted members of the decision-making classes with others who have previously been partly or completely converted to the democratic cause in question. In almost all the major events hosted by SDI, major politicians and policy makers are surrounded by other members of various elites who have already signed on to the cause of the urban poor. Their presence increases the comfort level for all actors, enhancing the sense of trust, intimacy, and sincerity attached to these contexts.

More empirical studies are needed to better understand the critical differences between truly failed performatives and performatives with the potential for a chain reaction in the future, so that this preliminary typology of what constitutes success as the potential product of a chain of deliberative failures can be refined.

Deliberative chains and the capacity to aspire

In a 2004 paper outlining a broad approach to the challenges of poverty reduction, I proposed that aspiration was a cultural and navigational capacity whose deliberate enhancement would positively affect the "terms of recognition." In proposing this approach, I was motivated partly by an interest in creating a new platform for combining "recognition-centered" approaches with "redistribution-centered" approaches to inequality and poverty. In that context, I pointed out the ways in which certain public forums for speech, debate, and persuasion offered occasions for slum dwellers to experiment with binding politicians and bureaucrats to make commitments to the urban homeless. At the time I had not looked more closely at the challenges of the conditions in which the poor are at a disadvantage in most deliberative contexts involving people in positions of greater power and privilege, and I had not realized that the conditions of success and failure for the performative speech acts of the poor were not well understood.

It might be useful to ask how the kind of context I have sought to identify—one in which (apparently) failed performatives have long-term potential for producing a generative deliberative chain—can be contrasted with some better-known examples of deliberative success, such as the participatory budgeting model first introduced in Porto Alegre, Brazil, and the process of political decentralization followed, with significant success, in Kerala, India. Both locales enjoyed special conditions, including remarkable commitments on the part of city authorities in Brazil and very high rates of adult literacy in Kerala. More important, these cases of deliberative success are top-down efforts and thus not characterized by the importance of performative actions and efforts on the part of the poor. Performative actions and efforts by the poor are my main concern in this chapter, because they contain elements of surprise, of success engendered by apparent failure. The two kinds of example—the bottom-up style and the top-down style—may need to be examined and harvested together, in order for some of the predictability, protocol, and transparency of top-down processes to be combined with the spontaneity, cultural resonance, and subaltern spirit of bottom-up processes, which are crucial to building the capacity to aspire. An exchange of properties between different sorts of context might greatly increase the potential of deliberative contexts in unequal societies to expand the number, variety, and power of various emergent public spheres.

In light of these arguments about frames, contexts, failed performatives, and the profile of deliberative chains that can produce success out of apparent failures, I am now in a better position to suggest why one should encourage the participation of the poor in forms of deliberative process that have one or more of the characteristics I have identified. Through the gradual change of contexts that the chain of performative failures may enable, even failed performatives can change the climate and the context in which the poor are able to develop their voices. If analysis of more evidence from developmental sites in which deliberative contexts are studied over time bears this conclusion out, the following maxim could be added to the inventory of ways in which the capacity to aspire might be strengthened: Let a thousand failures bloom—and the successes will take care of themselves!

Notes

1. For some close descriptions of deliberation, see Mansbridge (1980); Baiocchi (2005); Rao and Sanyal (2010); and Barron, Diprose, and Woolcock (2011).
2. The debates over the status of Austin's distinctions between performatives and constatives—the very heart of his theory of speech acts—have been the subject of a deep and ongoing set of debates that included thinkers as varied as Emile Benvensite, John Searle, and Jacques Derrida, all of whom sought to understand the distinctions between meaning and force in the social life of language. More recently, Judith Butler, Michel Callon, and others debated the nature of financial markets and instruments. For a fascinating contribution to these debates, see Felman (1983). I am grateful to my colleague Benjamin Lee (The New School) for many enlightening conversations and writings about this tradition (see Lee 1997).
3. *Mujra* is the stylized dance form that accompanies courtesanal cultures in North India. It is the model for certain production numbers ("item" numbers, in Bollywood parlance) in films, cabarets, and clubs in which a woman dances for a largely male audience with the subtext of subsequent paid sexual availability to the most generous patron.
4. A core term for the organizers and activists of the SDI network is *ritual*, which they use to emphasize their wish to create routines and precedents out of experiments and interventions. The creation and refinement of rituals (of enumeration, of savings, of house building, and the like) is part of the conscious politics of this movement. It reflects the understanding that rituals are not museums of habit but stages for social innovation, something about which professional social scientists have been much less clear.
5. I owe the term *performative chain* to José Medina (2006), who uses it to describe this sort of unpredictable but plausible chain of connections between performatives from different contexts that can help produce what he calls "felicitous subjects" as well as "felicitous statements" out of what were previously infelicitous ones.
6. I owe the image of "marking the territory" to a conversation with Benjamin Lee.
7. In using the term *deliberative chain*, I mean to link the sense of the "performative chain" as identified by Medina (2006) to the study of the failed performative and the growing literature on the commodity chain in economics and anthropology, in order to capture the global itineraries of common as well as unusual commodities.

References

Appadurai, Arjun. 2001. "Deep Democracy: Urban Governmentality and the Horizon of Politics." *Environment and Urbanization* 13 (2): 23–43. doi:10.1177/095624780101300203.

———. 2004. "The Capacity to Aspire: Culture and the Terms of Recognition." In *Culture and Public Action*, ed. Vijayendra Rao and Michael Walton. Stanford, CA: Stanford University Press.

Baiocchi, Gianpaolo. 2005. *Militants and Citizens: The Politics of Participatory Democracy in Porto Alegre*. Stanford, CA: Stanford University Press.

Banerjee, Mukulika. 2011. "Elections as *Communitas*." *Social Research: An International Quarterly* 78 (1): 75–98.

Barron, Patrick, Rachael Diprose, and Michael J. V. Woolcock. 2011. *Contesting Development: Participatory Projects and Local Conflict Dynamics in Indonesia*. Yale Agrarian Studies Series. New Haven, CT: Yale University Press.

Batliwala, Srilatha, and L. David Brown. 2006. *Transnational Civil Society: An Introduction*. Bloomfield, CT: Kumarian Press.

Butler, Judith. 1990. *Gender Trouble: Feminism and the Subversion of Identity*. New York: Routledge.

———. 1997. *Excitable Speech: A Politics of the Performative*. New York: Routledge.

———. 2004. *Undoing Gender*. New York: Routledge.

Cicourel, Aaron. 1992. "The Interpretation of Communicative Contexts: Examples from Medical Encounters." In *Rethinking Context: Language as an Interactive Phenomenon. Studies in the Social and Cultural Foundations of Language*, vol. 11, ed. Alessandro Duranti and Charles Goodwin. Cambridge: Cambridge University Press.

Coleman, Simon, and Peter Collins. 2006. *Locating the Field: Space, Place and Context in Anthropology*. A.S.A. Monograph, vol. 42. Oxford: Berg.

Culler, Jonathan D. 1981. *The Pursuit of Signs: Semiotics, Literature, Deconstruction*. Ithaca, NY: Cornell University Press.

Dilley, Roy. 1999. *The Problem of Context. Methodology and History in Anthropology*, vol. 4. New York: Berghahn Books.

Duranti, Alessandro, and Charles Goodwin. 1992. *Rethinking Context: Language as an Interactive Phenomenon. Studies in the Social and Cultural Foundations of Language*, vol. 11. Cambridge: Cambridge University Press.

Elster, Jon. 1998. *Deliberative Democracy*. Cambridge Studies in the Theory of Democracy. New York: Cambridge University Press.

Felman, Shoshana. 1983. *The Scandal of the Speaking Body: Don Juan with J. L. Austin, or Seduction in Two Languages*. Stanford, CA: Stanford University Press.

Goffman, Erving. 1974. *Frame Analysis: An Essay on the Organization of Experience*. Cambridge, MA: Harvard University Press.

Gutmann, Amy, and Dennis F. Thompson. 2004. *Why Deliberative Democracy?* Princeton, NJ: Princeton University Press.

Hirschman, Albert O. 1970. *Exit, Voice and Loyalty: Responses to Decline in Firms,Organizations and States.* Cambridge, MA: Harvard University Press.

Kopytko, Roman. 2003. "What Is Wrong with Modern Accounts of Context in Linguistics?" *Views: Vienna Working English Papers* 12 (1): 45–60.

Lee, Benjamin. 1997. *Talking Heads: Language, Metalanguage, and the Semiotics of Subjectivity.* Durham, NC: Duke University Press.

Mansbridge, Jane J. 1980. *Beyond Adversary Democracy.* New York: Basic Books.

Medina, José. 2006. *Speaking from Elsewhere: A New Contextualist Perspective on Meaning, Identity, and Discursive Agency.* Albany: State University of New York Press.

Needham, Rodney. 1975. "Polythetic Classification: Convergence and Consequences." *Man,* New Series, 10 (3): 349–69. doi:10.2307/2799807.

Rao, Vijayendra, and Paromita Sanyal. 2010. "Dignity through Discourse: Poverty and the Culture of Deliberation in Indian Village Democracies." *Annals of the American Academy of Political and Social Science.* 629 (1): 146–72. doi:10.1177/0002716209357402.

CHAPTER 5

Traveling to the Village of Knowledge

Gerry Mackie

Deliberative democracy—the idea that democracy is best justified and explained as the reciprocal exchange of public reasons—is the leading justification for democracy in normative political theory. Of what use is it for global development practice?

For about 15 years off and on now, I have studied and advised the nongovernmental organization (NGO) Tostan (www.tostan.org), its community empowerment program of basic education, and its remarkable activations of community development, notably in advancing the health and human rights of women and girls, in particular the collective abandonment of female genital cutting and early marriage (Mackie 1996, 2000, 2009; Mackie and LeJeune 2009; Cislaghi, Gillespie, and Mackie 2014). My social convention account of female genital cutting predicted that organizing the collective abandonment of the practice within an intramarrying community would be effective and stable—a prediction that seems to have been borne out.

Part of the process is revaluation of the alternatives of cutting and not cutting. In field observations of Tostan and similarly effective NGOs,

This chapter is part of my long engagement with the concept of deliberative democracy. Lessons learned from the Tostan example emerged from collaborations with Molly Melching (Tostan), Diane Gillespie (University of Washington-Bothell), and Beniamino Cislaghi (University of Leeds). I thank them and all who helped our research in Senegal, especially the villagers studied. I also thank Patrick Heller, Karla Hoff, Jane Mansbridge, and Vijayendra Rao for advice. The larger research program is supported by grants from the Wallace Global Fund, the UNICEF Child Protection Office, and the University of California San Diego Academic Senate.

I learned that values deliberations within the community were another essential part of the change. In the spring of 2010, Cislaghi, Gillespie, and I began collecting data on the content of those values deliberations. When testing interview questions in the target villages, I had time to quiz people about issues that interested me: social conventions and social norms, positive and negative social sanctions. My questions provoked bafflement among the respondents. Eventually, they were able to come up with a single important local rule (respect for elders) and a single sanction (rebuke before the whole village), although that sanction had never been imposed, as far as anyone could recall.

John Dewey said, "If you want to know what a man's values are do not ask him. One is rarely aware, with any high degree of perception, what are the values that govern one's conduct" (quoted in Ralston 2010). Dewey would not put it this way, but values are implicit, automatic, and only rarely explicit and controlled; they are embodied in practices. When reviewing videotapes of Tostan education sessions involving the villages, I saw participants manifest in detail values, norms, reasons, and sanctions when they put on skits about moral conflicts. Participants easily took on the role of one parent wanting to keep a child in school and another wanting to put the child to work they understood exactly what each would say and what family and friends would say in the exchange. When it comes to everyday values, they, and the rest of us, have more "know how" than "know that."

People are capable of practical reason, of individual and collective deliberation over what to do. We have inherited from our intellectual grandparents, however, models of deliberation that are not only too abstracted from essentials but also in some ways are false. To the extent that our models are defective, we are unable to describe and prescribe effective public deliberation. The empirical research on the instrumental values of deliberation is inconclusive, I suggest, because we need a more empirical account of legitimate persuasion and attitude change. I identify the reciprocal exchange of public reasons as the distinct and intrinsic value of deliberation. I call the traditional account of deliberation the "formal-argumentation" view. The "subaltern challenge" to the formal-argumentation view argues that the insistence on formal argumentation excludes people who are less adept at it and thus violates the ideal of equal inclusion of all. Deliberative democracy has accommodated the subaltern challenge but still subordinates emotion and intuition to formal argument.

I state the empirical challenge to the formal-argumentation view. Moral interaction is not an imperfect approximation of formal argumentation. Rather, formal argumentation is a defective model of moral interaction. Like many others before me, I point to the importance of emotion and intuition in public deliberation. I propose that we understand public deliberation entirely as a matter of the reciprocal exchange of reasons, that we drop the controversial and exclusionary model of formal argumentation.

Public deliberation as exchange of reasons concerning a proposed moral judgment is still an incomplete model of moral interaction, however. Also needed are better descriptions of moral sensitivity, moral focus, and moral action and better prescriptions for advancing these neglected aspects of moral interaction.

The foregoing considerations should guide the implementation of public deliberation in global development practice. In that practice, indirect promotion of deliberation could more efficiently advance valuable processes and outcomes, as could nondeliberative methods such as exemplarity, performance, and pedagogy. I illustrate these ideas in three brief case studies. In each, these methods are used to midwife deliberation: creating deliberators, creating deliberation, and expanding the public sphere.

Public deliberation and the problem of the second best

There is an ongoing quandary at the core of the deliberative-democratic ideal, dating back to its genesis in Jürgen Habermas. On the one hand, Habermas identifies an ideal process that would define the true or the right based on the unavoidable presuppositions of argumentation: "freedom of access, equal rights to participate, truthfulness on the part of participants, absence of coercion in adopting positions, and so on" (Habermas 1993b, 31). Habermas seeks to bring Kant's categorical imperative down to earth by reformulating it as a discourse principle: "Just those action norms are valid to which all possibly affected persons could agree as participants in rational discourses" (Habermas 1996, 107). A more specific democracy principle states that "only those statutes may claim legitimacy that can meet with the assent of all citizens in a discursive process of legislation that in turn has been legally constituted" (110).

On the other hand, Habermas insists that moral questions can be decided only in an actual discourse (Habermas 1993b). Deliberative democracy confounds a hypothetical procedure for defining rightness with an institutional prescription for more discussion on more issues by more people.

Habermas (1993b) defends the usefulness of his idealization of communication using the analogy that a number can be ever more closely approximated (I suspect that what he is referring to is the asymptotic value of a function). In an influential review article, deliberative-democracy theorist Dennis Thompson (2008, 505) talks about standards for evaluating deliberative quality that are implicit in political practice and presupposed by the communication that takes place in actual democracies. "The closer the actual deliberation comes to meeting the standards," he writes, "the better it is in terms of deliberative theory." The hidden metaphor here is a journey from a source along a straight line to the ideal destination; all we need to know is whether we are farther from it or closer to it.

Asymptotic approximation is the usual understanding of the ideal in political theory, but it is a mistaken one. Even something as simple as Habermas's deliberative ideal contains more than one dimension of value. If perfect realization of any one of those dimensions is infeasible (and all of them always are), then those dimensions must be weighed and traded off against one another—and feasibility constraints themselves can be both complicated and uncertainly known. Knowing the ideal is far from sufficient to decide whether one feasible arrangement is better than another feasible arrangement in bringing about the better democratic or development process and outcome (see Sen 2009). The ideal fails to guide.

To illustrate further, Joshua Cohen (1989) proposes that actual democratic institutions should mirror and approximate some version of ideal deliberation. The problem, as we know from the problem of the second best, is that the recommendations that emerge from mirroring may strongly diverge from the recommendations that emerge from approximation (Estlund 2007). The theory of the second best says that if it is not feasible to satisfy the optimal value of one or more of some set of conditions required for attainment of some first-best ideal state, then attainment of the second-best state may require departure from the optimal values of one or more of the remaining conditions. I use this formal theorem metaphorically, just as Habermas (perhaps) appealed to the asymptotic value of a function as a metaphor to explicate his view. To mirror ideal deliberation in an actual institution would be to approach each of its several conditions separately as closely as practical. For example, ideal deliberation requires a unanimous conclusion; mirroring would thus recommend an actual decision rule closest to unanimity. Ideal deliberation suspends power; mirroring would thus recommend responding to power not with power but only with sincere argumentation. To approximate ideal deliberation in an actual institution would be to approach its several conditions together as closely as practical, with sensitivity to problems of the second best. Ideal deliberation is atemporal, with no status quo. In the temporal world, there is a status quo, and adoption of a unanimity rule would wrongly entrench it. In the actual world, with its status quo, the best approximation of unanimity is majority rule. It may be better to respond to colonial occupation with Gandhian civil disobedience than with a moral philosophy seminar.

Maximizing deliberation?

Delegation, voting, and discussion are the three main mechanisms of modern political democracy. Delegation is well theorized and studied: it can go wrong in many ways and works correctly only under tightly specified conditions. The Italian scholar Marsilius of Padua (1275–1342) thought mere election to lifetime terms would be sufficient for accountable delegation. In contrast, James Madison and other founders of representative democracy showed that repeated elections to limited terms are essential for proper delegation.

The number of possible voting rules is infinite, but only about a dozen are useful in political practice. The institutional recommendations of deliberative democracy often do not go far beyond the injunction to increase group discussion in its sites, in its duration, and in the number of people and issues involved. Delegation and voting are each valuable only in optimal quality and quantity, however; in practice, more of either would often be worse. Why should public deliberation be any different? Citizens delegate to accountable representatives in order to economize on the costly burdens of public discussion and decision. Should they delegate more to them, increasing the length of their terms from, say, 2 years to 24, or allowing them to make not just political decisions but also decisions about what people should do in their personal lives? Citizens vote to hold representatives accountable, but if they voted every day on retaining representatives, their representatives would have no slack to carry out policies they are better informed about and that take more than a day to yield beneficial outcomes. Citizens could vote directly on every political issue, several times a day, but doing so would reduce the epistemic value of outcomes. Voting on every issue or voting every day on retaining representatives would also drastically reduce the number of people participating in voting, because citizens would know less about each issue and because they have many more purposes in life other than participating in political decisions. Citizens need the right kind of discussion, in the right institutional formats, and in the right amounts, not simply more.

Deliberative democrats hypothesize a number of beneficial effects of public deliberation. It is, for example,

> expected to lead to empathy with the other and a broadened sense of people's own interests through an egalitarian, open-minded and reciprocal process of argumentation. Following from this result are other benefits: citizens are more enlightened about their own and others' needs and experiences, can better resolve deep conflict, are more engaged in politics, place their faith in the basic tenets of democracy, perceive their political system as legitimate, and lead a healthier civic life (Mendelberg 2002, 154).

It might "shape preferences, moderate self-interest, empower the marginalized, mediate differences, further integration and solidarity, enhance recognition, produce reasonable opinions and policy, and possibly lead to consensus" (Chambers 2003, 309). Actual deliberation, let's say, is an institution of group discussion generally expected to yield benefits, in terms of all relevant values, that are more worthy than the costs. Who could be against that? Increasing discussion, however, is not the same as increasing deliberation: group discussion, if positive in effect, can still cost more than it's worth and can even have quite undesirable effects. One problem is that theorists of deliberative democracy sometimes have defined deliberation in a question-begging manner: deliberation is discussion that is beneficial; discussion that is not beneficial is not deliberation.

Several reviews summarize the empirical research on collective deliberation. These review articles are summarized by Thompson (2008, 499), who reveals a second problem: "taken together the results are mixed or inconclusive." The two problems in combination could tempt one to explain any disconfirming result as not really about deliberation (as Mutz 2008 complains). There is a bustle of conceptual revision and empirical investigation among deliberative democrats today (see, for example, Habermas 2006, Rosenberg 2007, Thompson 2008, Mansbridge and others 2010, Bächtiger and others 2010), much of it wrestling with the sorts of concerns I raise here.

Some discussion does not result in legitimate moral influence; the discussion that does can be called deliberation. But there is also legitimate moral influence, such as exemplarity, which does not involve discussion. It is also possible that the right kinds of education, economic development, mechanisms of political delegation and voting, and other factors could more efficiently promote one or more of the beneficial effects claimed for deliberation.

What is distinctive about public deliberation, and worthy of special attention, however, is the reciprocal giving of reasons. This quality is intrinsically valuable, regardless of its positive (or negative) effects. It is important that all have the right to exchange reasons for and against proposals for authoritative collective action. As with many rights, one should possess the right even if one chooses not to exercise it.

Democratic deliberation is the reciprocal giving of reasons, and reasons should be of the kind that all could accept—not that all would accept. What is meant is that reasons offered should be public—for example, not based on divine revelation not available to all. Public reasons should also not be based on threats of material reward or punishments and not be based on merely private interests.

Reasons are difficult to define with necessary and sufficient conditions. Scanlon (1998) takes reasons as a primitive, a consideration that counts in favor of something. Counts how, he asks. By providing a reason for it. Even though we cannot say what a reason is, we know a reason when we hear one.

Formal argumentation

Because of the accident of its origins in German philosophy, deliberative democracy in its formative years assumed the reciprocal giving of reasons to mean rational argumentation—sometimes moral argument at the highest level of formality, such as would be found in a graduate

rational

philosophy seminar or the judgments of a constitutional court. This view of deliberative democracy can be called the formal-argumentation view. Habermas's prose is ruthlessly formal and abstract, in the tradition of German idealism and Frankfurt critical theory. John Rawls (2005), who in later days called himself a deliberative democrat, declared that in a constitutional regime with judicial review, the constitutional court—not the parliament, not civil society, not the people—is the exemplar of public reason.

Subaltern challenges to the formal-argumentation view

The formal-argumentation view faces what I'll call the subaltern challenge. Dryzek (2000, 57) portrays the contrast as the gentlemen's club challenged by the consciousness-raising group. The ideal of public deliberation assumes, among other things, equal inclusion of all affected individuals. But an insistence on formal argument is likely to exclude people less adept at it, people from more oppressed gender, class, race, and caste groups. It is also likely to exclude the more passionate and embodied styles of communication that might be offered by the oppressed, such as the rhetoric of Martin Luther King, Jr. ("I have a dream that one day every valley shall be exalted, every hill and mountain shall be made low, the rough places will be made plain, and the crooked places will be made straight, and the glory of the Lord shall be revealed, and all flesh shall see it together").

Iris Marion Young proposed that deliberative democracy be understood as inclusive communication rather than inclusive argument:

> The ideal of disembodied and disembedded reason that [formal argumentation] presupposes is a fiction. What such privileging takes to be neutral, universal, and dispassionate expression actually carries the rhetorical nuances of particular situated social positions and relations, which social conventions do not mark as rhetorical and particular in the same way that they notice others (2000, 63).

She would supplement argument with greeting, rhetoric, and narrative.

Deliberative democrats accommodated the subaltern challenge. Dryzek (2000) added that argumentation itself can be coercive, as when there is not equal communicative competence in a group. Argument can fail to connect the particular to the general, as when a supreme court voids a law only because it contravenes a constitution or an argument ultimately appeals to the authority of tradition. I would add that aggressive argumentation (the form engaged in by Plato's Socrates in certain moods or Dostoyevsky's Grand Inquisitor), although formally pure, can be as domineering as force or deception. Most of us have encountered the bullying sophist, whose arguments we cannot answer at the moment but whom we know to be in error. He or she often argues in bad faith, but the sincere zealot is just as deplorable.

Dryzek proposes two tests for political communication. First, coercion should be excluded. Second, communication that cannot connect the particular to the general should be excluded. Greeting can be contemptuous and subordinating. Rhetoric can be manipulatively deceptive and can fail to move beyond the particular audience to wider humanity. If narrative is exclusively about an individual's experience, there is no political point in hearing it, because it does not appeal to generalizable interests and rights relevant to others.

Dryzek is fair in applying his criteria equally to more privileged argument and to less privileged subaltern modes of communication. Nevertheless, the impression lingers in the deliberative democracy literature that formal argumentation is king, supplemented by communicative handmaidens. Storytelling, personal experiences, humor, and rhetoric are "nonrational," according to an authoritative review of the state of deliberative democracy by five of its leading theorists (Bächtiger and others 2010).

The empirical challenge to the formal-argumentation view

I offer the empirical challenge to the formal-argumentation view. The problem is not that the view neglects nonformal modes of persuasion and attitude change among subalterns but that it neglects them among all people, subaltern and otherwise. Actual and legitimate persuasion and attitude change are not an imperfect approximation of formal argumentation. Rather, the model of formal argumentation is an imperfect approximation of actual and legitimate persuasion and attitude change. Although its rigorous standards are undeniably valuable, and essential inside its domain, formal argumentation is a defectively incomplete model of individual and public deliberation, as well as of many other neglected aspects of moral interaction. Formal argumentation always begins from premises, axioms, assumptions, intuitions, and sentiments, often tacit and unacknowledged. In political theory, for example, justifications of modern political liberalism and democracy are usually rooted in an appeal to intuitions about the value of equal respect or the values of free and equal citizenship. Assessment of such justifications depends not only on their qualities of formal argument but also on the plausibility and appeal of both their premises and their conclusions. Formal argument can improve our views, but it is sourced on understandings from outside of its domain.

Habermas (2001a, 31) says that the human sciences should aim at the "rational reconstruction of the know-how which is spontaneously expressed in the everyday practice of subjects who are capable of speech and action." Everyday communication coordinates social action, with an implicit warrant that the speaker can redeem validity claims of truth, rightness, and sincerity upon demand by any listener. The claim that formal argumentation is the best rational reconstruction of the warrant for everyday know-how is in error, I submit. For Habermas, ideal discourse does not have content that can be specified in advance: "what constitutes a good reason or a bad argument can only be judged from the point of view of the participants themselves" (Bächtiger and others 2010, 40). I turn this point against any Habermasian who assumes that formal argumentation is the correct model of human deliberation.

Empirical moral psychologist Lawrence Kohlberg combined Piaget's theory of cognitive stages in the development of children with the ideas of neo-Kantian moral and political philosopher John Rawls. He hypothesized six stages of moral development, the highest stages being "postconventional" levels five and six, which correspond to Rawls's exemplary supreme court or Habermas's ideal argumentation. Habermas (1993a, 2001b) has written at length about the relationship between his discourse ethics and Kohlberg's experimental program.

Certain neo-Kohlbergians, among them Darcia Narvaez (2005), find limitations in Kohlberg's approach. Recognition of these limitations illuminates why deliberative democracy has problems with both empirical evidence of benefit and concrete institutional prescription. Unfortunately, as tested by interview questions, Kohlberg found that almost none of the respondents in the many populations sampled by his research program functions at levels five or six (able to offer abstract and universalizing argumentation about a moral judgment in response to hypothetical moral dilemmas).

Neo-Kohlbergians revised Kohlberg's experimental protocol. Instead of asking subjects to generate argument about a moral dilemma, they asked them to rate on a five-point scale their assessment of 12 issues relevant to deciding a dilemma and to rank the four most important issues. About half the population is able to function at the postconventional stage of moral judgment when tacit judgments are measured by recognition memory—that is, when they are reminded of potentially relevant arguments. Data like these suggest that having experts debate a moral issue before an audience is more beneficial than having everyone in a community engage in the debate, as ideal deliberation would prescribe.

The most powerful demographic correlate of better moral judgment is education, which accounts for 50 percent of the variance: the quality of moral judgment improves with undergraduate and graduate education (Narvaez 2005). Another strong factor is wider social experience. As far as I know, the neo-Kohlbergians have not studied participation in political deliberation as an explanatory variable, but I suspect it would be much weaker than education and that education would more likely cause participation than participation cause education. If postconventional political deliberation is valuable, perhaps it could be more efficiently promoted indirectly by education in general and moral education in particular than directly by more public discussion by more people about more political issues.

Narvaez (2005) also urges that moral judgment, emphasized by neo-Kantians like Rawls and especially Habermas, is only one slice of human moral life and its corresponding psychological processes. Practical reason depends on moral judgment (reasoning about the best moral choice), but it also depends on moral sensitivity (noticing morally relevant cues, who is involved, what actions to take, what might ensue); moral focus (placing moral aims above other goals and needs, situationally or as a habit); and moral action (knowing how to carry out a moral action and actually doing so). One finding coming out of the Kohlberg research program is that the empirical relationship between better moral judgment and better moral action is quite imperfect (Blasi 1980): there is an influence but not a determination. Moreover, studies of people nominated by their communities as moral exemplars indicate that they were singled out not for their moral judgment but for a variety of expert skills across the terrain of moral experience (Narvaez 2005). Like 99 percent of the population, they do not evidence the postconventional stage of morality (although they would likely score high if measured on tacit judgment).

There is a conceptual problem of moving beyond mere judgment. There is an empirical question of whether more public deliberation about more issues develops a variety of skills that elicit moral sensitivity, moral judgment, moral focus, and moral action. And there is a further empirical question of whether deliberation is the best way to develop those skills.

According to Habermas, "moral issues are never raised for their own sake; people raise them seeking a guide for action. For this reason the demotivated solutions that postconventional morality finds for decontextualized issues must be reinserted into practical life" (2001a, 179). His gestures in this direction are unpersuasive, however. In order to restore context to his discourse ethics, he proposes another ideal discourse of application, in which everyone agrees on which one of some vast number of already agreed-on and hence universally valid norms applies to the particular situation. He also adds on existential-ethical deliberations, in which individuals or groups clarify their identities, an obscure and undefended notion, and pragmatic discourses in which people balance opposing but not generalizable interests.

Although Habermas concedes that the contents of arguments cannot be explicated solely in terms of argumentation, he dogmatically counters that no experiences or moral feelings are completely prior to argumentation (1993, 59). A simple reply to his assertion is that no moral arguments are completely prior to experiences or feelings. There is no good reason to insist that the relationship between the forms of argumentation and the contents of argumentation is hierarchical rather than mutual. It is baffling that the Kantian tradition singles out one aspect of the moral life—moral judgment—for sacralization. If a demon forced us to privilege one aspect of morality above all others, surely moral action would outrank moral judgment.

Practical reason: cognitive and emotional, controlled and automatic

Political philosophers typically understand and conceptualize practical reason, including morality and politics, exclusively as a matter of controlled cognition. It is not. Practical reason also involves emotion and automatic processes. Advances in cognitive science have made obsolete the notion that reason and emotion are in opposition. Yes, sometimes hot passions can distort judgment. But cold judgment can be distorted by the absence of the appropriate emotions. Cognition and emotion are interdependent in decision processes, and the proper blend of judgment and emotion is essential to a good result.

Bechara and Damasio (2005) studied patients with brain lesions that impaired their judgments and decisions in real life, even though their formal problem-solving abilities in laboratory tests were normal. The patients could estimate immediate and future consequences of alternative actions and carry out cost-benefit analyses, but they were unable to reach decisions or made extremely poor ones. The lesions had sundered the connection between the executive and emotional features of their brains. Krause (2008) wrote a book on the topic of moral sentiment and democratic deliberation, arguing that emotions generate the impartial standpoint needed for proper public deliberation.

Psychologists are rapidly refining dual process theories of the mind (Evans and Frankish 2009). Humans know much more than they can say. Type 1 processes are fast and automatic; they involve substantial processing capacity but require low effort. I dub them *automatic processes*. Type 2 processes are slow and controlled; they involve limited capacity and require substantial effort. I dub them *controlled processes*. Powerful intuitions inform thoughts and actions. With little or no effort, they emerge as appropriate from large banks of implicit knowledge, much of it implicitly learned (Narvaez 2010).

According to Narvaez, a basic system regulates bodily functions. A primitive system involves subsymbolic processing of stimuli, including nondiscursive inductions from experience. A sophisticated unconscious, built from experience, attends to meaning and emotion. Experiences can inform a present task, even though the wealth of previous learning is not consciously available to the actor. Moral intuitions often prompt action (and one account of moral philosophy is that it systematizes such intuitions). Tacit knowledge is not typically irrational or impulsive. Intuition can be more naive (a novice at a craft) or more sophisticated (an expert), according to Narvaez. Intuition guides one's moral course far more often than does controlled cognition.

Any aspect of political practical reason can be legitimate or illegitimate in one of its instances (table 5.1), and any aspect can correct another. For example, automatic emotion can identify and motivate right action when controlled cognition fails. Huck Finn had been taught discursively the

TABLE 5.1 Four aspects of political practical reason, with examples

Aspect of reason	Controlled	Automatic
Cognition	Public-spirited argumentation (legitimate)	Belief that others are moral equals (legitimate)
	Bullying sophistry (illegitimate)	Surrender to negative or false stereotypes (illegitimate)
Emotion	Reciprocal sympathy (legitimate)	Habituated empathic concern (legitimate)
	Distorting passion (illegitimate)	Tacit contempt for social inferiors (illegitimate)

universal and abstract right of property and knew that it was morally wrong for him to allow his runaway companion Jim to escape from slavery. (According to some theories of the day, Jim was not a rational agent to be included in any Kantian universalization.) When Huck decides to turn Jim in and composes a letter disclosing Jim's whereabouts, he feels washed clean of sin for the first time in his life and is about to commence a prayer. He is halted, however, by a cascade of emotional memories about his life on the river with Jim:

> I was a-trembling, because I'd got to decide, forever, betwixt two things, and I knowed it. I studied a minute, sort of holding my breath, and then says to myself: "All right, then, I'll *go* to hell"—and tore it up. . . . For a starter I would go to work and steal Jim out of slavery again; and if I could think up anything worse, I would do that, too; because as long as I was in, and in for good, I might as well go the whole hog (Twain 1994 [1912]).

Controlled cognition can identify the right moral judgment when automatic emotion fails. Haidt and Hersh (2001) ask subjects whether the actions described in various scenarios are morally wrong. For example, suppose an adult brother and sister consensually engage in incest once, using contraception, and no emotional complications ensue. Many subjects (more among the less educated) judge their action as morally wrong, even though neither sibling is harmed. Even when the absence of harm is fully reiterated, subjects tend to persist in their judgment of moral wrong and can offer no reasons for their judgment, which Haidt and Hersh call "moral dumbfounding." Nussbaum (2004) argues at length for the proposition that disgust is an unreliable guide to moral judgment and the coercive prohibition of actions.

The formal-argumentation account of attitude formation, persuasion, and attitude change is empirically defective. Attitudes are built from experiences summarized in tacit schemata; shared attitudes are built from experiences shared in groups. Formation of shared schemata is mostly automatic, based on implicit observation of and induction from public objects and public practices, occasionally clarified or corrected by controlled processes of instruction or discussion.

Deliberation as the reciprocal exchange of public reasons

Young (2000) proposed moving from inclusive argumentation to inclusive communication as the deliberative ideal. But communication is too broad a category, including as it does morally offensive content, such as threat, insult, sarcasm, and morally irrelevant content. Public deliberation is the reciprocal giving of reasons that all could accept; reasons are considerations that count for or against something. Formal argument, figurative argument, emotion, rhetoric, individual testimony, dance, song, proverb, humor—all can genuinely contribute considerations that count for or against something, outside the austere precincts of graduate seminars and constitutional courts. The subaltern challenge to deliberative democracy dissolves if one views public deliberation not as formal argumentation but as the exchange of reasons. To deliberate is to weigh the reasons for and against something. Rooted in *libra* (a scale), it is the broad and intuitive idea that the various descriptive and prescriptive theories of decision making attempt to model.

Deliberation can be understood entirely as the reciprocal exchange of reasons; there is no need to insist on a controversial and exclusionary model of formal argumentation as the only legitimate or even the privileged aspect of the process. An apostle of formal argumentation is correct to claim that simplifying abstractions and maintaining logical consistency can improve the understanding of reasons, but they are not the ultimate source of those reasons; they are one of the servants of morality, not its master. I agree with Dryzek (2000, 167) that "emotions must in the end be capable of rational justification" but add that rational justification must in the end be capable of support by appropriate emotions. Dryzek writes that "the problem with these alternative forms of communication is that they are incomplete." The problem with formal argumentation is that it is incomplete as well.

Deliberation simply as the exchange of reasons, however, continues to erroneously divert theoretical and practical attention toward moral judgment and away from moral sensitivity, moral focus, and moral action. True, deliberation is hypothesized to promote sensitivity, and within a deliberation, methods for promoting sensitivity, focus, and action could be discussed. But those other methods—education, exemplarity, habituated empathic concern, strength of will, instrumental expertise—need not be deliberative themselves.

One should keep the following considerations in mind when proposing to implement public deliberation among a group. The hypothetical ideal of deliberation is distinct from institutional prescriptions for more deliberation because of the problem of the second best. It is very unlikely that maximizing deliberation would maximize the realization of morally desirable processes and outcomes. Institutional prescriptions for more deliberation sometimes beg the question by defining deliberation as any discussion that proves valuable. Deliberative democracy's origins in theories of formal argumentation neglect not only the subaltern but also the empirical processes of legitimate persuasion and attitude change among people in general.

Midwifing deliberation

Almost no one in the developed world is able to argue at the abstract level assumed by ideal deliberation; one may assume the same is true for people in the developing world. Indirect promotion of deliberation could more efficiently advance valuable processes and outcomes, as could nondeliberative methods such as exemplarity, performance, and pedagogy. Deliberative judgment is only part of moral life; nondeliberative methods could also advance moral sensitivity, moral focus, and moral action.

In this section I examine three examples: Gandhi's salt *satyagraha* in colonial India, Antanas Mockus's successes as mayor of Bogota, and Tostan's community empowerment program in rural West Africa. Each of these experiences midwives deliberation by creating deliberators, creating deliberation, and expanding the public sphere.

Gandhi in India

Lloyd and Susan Hoeber Rudolph (2015) contrast the young Habermas's account of a bourgeois public sphere emerging in early modern European coffee houses with Gandhi's use of the ashram and *satyagraha* to expand and democratize the public sphere in colonial India. Gandhi founded several ashrams, core groups where new moral models were discussed and practiced. Moral practices and deliberations were actively diffused from the core via *satyagrahas* to the population. According to the Rudolphs, Gandhi recognized that public deliberations and cultural performance could "reach high levels of complexity under conditions of low literacy" (163). Traveling theater, grandmother's tales, and public oratory in village meetings "regularly engage ordinary nonliterate people in complex and sophisticated . . . communication" (163). In conditions of nonliteracy, exemplification and performance play a much stronger role than coffee houses, literary societies, or political journals. These activities are cognitive, emotional, controlled, and automatic in their content, not simply a matter of controlled cognition.

Gandhi did not punctiliously dispute constitutional law in an appearance before the British Law Lords; he did not convene a graduate seminar on the question of British colonial rule to be held next Wednesday, refreshments to be provided. He and his followers marched 240 miles in 24 days, from ashram to sea, to produce salt from the ocean in protest over the British salt tax. After his arrest, his followers continued down the coast.

Their action prompted millions of Indians to engage in civil disobedience and changed British, Indian, and world attitudes toward independence.

The British tax on salt hurt the poorest, salt was needed by every Indian, the unilateral British power to tax highlighted India's colonial status, and the ability of anyone to make salt (an essential of life) from seawater alluded to the capacity for independence. Gandhi's speeches and publicity on the march were not public deliberation in the ideal sense—but so much the worse for the supposed ideal (one could say that in the circumstances it was the best feasible approximation of ideal deliberation under the constraints faced, but that description abstracts away from essential features of the case). Gandhi's actions created deliberators and deliberation in many corners of India; greatly expanded the Indian public sphere; and enhanced moral sensitivity, moral judgment, moral focus, and, most important, moral action in the short and the long run. A mirroring of the deliberative ideal—discussion among the British and the Indians on the basis of abstract and universalizing argumentation—would not have had the same results.

Antanas Mockus in Bogota

Antanas Mockus, a philosopher influenced by Habermas and Jon Elster, was mayor of Bogota, Colombia, in 1995–97 and 2001–03. He relied not only on conventional political authority and its coercive power but also to an unprecedented degree on exemplarity, performance, and pedagogical devices intended to change mutual expectations in the population and thereby alter social norms. During his years of governance, water usage in Bogota went down 40 percent, homicide fell 70 percent, and traffic fatalities declined 50 percent; water and sewer services were extended to nearly all households (Antanas Mockus, Wikipedia, accessed February 22, 2015; the remainder of the information is from Mockus n.d.).

One of his central doctrines is the harmonization of moral, legal, and social norms (Mackie 2015). Law is upheld by legitimacy more than by coercive menace. In Bogota, according to Mockus, there was among some a short-cut culture that took pride in defying the law; members of this subculture subscribe to a social norm that prescribes defiance of legal norms. Yet public policy and administration seldom venture beyond enactment of legal norms. Many legal norms are enacted to enforce ultimately moral norms, and legal norms can be ineffective if they are not supported by social norms and their social sanctions. (Mockus's municipal reforms were also based on more conventional methods of good policy and good administration, but they are not the topic of this chapter.)

One major accomplishment was the revision of the police code from a harmonization of norms standpoint. Each person is morally responsible for compliance, he argued. All are responsible for applying social sanctions to support compliance; the state's legal power is the last remedy to be applied. The code was revised in a conventional process of citizen participation involving consultation by elected and appointed officials with 917 entities and associations in the city. An innovation was the distribution of 350,000 thumbs-up and thumbs-down cards for citizens to display spontaneously in the regulation of social norms in traffic encounters and other areas of everyday life. The thumbs-down cards were sometimes too provocative; later, a question-mark card was offered as well.

Is this public deliberation? Perhaps it is an approximation of it, perhaps it is something else. Nevertheless, the attention-getting innovation inspired multiple informal deliberations, large and small, on the topic of the harmonization of norms intended to contribute to the beneficial revision of social norms.

Bogota had unusually high levels of gun violence. It was not politically practical to forbid the carrying of firearms. Instead, the city banned the carrying of firearms on weekends and in the month of December. The partial ban had the direct effect of reducing firearm fatalities, but it also had the indirect effect of prompting deliberations about the connection between easy access to firearms and a high level of lethal violence. It may have shifted social norms among some portions of the population.

Bogota suffered from high tax noncompliance. In 2002 Mockus opened a "110 percent with Bogota" campaign, in which citizens were asked to make a voluntary overpayment of 10 percent on their municipal taxes. The direct effect would surprise an economist: 63,000 citizens did so. But Bogota was a city of 7 million, a sceptic would reply. The sceptic, though, fails to notice a larger indirect effect: the increase in overall tax compliance. The campaign highlighted the connection between tax collection and city services, leading taxpayers were taken on public tours of less visible municipal services, and the provocative 110 percent challenge prompted multiple deliberations throughout the city on the purposes of taxation and governance. According to Mockus:

> Voluntary contributions are . . . the basis of pedagogy by example. . . . There is a shift from a situation where paying taxes is a tiresome obligation to one where there are reasons to feel proud and to congratulate people who contribute. The strategy of mobilizing pride and social approval is a useful alternative to legal sanctions. . . . In fact a good part of the collection strategy for the tax office . . . was based on persuasion, not on coercion.

The FARC narco-guerillas threatened Mockus's life, forcing him to wear a bulletproof vest. Rather than wear it discreetly under his clothing, he wore it over his clothing, and in public and media appearances he explained that the FARC was ready to kill but not ready to reason. He cut a hole in the vest over his heart to symbolize that his heart was still open to communication with the FARC. Were Mockus's actions merely a sullied approximation of ideally rational argumentation? Or is rational argumentation an incomplete model of moral interaction?

The Tostan Community Empowerment Program in West Africa

The NGO Tostan in Senegal is well known for supporting the organization of community abandonment of female genital cutting and early or forced marriage. One essential factor behind its success is a process of organized diffusion from a small core group through the rest of the community, culminating in a public declaration of coordinated abandonment (Mackie 1996, 2000). Another essential factor, consistently observed in effective abandonment programs across Africa, is human rights discussions within the community about the pros and cons of some of its social practices (Mackie 2009).

Tostan developed a democracy and human rights module of its nonformal education program in rural African villages (Gillespie and Melching 2010). An unexpected result in the first village where the module was added was heightened community organization and social action. At the end of the program, participants are asked to undertake a project. Unprompted by Tostan, participants in Malicounda Bambara decided to organize an end to female genital cutting. The community controversy was tough and prolonged, but eventually a decision to abandon was made. That decision interested nearby villages, and the process of organized diffusion of community abandonments began.

The independent and pioneering organized community abandonment of female genital cutting supported by the NGO CEOSS in the Coptic town of Deir Al Barsha also shifted from health discourse to a human rights discourse. KMG Ethiopia—which has organized an end to female genital cutting and marriage by abduction and attained other beneficial results across an Ethiopian province of 800,000— started with women's rights discourse. It then moved to a human rights discourse and added community dialogue and organized community abandonment (Mackie 2009). Abandonment of female genital cutting is only one of many consequences of these programs, and it is not their primary goal.

Much is known about the input of human rights discourse and the output of dramatic community action. What happens in between? Is it an instance of public deliberation, as recently conceptualized by democratic theorists?

Cislaghi, Gillespie, and I (2014) document the content of the Tostan democracy and human rights curriculum and the responses of participants in three villages over 21 months. To describe and explain the process of change with the standard deliberative-democracy model would be incomplete and even misleading. We observed an explicit exchange of reasons and reasoning about the consistency of values, beliefs, and practices. But changing moral interactions in the community were not narrowly confined to formal argument or controlled cognition. We also observed in greater abundance pedagogy, exemplarity, and performance; emotions and indications of automatic processes; and changes in moral sensitivity, moral focus, and moral action.

In addition to formal argument, Tostan relies on the figurative argument of image, proverb, song, dance, story, and poem. It does so not just out of respect for West African customs or as a way to "meet people where they are." Appropriate emotions are best coordinated by local conventions of expression. Figurative argument is well suited to the task of bringing together differing domains—local tradition, local religion, national government, democracy, international human rights, methods of inquiry and collective problem solving, literacy and numeracy—in unexpected and creative ways. The fusion of the traditional and the new in the figurative mode by the core group more readily diffuses to friends and neighbors than do formal and alien messaging campaigns.

The changes seen in Tostan villages take time to emerge. The first session of the program contains a story (Melching 2009). In it, four people travel together to the village of knowledge. After a while, the way becomes hilly, and one villager complains that walking is too hard. Later, a second villager complains that the trip is taking too long, adding that the old village was okay, even with its problems. Then a third villager becomes very tired of the travel. In each case, the others urge the villagers on. A fourth villager keeps her eye on the goal; knowing that she will be proud to reach the village of knowledge eases her way.

Participants are asked five discussion questions about the story. The content of the story and the ensuing discussion are equivalent to the formal idea that a larger reward in the future justifies a smaller sacrifice in the present. But passive receipt of the formal injunction and active discussion of the vivid story differ in cognitive depth and motivational force, in the force of their supporting reasons.

In session 3 of the program, class members are asked to close their eyes and imagine what they would like their community to be like five years later. A large paper is posted, and each is asked to draw in one of those items, such as "a health center, school, village market, trees, water source, garden project, two people holding hands, nice houses, light and electricity, factories, mosque, playgrounds, sports areas, a dove of peace, carpenter shops, etc." (Melching 2009). Then they are asked to think of what resources they have in hand and what they would have to change and add to achieve the ideal community. Points are discussed and the top eight are listed. Formal argumentation would conclude and declare "We must strive for a better community," reminiscent of the empty Soviet slogans of yore. The Tostan process activates concrete images of community improvements and pools them in the public of the class into a common aspirational vision with motivating concrete detail. Such considerations have more force than their formal equivalents.

Sessions 5–10 are about justifications for government and law, constitutionalism, majority rule and minority rights, and the governmental structure of the country. Session 11 inaugurates a 13-session series on about two dozen international human rights.

Session 14, on the right to be protected against discrimination, is the most powerful and motivating session. It begins with an image containing a variety of people: young, old, male, female, Muslim, Christian, disabled, European, African, Asian. Participants are asked what they see in the image and then asked what the figures have in common. They answer that the figures are all humans. Participants are asked if all are needed to create a better society; after discussion, they conclude that all are needed. They are asked what would happen if some people were excluded; they respond that the excluded could hinder the progress of the community.

Latent values are activated and some of their presuppositions and entailments brought out. Other values and experiences—from anywhere from nearby communities to international human rights instruments—are introduced. The meaning of values is elaborated on and expanded by the pooling of local and global experiences in class interactions. Manifested and extended values are brought into coherence · /ith one another, and new values coherent with extended old values are derived. Through precept, example, participation in and watching of skits, and community projects of escalating scope, participants learn how to put knowledge into action.

The program itself is not deliberation. At most, it midwifes deliberation with a pedagogy that helps create a public and agents capable of being public actors. For the community to change a harmful social practice, enough people must come to believe that enough people are willing to change and be able to coordinate that change. Community change requires that the public sphere expand beyond male elders to women, young men, and outcastes. Expansion of the public sphere requires that previously excluded individuals model, rehearse, and enact new roles as public actors. The psychological and social processes of change involve much more than deliberative consensus (Cislaghi, Gillespie, and Mackie 2014).

Conclusions

Local, regional, and national movements to curb violence against women have enthusiastically appropriated the international human rights framework. But to be effective, human rights ideas need to be actively remade in the local vernacular. "Human rights ideas, embedded in cultural assumptions about the nature of the person, the community, and the state, do not translate easily from one setting to another," writes Merry (2006, 3). "Nor do ideas move readily the other way, from local to global settings." Activists, she adds, frame local stories in terms of international human rights language, translating between two worlds.

Deliberations about local values in developing communities can and should improve global understandings of international human rights as well. People from Cambridge and New York need to travel to the villages of knowledge, to human rights communities such as Malicounda Bambara in rural Senegal.

References

Bächtiger, Andre, Simon Niemeyer, Michael Neblo, Marco R. Steenbergen, and Jürg Steiner. 2010. "Disentangling Diversity in Deliberative Democracy: Competing Theories, Their Blind Spots and Complementarities." *Journal of Political Philosophy* 18 (1): 32–63.
Bechara, Antoine, and Antonio R. Damasio. 2005. "The Somatic Marker Hypothesis: A Neural Theory of Economic Decision." *Games and Economic Behavior* 52 (2): 336–72.
Bicchieri, Cristina. 2006. *The Grammar of Society*. Cambridge: Cambridge University Press.
Blasi, Augusto. 1980. "Bridging Moral Cognition and Moral Action: A Critical Review of the Literature." *Educational Psychology Review* 11: 343–60.
Chambers, Simone. 2003. "Deliberative Democratic Theory." *Annual Review of Political Science*. 6: 307–26.
Cislaghi, Beniamino, Diane Gillespie, and Gerry Mackie. 2014. *Values Deliberation and Collective Change in Rural Senegal*. Report to Wallace Global Fund. https:// sites.sas.upenn.edu/penn-unicef-summer/files/values_deliberations_full.pdf.
Cohen, Joshua. 1989. "Deliberation and Democratic Legitimacy." In *The Good Polity*, ed. Alan Hamlin and Philip Pettit. Oxford: Basil Blackwell.
Dryzek, John. 2000. *Deliberative Democracy and Beyond*. Cambridge: Cambridge University Press.
Estlund, David. 2007. *Democratic Authority*. Princeton, NJ: Princeton University Press.
Evans, Jonathan St. B. T, and Keith Ed Frankish. 2009. In *Two Minds: Dual Processes and Beyond*. New York: Oxford University Press.
Gillespie, Diane, and Molly Melching. 2010. "The Transformative Power of Democracy and Human Rights in Nonformal Education: The Case of Tostan." *Adult Education Quarterly* 60 (5): 477–98.
Habermas, Jürgen. 1993a. "Lawrence Kohlberg and Neo-Aristotelianism." In *Justification and Application: Remarks on Discourse Ethics*, ed. Jürgen Habermas. Cambridge: Cambridge University Press.
———. 1993b. "Remarks on Discourse Ethics." In *Justification and Application: Remarks on Discourse Ethics*, ed. Jürgen Habermas. Cambridge: Cambridge University Press.
———. 1996. *Between Facts and Norms*. Cambridge, MA: MIT Press.
———. 2001a. "Moral Consciousness and Communicative Action." In *Moral Consciousness and Communicative Action*, ed. Jürgen Habermas. Cambridge, MA: MIT Press.

———. 2001b. "Reconstruction and Interpretation in the Social Sciences." In *Moral Consciousness and Communicative Action*, ed. Jürgen Habermas. Cambridge, MA: MIT Press.

———. 2006. "Political Communication in Media Society." *Communication Theory* 16 (4): 412–26.

Haidt, J., and M. Hersh. 2001. "Sexual Morality: The Cultures and Emotions of Conservatives and Liberals." *Journal of Applied Social Psychology* 31: 191–221.

Krause, Sharon. 2008. *Civil Passions*. Princeton, NJ: Princeton University Press.

Mackie, Gerry. 1996. "Ending Footbinding and Infibulation: A Convention Account." *American Sociological Review* 61 (6): 999–1017.

———. 2000. "Female Genital Cutting: The Beginning of the End." In *Female Circumcision: Multidisciplinary Perspectives*, ed. Bettina Shell-Duncan and Ylva Hernlund, 245–82. Boulder, CO: Lynne Reinner Publishers.

———. 2009. "Lessons Learned: The Social Convention Theory of FGM/C and Abandonment Projects in Five Practicing Countries." Background paper for UNICEF Innocenti Research Centre, Florence, Italy.

———. 2015. "Effective Rule of Law Requires Construction of a Social Norm of Legal Obedience." In *Cultural Agency Reloaded: The Legacy of Antanas Mockus*, ed. Carlos Tognato. Cambridge, MA: Harvard University Press.

Mackie, Gerry, and John LeJeune. 2009. "Social Dynamics of Abandonment of Harmful Practices: A New Look at the Theory." Innocenti Working Paper, UNICEF Innocenti Research Centre, Florence, Italy.

Mansbridge, Jane, James Bohman, Simone Chambers, David Estlund, Andreas Føllesdal, Archon Fung, Cristina Lafont, Bernard Manin, and José Luis Martí. 2010. "The Place of Self-Interest and the Role of Power in Deliberative Democracy." *Journal of Political Philosophy* 18 (1): 64–100.

Melching, Molly. 2009. *Kobi I: Democracy, Human Rights, and Problem Solving*. Dakar: Tostan.

Mendelberg, Tali. 2002. "The Deliberative Citizen: Theory and Evidence." In *Political Decision Making, Deliberation and Participation: Research in Micropolitics*, vol. 6, ed. Michael X. Delli Carpini, Leonie Huddy, and Robert Y. Shapiro. Greenwich, CT: JAI Press.

Merry, Sally Engle. 2006. *Human Rights and Gender Violence*. Chicago: University of Chicago Press.

Mockus, Antanas. n.d. "Bogota's Capacity for Self-Transformation and Citizenship Building." Informal policy document for the city of Bogota, Colombia.

Mutz, Diane C. 2008. "Is Deliberative Democracy a Falsifiable Theory?" *Annual Review of Political Science* 11: 521–38.

Narvaez, Darcia. 2005. "The Neo-Kohlbergian Tradition and Beyond: Schemas, Expertise and Character." In *Nebraska Symposium on Motivation, Vol. 51: Moral Motivation through the Lifespan*, ed. C. Pope-Edwards and G. Carlo. Lincoln: University of Nebraska Press.

———. 2010. "Moral Complexity: The Fatal Attraction of Truthiness and the Importance of Mature Moral Functioning." *Perspectives on Psychological Science* 5 (2): 163–81.

Nussbaum, Martha. 2004. *Hiding from Humanity*. Princeton, NJ: Princeton University Press.

Ralston, Shane J. 2010. "Dewey and Goodin on the Value of Monological Deliberation." *Etica & Politica/Ethics & Politics* 12 (1): 235–55.

Rawls, John. 2005. *Political Liberalism*. New York: Columbia University Press.

Rosenberg, Shawn W., ed. 2007. *Can the People Govern? Deliberation, Participation, and Democracy*. Basingstoke, United Kingdom: Palgrave Macmillan.

Rudolph, Lloyd I., and Susanne Hoeber Rudolph. 2015. "The Coffee House and the Ashram: Gandhi, Civil Society and Public Spheres." In *Politics in South Asia: Culture, Rationality and Conceptual Flow*, ed. J. Schöttli, D. Frommherz, K. Fürstenberg, M. Gallenkamp, L. König, and M. Pauli. Berlin: Springer.

Scanlon, Thomas. 1998. *What We Owe to Each Other*. Cambridge, MA: Harvard University Press.

Sen, Amaryta. 2009. *The Idea of Justice*. Cambridge, MA: Belknap Press.

Thompson, Dennis. 2008. "Deliberative Democratic Theory and Empirical Political Science." *Annual Review of Political Science* 11: 497–520.

Scanlon, Thomas. 1998. *What We Owe Each Other*. Cambridge, MA: Harvard University Press.

Twain, Mark. 1994 (1912). *The Adventures of Huckleberry Finn*. New York: Dover Publications.

UNICEF (United Nations International Children's Emergency Fund). 2005. "Changing a Harmful Social Convention: Female Genital Mutilation/Cutting." *Innocenti Digest*, UNICEF Innocenti Research Centre, Florence, Italy.

———. 2007. *Coordinated Strategy to End Female Genital Mutilation/Cutting in One Generation*. New York.

———. 2008. *Long-Term Evaluation of the Tostan Programme in Senegal: Kolda, Thies, and Fatick Regions*. New York.

Young, Iris Marion. 2000. *Inclusion and Democracy*. New York: Oxford University Press.

CHAPTER 6

But Who Will Speak for the People? The Travel and Translation of Participatory Budgeting

Gianpaolo Baiocchi

The global travel and adoption of participatory budgeting is a remarkable story. A relatively simple idea—that ordinary citizens should have a direct say in public budgets that affect them—has traveled the world by the most unexpected routes, landing in unlikely sites. Some 26 years after its shaky start under the leftist government of the Workers' Party (Partido dos Trabalhadores [PT]) in Porto Alegre, Brazil, and 28 years after its first mention by neighborhood activists in that city, the idea and basic blueprint of participatory budgeting have circled the world, having been implemented in hundreds of cities on seven continents.[1]

The idea of participatory budgeting first circulated through Workers' Party networks in Brazil in the 1990s, before becoming popular throughout Latin America, through political party networks and then nongovernmental organizations (NGOs). Hundreds of municipal participatory budgets were developed in Argentina, Chile, the Dominican Republic, Ecuador, Guatemala, Peru, Uruguay, República Bolivariana de Venezuela, and elsewhere in Latin America.

In the 2000s, participatory budgeting attracted the attention of international development agencies as well as activists in the global North, who learned about it through the World Social Forum. Since 2000 the World Bank and agencies of the United Nations have helped bring participatory

This chapter draws on an ongoing research project with Ernesto Ganuza (Instituto de Estudios Sociales Avanzados [IESA], Spain). The account of Camaragibe and Gravataí draws on a research project with Patrick Heller and Marcelo K. Silva that is discussed at length in Baiocchi, Heller, and Silva (2011).

budgeting to Asia and Africa, in countries such as Fiji, Mozambique, Senegal, Turkey, and Zimbabwe.

At the same time, European cities began to implement this idea.[2] Dozens of cities in Albania, France, Germany, Italy, Portugal, Spain, and the United Kingdom now use participatory budgeting.[3] It has become official government policy in the Dominican Republic, Peru, and República Bolivariana de Venezuela and been actively promoted by Labour governments in the United Kingdom. It has even been used in the United States, where it has been implemented in Chicago's 49th Ward since 2009.

Something about participatory budgeting is clearly attractive; something about the idea resonates with the current moment of retrenched national states and dissatisfaction with mainstream development ideas. The ethos of participation, creativity, and decentralization is also part of what might be called a "new spirit of government" characteristic of entrepreneurial states in the current era (Jessop 2000). Its spread no doubt also reflects the rapid communications and increasingly intermeshed networks of the globalized era.

Looking at this diffusion raises questions about how ideas—and specifically ideas about governing and running social affairs—travel, how they are translated and conveyed by different actors and ultimately received and put into practice. At the very least, the story of participatory budgeting challenges the notion that the sole mechanisms for development today are institutional blueprints from North to South and the dominance of North-based actors and institutions in generating those blueprints. Indeed, the story also bears the mark of "counter-hegemonic globalization," the notion that "transnational connections can potentially be harnessed to the construction of more equitable distributions of wealth and power" (Evans 2004, 1).

This chapter addresses deliberation not as an institutional arrangement or a communicative practice but as a policy instrument that travels and is adopted and translated as it moves along different conduits, with possible unintended effects. A policy instrument is a "device that is both technical and social, that organizes specific social relations between the state and those it is addressed to, according to the representations and meanings it carries" (Lascoumes and Le Gales 2007, 4).[4] This view rejects what has been described as the "pragmatist" view. It suggests that instruments do not "land from heaven" and that when they do "land" they represent the play of interests and arrays of actors interested in (or opposed to) the device. Policy instruments "are not neutral devices: they produce specific effects, independently of the objective pursued (the aims ascribed to them), which structure public policy according to their own logic" (2007, 5).

The idea of policy instruments borrows from science and technology studies, which made a strong case for bracketing the question of whether ideas are in any way "good" in trying to understand how they travel.[5] Understanding that the evaluation of the inherent goodness of an idea or technique is often a retrospective evaluation based on its adoption and not the other way around, these scholars chose not to "look for the intrinsic qualities of any given statement but to look instead for all the transformations it undergoes later in other hands" (Latour 1987, 59).

For people who overlap in their roles as scholars, advocates, promoters, and implementers of deliberative democracy, this corrective is important for two main reasons. First, deliberative democracy is a vague idea that is open to interpretation. Even something like participatory budgeting can be ambiguously interpreted. What travels in the name of deliberative democracy can be radically different and take on very different meanings in different places.

Second, the political play around the adoption and transformation of deliberative institutions is inseparable from the eventual content of those institutions. The emergent discussion about conditions that are "favorable to deliberative democracy" too often brackets this element of transmission and translation. A common finding is that a "strong civil society" and a "willing government" are ideal conditions for robust participatory governance. Attention to instruments and their transformations should at least raise the question about the content of the institution as interpreted in a particular setting. In the absence of a local coalition to demand that the interpretation of a vague idea of participation should include binding decision making, why should one expect such a robust interpretation of deliberative democracy in the first place?

This chapter connects the dots between the early moments of participatory budgeting and its later incarnations in three settings (in Brazil, Peru, and Spain), drawing on approaches from science and technology studies and critical studies of globalization. It examines chains of actors and institutions that pass along the idea, as well as the dynamics of translation and adaptation as it is passed along. Scholarly work on international linkages has examined the promotion of legal expertise (Dezalay and Garth 2002), advocacy networks (Keck and Sikkink 1998), by "following the actors" (Latour 1987).

 The translation process can occur in three ways. First, it can take the form of what Evans (2004) calls "institutional monocropping"—a rigid kind of blueprintism. Second, it can resemble "democratic experimentalism" or "bootstrapping," as Sabel (2004) calls on the ground learning and trial and error. Third, it can fail to interest local actors or generate so much opposition that the transmission is simply blocked. Central to each negotiation, and specific to the travel of deliberation, is the symbolic role of "the people"—what part they play and who is authorized to speak for them. Before describing each of the cases, I briefly address participation in the current context.

What is at stake?

This chapter tries to understand deliberative democracy in "a world of objects in motion" (Appadurai 2000).[6] If one characteristic of the current moment is that globalization raises new democratic dilemmas between forms and scales of governance and representation (Held 1999; Habermas 2001), one potentially hopeful sign is the evocation of deliberative democracy in so many contexts (Melo and Baiocchi 2006). Deliberative proposals have appeared not in the context of transnational institutions but rather at local and regional levels, precisely as the nation-state has "hollowed out" (Jessop 2000). The global spread of electoral democratic norms, "in the 'thin' sense of electorally sanctioned transfers of formal political power," has nonetheless paved the way for "experiences with participation at the micro level of projects and communities" (Evans 2004, 37). With the multiplication of these experiences, enthusiasm for citizen participation has grown—in practitioner communities and academic circles alike—and the apparent paradox of the concomitant spread of "thin" democracy, hollowed out nation-states, and local participatory experiences has prompted a great deal of critical reflection.

As a result of these changes, local processes of regulation and coordination have become increasingly complex, and local governments have had to reposition their strategies and practices within entirely new territorial divisions of labor and institutional arrangements, as well as within much more competitive economic environments. Urban governance itself has undergone a number of changes as a result of the restructuring of national economies and the transformation of national states and their relationships to local units. Local administrators have found cities and regions to be of increasing economic importance, and many city governments have been able to rely less on unconditional transfers from central units. These trends have generally been accompanied by an increase in local autonomy for local governments and a shifting downward of the spheres of decision making.

Critical scholarship has challenged the heroic claims made on behalf of participatory approaches while taking participatory boosterism to task for failing to address questions of power, inequality, and politics (Cleaver 1999). More broadly, scholars have begun to point to participation, and participatory prescriptions in particular, as part of neoliberal governmentality. Participation emphasizes some of the most important characteristics of the entrepreneurial citizen being promoted as part of the move toward more rational government: self-regulation, responsibility for one's own problems, and a nonconflictive partnership with the state (Li 2007) Because participation in government is seen as an alternative to conflictive mobilization and disruption, it is argued, it becomes part of a set of strategies that depoliticize conflicts, paving the way for ever more aggressive neoliberal reforms of the state.

Perhaps the central criticism of participation has been that as a mainstream development prescription it is depoliticizing. Cleaver (1999, 598), for example, argues that belief in participation is based on three postulates: "that participation is intrinsically a 'good thing' (especially for the participants), that a focus on 'getting the techniques right' is the principal way of ensuring the success of such approaches, and that considerations of power and politics on the whole should be avoided as divisive and obstructive." According to Leal (2007, 543), "For participation to become part of dominant development practice, it first had to be modified, sanitized, and depoliticized. Once purged of all the threatening elements, participation could be reengineered as an instrument that could play a role within the status quo, rather than one that defied it."

Participatory budgeting represents the evolution of ideas about "participation in government" from something that could "defy" the status quo to something that could maintain and improve it. But the story is much more complicated than the "sanitized" versions adopted by development agencies. The evolution of participatory budgeting as a privileged tool for the dual goals of good governance and redistribution was a result of the changing fortunes of the PT. As the party won its first elections and its leaders embarked on running administrations that delivered results and brought them reelection, the calculus about the usefulness of different participatory strategies changed. In this way, participatory budgeting as something that enhances governance dates to discussions within the PT in the late 1980s, not discussions by a cabal of neoliberal development technocrats in the 2000s, as is sometimes implied. What is missing is an account of the translation and travel of deliberative democracy in a world of flows.

Understanding the travel of instruments

New policy instruments can be adopted in two ways: institutional monocropping and democratic experimentalism. Institutional monocropping refers to "the imposition of blueprints based on idealized versions of [Anglo-American] institutions" (Evans 2004, 32). A single institutional blueprint is applied regardless of context, often against the interests of local populations and to the detriment of their developmental possibilities.

A number of scholars have studied the way that institutional imperatives, the logic of expertise, and (usually) North-South hierarchies interact to reproduce blueprintism, even in the face of stated interests in not doing so and evidence that the blueprint does not work. Ferguson (1994) argues that development projects are important not necessarily for what they do or do not do but for their side effects—namely, the continued application of the same failed schemes. In the context of poverty-reduction schemes in Lesotho, Ferguson (1994, 274) describes the way the "reduction of poverty to a technical problem serves to depoliticize it" while crystallizing local "power relations, not to rationalize or coordinate them, so much as to cinch them all together into a knot."

Goldman (2005) argues that the institutional imperatives of the World Bank propel knowledge production (and the enrollment of technocrats and scientists) to justify the interventions it seeks to carry out. Scott (1998, 6) discusses the straitjacket of "monotonic regimes of centralized rationality" in planning schemes that rely on simplification of complex relationships into legible scripts. In the end, the "high-modernist, planned social order . . . excludes the necessary role of local knowledge and know-how."

Other scholars discuss the possibilities of learning, pragmatic experimentation, and creativity on the part of people in charge of public institutions. "Democratic experimentalism" refers to the way local actors "utilize their local knowledge to fit solutions to their individual circumstances" but rely on the information pooling of "others facing similar problems" (Dorf and Sabel 1998, 1). Sabel (2004, 7) uses the term as a metaphor that suggests a process of building institutions that are capable of constant adjustment and benefit from social learning, a process in which "each move suggests the next." He argues that such bootstrapped institutions "are as much the outcome as the starting points of development." According to Sabel (2004, 7), bootstrapping is the process by which institutions "can be rebuilt, again and again, by changing combinations of public and private actors, in light of the changing social constraints."

Scholars often laud the creativity of social movements and civil society actors. Attention to these forms of democratic experimentalism points to both the partial viewpoints and creativity of actors within government. Tendler's 1998 account of the administrators in Ceará, Brazil, for example, emphasizes the creative and pragmatic crafting of "good government in the tropics." Grindle (2007) emphasizes the way cadres of local government bureaucrats in Latin America have engaged in cross-learning and novel forms of partnerships with the private sector and key stakeholders alike. Borraz and John (2004) examine the ways new managerial local authorities have sought partnerships and the concertation of interests with private actors in the process of innovation.

Insightful as they are, accounts of both monocropping and experimentation suffer from parallel problems. Both are retrospective accounts that suppress moments of uncertainty and tend to describe a series of inevitable stages moving from the abstract to the concrete. The account of monocropping tends to ignore the collective nature of projects; the experimentation account tends to underplay power and conflict.

Monocropping is almost never the work of a single omnipotent actor; development projects are often framed as partnerships and usually involve more than one international actor, government actors from different levels, stakeholders of different sorts, and various experts. Projects may indeed have a logic of their own, but it is unwarranted to assume that this logic is simply a reproduction of the logic of the most powerful actor. The construction of facts is always a collective process (Latour 1987). Policy instruments become a "point of inevitable passage" and play a part in what Callon (1987) has called the stage of problematization, which allows heterogeneous actors to come together around issues and agree to work on them jointly.

For their part, experimentalists have been justifiably criticized for not paying enough attention to power dynamics. The very definition of a government's goals reflects the power of some agents to define the agenda, as does determination of who gets to be a "stakeholder" in these discussions. "There is appeal to social factors only when the true path of reason has been 'distorted' but not when it goes straight" (Latour 1987, 136).

A central argument of this chapter is that there is a fundamental open-endedness to some of the processes of the transmission of ideas. To ask about the "conditions of possibility" for monocropping or experimentalism, therefore, means to be attentive to instability and processes of translation, a term I use here in the sense of creating a new network of allies for a project while changing its meaning to fit the network. "Translating interests means at once offering new interpretations of these interests and channeling people in different directions" (Latour 1987, 117). Every translation is thus a transformation and a displacement (Callon 1987, 224), "a constant process of relating information and actors, and of regularly reinterpreting the systems thus created" (Lascoumes and Le Gales 2007, 7). Scholars of translation are attentive to the politics of instrumentation: the creation of a network of "allies and associations," the negotiation around interests of different actors, and the crystallization (or lack of crystallization) of those identities around the project.

Four sets of questions guide me as I examine the travel of the idea of participatory budgeting:

- What is it that actually travels? As the idea moves, how does the instrument change? As a set of institutional designs, how does it change?
- How is participatory budgeting justified? What reasons are given for its implementation?
- How is participatory budgeting implemented? Does its implementation resemble monocropping or experimentalism?
- How does the politics of instrumentation account for these different processes?

Conduits matter: Global translations and international networks

The spread of participatory budgeting took place in at least two phases. The first was diffusion through Brazil—and to a lesser extent Latin America—up to the mid-1990s. During this period it was through networks associated with the PT and allied NGOs that the idea travelled as a blueprint of a success story of "how the left can govern." The "Porto Alegre Story" became emblematic of the way the PT could govern and govern well.

By the later 1990s, the idea began to travel farther afield, through various conduits. International agencies conferred on participatory budgeting the legitimacy of an international best practice, and the concept garnered recognition in many different settings as a strategy for good governance. A number of networks developed to promote its implementation, and many consultancy-oriented NGOs—often funded by international agencies—started work on participatory budgeting in the late 1990s. The PT administration in Porto Alegre played no small role in this diffusion, actively promoting participatory budgeting in a variety of places, such as the World Social Forum. By 2015 more than 1,500 cities claimed to be practicing participatory budgeting.

Brazilian networks and the travel of participatory budgeting

The story of the translation of participatory budgeting throughout Brazil begins with the success of the Porto Alegre administration and a national network on participation. By the end of the 1980s and the second generation of popular administrations, experience had accumulated about participatory reforms. Little systematic theorizing had been done, however.

Led by a small number of important NGOs, a national forum—the National Forum on Popular Participation in Democratic and Popular Administrations (FNPP)—was created in 1990 as a place for people to meet and exchange experiences and ideas about participation. People from NGOs, social movement organizations, PT administrations, and academia debated the merits of various forms of participation.

Early on in the FNPP, there was a debate between people who advocated for "popular councils" and people who supported "institutional channels" of participation, such as participatory budgeting. Informed partly by the experiences of the next few years, when several PT administrations failed, some spectacularly, and partly by the shifting of the composition of the FNPP, which by 1996 had become almost exclusively controlled by administrators from PT administrations, the Forum settled on participatory budgeting as a preferred prescription and became involved in tracking and disseminating participatory budgeting practices.

Porto Alegre's model of participatory budgeting, which emerged out of a combination of experimentation, responses to external pressures, and a search for legitimacy in the absence of a reliable social movement base, became the model administration and the central point of reference for other participatory budgeting experiments, as it seemed successful in both delivering good governance and garnering legitimacy. A range of research and indicators confirms that participatory budgeting has indeed been a very successful innovation to governance and municipal decision making.[7]

One of the central features of the Porto Alegre model is its deliberate move away from civil society representation, which had been dominant in many PT administrations, toward a formula of direct (individual) participation. Civil society–mediated participation was prone to political difficulties and crises of legitimacy, when PT administrators were caught between charges of "clientelism of the left" (as seen by local media) when they met the demands of civil society and "class treason" (as seen by their allies) when they did not. Open participation, or citizen (as opposed to civic) participation in the local forums that decided on the budget, became a way for the administration to generate legitimacy for its redistributive platforms among the broader voting public as well as with allies.

The other two important elements of the Porto Alegre model were self-regulation (the setting of the rules of the process by participants themselves) and self-determination (the fact that participants, not administrators, make decisions about the capital budget). The net result in Porto Alegre was a transparent participatory system with broad participation from the city's poorer citizens that was widely perceived as legitimate and citizen run and that was successful at managing conflicts over demands.

Participatory budgeting became widely recognized as central to the "PT formula" of combining redistribution with broad-based participation. By the mid-1990s, the PT had become more adept at solving certain endemic problems. The "PT way of governing" combined social justice goals with transparency, broad participation, and effective governance. It was on this basis that the party expanded its electoral influence in municipal governments throughout Brazil in the late 1990s. Far from destabilizing the bourgeois political system, as some observers in the mid-1980s had predicted, participation became a central piece in a strategy of running government well. Good governance for the thinkers and activists of the PT, of course, meant something other than reducing deficits and improving the delivery of public services, but it certainly included that as well.

Participatory budgeting reforms were copied, and transformed in the process of being copied, throughout Brazil. Twelve cities introduced participatory budgeting in 1989–92, 36 did so in 1993–96, at least 103 did so in 1997–2000, and at least 150 did so in 2001–04, according to surveys conducted by the FNPP. Many experiments begin as exact copies of the Porto Alegre experiment, down to the names of the municipal departments responsible for the process, only to be modified after a year or two (Teixeira 2002).

Participatory budgeting was widely adopted throughout Brazil for a variety of reasons. In addition to the FNPP, NGOs such as the Instituto Brasileiro de Análises Sociais e Econômicas (IBASE) were instrumental in monitoring and promoting participatory budgeting to progressive administrators. Fundação Getúlio Vargas, Brazil's elite public policy institute, and Pólis, in São Paulo, were instrumental in documenting and promoting best municipal practices. Participatory budgeting programs, alongside a bundle of other municipal best practices, were diffused in a period of intensive creativity and experimentation.

The basic structure adopted generally included a yearly cycle of district-level meetings, concurrent meetings of a main budget council, and, somewhat less commonly, municipal thematic meetings. The majority of cases included a system of representation of delegates based on numbers of participants at some meeting or, less commonly, the number of residents per district, as well as a second tier of councilors who were elected by the delegates. Less common features involved meetings with civil society groups and group visits to sites of interest.

The purpose of meetings varied. District-level meetings often elected delegates, deliberated over priorities, raised needs, and accounted for previous years' projects.

A 1996 "How To" guide from the FNPP (1996, 5) proposes that participatory budgeting can be an efficient instrument for important political, economic, and social achievements: greater transparency in the elaboration and execution of the budget; more social control of the budget and of public finances; the creation of a new standard for distribution of resources that would permit meeting the needs of the poorer population; the increase of municipal resources; fighting clientelism and corruption; the increase of legitimacy of municipal administration; the sharing of power between authorities and society; the strengthening of cooperation and solidarity; the affirmation of the culture of dialogue and of the mutual commitment between government and population; mobilization of organized and unorganized social sectors; education for citizenship; and the broadening of the public sphere.

The benefits of participatory budgeting in this version are a mix of good governance (transparency, increased resources, reduction in clientelism); social justice (redistribution of resources); and civic goals (legitimacy, dialogue, cooperation, and solidarity). Motivations for administrators to pursue these types of projects include building a base of support, legitimating redistribution, increasing the awareness of the population, and increasing transparency (Wampler 2007). As the audience for a how-to guide no doubt includes administrators, it therefore make sense for it to emphasize governance-enhancing benefits.

Global networks

Participatory budgeting became a global phenomenon in the late 1990s. In 1997 the United Nations Development Programme (UNDP) declared it a best practice; in 2001 it featured participatory budgeting prominently in its flagship *Human Development Report*. The "exchange and emulation programs" funded by the European Union (Network 9 of the URB-AL cooperation program) were important in the dissemination that followed (Allegretti and Herzberg 2004). Direct exchanges were responsible for some of the first examples outside of Latin America, many of them linked to the political left. Academic institutions, such as the Institute of Development Studies in the United Kingdom, were also prominent.

Many international initiatives track and disseminate participatory budgeting, often partially supported by municipal administrations themselves. They include the International Budget Network; the UNDP–funded International Observatory of Participatory Democracy; the European-based Budget Participatif network; the International Forum of Local Authorities, which convenes with the World Social Forum; and countless workshops at social forums dedicated to participatory budgeting. The World Social Forum is probably among the most important engines of diffusion of the idea, although its impact has not been documented. Many networks meet to share ideas and templates in this "space of mutual encounter and learning, of multiple discourses, modes and activities." Progressive activists have travelled long distances to learn and diffuse this learning about participatory budgeting.

In the developing world, dissemination of participatory budgeting has come largely from development agencies. The World Bank Institute tracks participatory budgeting best practices in supporting NGOs involved in promotion. The U.S. Agency for International Development (USAID) has been active in directly promoting participatory budgeting, playing direct consultancy and training roles, particularly in Latin America.

As a result of the involvement of development agencies, participatory budgeting diffused quickly. Two important elements helped participatory recipes and blueprints "jump" to the terrain of multilateral agencies. First, participation became seen as a technical fix. Second, the development discourse was changing, as were the roles and functions of national states, with lower levels of government attracting attention as strategic sites.

The success and diffusion of participatory budgeting took place alongside growing interest in participation by multilateral agencies in the 1990s. The United Nations and other institutions advocated participation as early as the 1970s, developing several "participatory methodologies. But the late 1990s were a period of intense interest in the role of civil society and community-based development among development agencies, partly as a result of reformers and progressives within these institutions who gained influence during this period. The change also reflected a shift in thinking that culminated with the recognition that "structural adjustment" had failed to either provide benefits to the majority of populations in question or even promote development and that "state-dominated development has failed, but so will stateless development" (World Bank 1997, 25). This period witnessed a shift toward good governance, or the idea that "the state itself does not inhibit development, but its manner of governance can" (Grindle 2007, 25). Good governance complements a slightly earlier emphasis on decentralization, a 1980s catchphrase used by policy makers who argued that a less centralized state would be less bureaucratic, more responsive, and more efficient.

It is in this context that participation came to be valued as a complement to good local governance and an alternative development prescription, a means to achieve "greater efficiency and effectiveness of investment and of contributing to processes of democratization and empowerment" (Cleaver 1999, 597). Participatory development practitioners recognized the "necessity of engagement with the state" (Gaventa and Valderrama 1999, 3), and the "good governance agenda" more and more emphasized transparent, accountable, and participatory institutions. Participatory budgeting was one of several contending best practices that were adopted and actively promoted in the period.

There is a notable difference in the strategies used to promote participatory budgeting by participatory budgeting networks on the one hand and NGOs and donor organizations on the other. Participatory budgeting networks almost always make a normative argument for participatory budgeting. For NGOs participatory budgeting not only helps redistribute resources in ways that help reduce poverty, it also advances a democratic form of governance that is right on its own terms, independent of the outcomes it produces. The redistribution of power (supposedly advanced by participatory budgeting) is a desirable goal in and of itself. NGOs thus frequently make passionate and emotional arguments concerning the value of giving voice to the poor.

In contrast, for donor organizations, such as the World Bank, USAID, the Department for International Development (DFID), and UN-Habitat, participatory budgeting is a "tool" or "best practice" to help advance specific ends, such as poverty reduction, improved public accountability, and "good governance." Although these organizations recognize the political nature of participatory budgeting and its redistributive function, they appear to value participatory budgeting only insofar as it has been proven effective. Accordingly, donor organizations have shown significant interest in technical training programs for participatory budgeting and the dissemination of best practices materials. For example, World Bank materials describe participatory budgeting as

> an innovative mechanism which aims to involve citizens in the decision-making process of public budgeting. By creating a channel for citizens to give voice to their priorities, participatory budgeting can be instrumental in making the allocation of public resources more inclusive and equitable. By promoting public access to revenue and expenditure information, participatory budgeting effectively

increases transparency in fiscal policy and public expenditure management, reducing scope for clientelistic practices, elite capture, and corruption, thereby enhancing the government's credibility and the citizens' trust. (World Bank n.d.)

The World Bank also recognizes that participatory budgeting enhances social accountability and promotes active citizenship and social learning. However, it views participatory budgeting primarily as a tool to achieve specific ends, not as something valuable in and of itself.

The introduction to UN-Habitat's *Participatory Budgeting in Africa: A Training Companion* discusses participatory budgeting as an "innovative urban management practice with excellent potential to promote principles of good urban governance" (2008). It describes participatory budgeting as an "important tool in the democratization of cities . . . and in support of decentralization and social accountability." This training companion serves as a technical guide for implementing participatory budgeting, highlighting examples of best practices from eastern and southern Africa.

In 2007 the Bank-Netherlands Partnership Program (BNPP) and the World Bank Institute financed a radio course on participatory budgeting as part of the Africa Good Governance Program on the Radio Waves project. The program, which consisted of 10 broadcasts, can be accessed online (World Bank 2007).

Several lessons emerge from this diffusion. First, the institutional design promoted in different networks is often vague, making it difficult to see that the participatory budgeting promoted by USAID is different from the participatory budgeting promoted by the World Social Forum. Second, and more important, different actors often come together on projects. In many contexts, a combination of networks is present. These overlaps are so common that one recent review of experiences in Latin America noted that Bank-funded participatory budgeting projects are most empowering when indigenous or leftist movements challenge the terms of the debate (Goldfrank 2007; Van Cott 2008).

Context matters, too: Local mediations

This section describes the ways in which the idea of participatory budgeted reached three different parts of the world in the late 1990s and early 2000s. The case studies document the experiences of Camaragibe and Gravataí, in Brazil; Ilo and Villa El Salvador, in Peru; and Cordoba, in Spain.

Bootstrapping democracy: Reforms in Camaragibe and Gravataí, Brazil

Participatory budgeting expanded in Brazil between 1997 and 2000, when administrators carried out many variations on the theme. PT administrators were expected to introduce mechanisms of participation; by 1996 participatory budgeting had become the principal PT formula for doing so.

As a blueprint, participatory budgeting had been applied successfully in dozens of cities by the time of the conferences and discussions of late 1996. Its central innovation—open meetings leading to binding decisions on urban infrastructure—seemed to have travelled well, often extending support for PT administrations' redistributive platforms among the broader voting public while shielding administrators from charges of "clientelism of the left." The idea that local PT governments should be instruments of popular mobilization had given way to more pragmatic understandings that the PT should focus on governing well.

Two Brazilian cities—Camaragibe, in Pernambuco in the Northeast, and Gravataí, in Rio Grande do Sul, in the South—adapted these blueprints in different ways, as described in detail elsewhere (Baiocchi, Heller, and Silva 2011). Both cities creatively adapted the participatory budgeting blueprint while staying close to the principle of direct, binding participation mixed with delegated participation via elected representatives. Of importance here is the nature of the experimentalism and adaptation of the institutional blueprint in the different contexts.

Both Camaragibe and Gravataí are medium-size, poorer municipalities with weak histories of social movements and civil society—in other words, inauspicious settings for the transplant of a model fine-tuned in a city like Porto Alegre, with its oppositional history and fuller coffers (Baiocchi 2005). Moreover, fiscal 1996 and 1997 were especially difficult for Brazilian municipalities; the mayors in both cities faced difficult tasks delivering on their campaign promises.

Gravataí originally modeled its participatory budgeting on Porto Alegre, but it modified its approach significantly after a few months. Organized civil society was essentially absent from the process, if not openly antagonistic; it played little or no role in drawing participants or processing demands. The participatory process relied instead on the active and intensive intervention of city government to make it work.

City Hall employees divided the town of 230,000 into 85 micro-districts and coordinated meetings in each at the beginning of the cycle. Their effort was a massive and complex experiment in inclusive participation that depended on a concerted effort by administrators, who had to facilitate hundreds of meetings a year.

Participation in the first year was high (6,900 participants). It dropped to 3,500 the second year before climbing to 13,000 the third year. On a per capita basis, this rate of participation was four times as high as in Porto Alegre. In promotional materials in the third year of the process, Gravataí administrators started to call themselves the "champion of popular participation."

Camaragibe represents an important departure from the basic blueprint. In a town far less plugged into national circuits than Gravataí, the participatory blueprint for the participatory administration was a highly local

invention based on the previous experiences of health councils and a pragmatic response to a lack of funds for investments. The mayor-elect—a
doctor and highly respected activist from the health movement—had
headed the municipal health department and launched a municipal health
conference. Once elected, he sought partnerships with several advisory
institutions, including the Recife-based Josué de Castro Center, a progressive social science research institute.[8] These advisors helped further the
earlier diagnostic work of the campaign process by continuing to carry out
research in the town's five districts. Rather than controlling the budget, the
process that emerged out of the diagnostic process intervened in the
governance of all the municipal departments that served citizens directly.
The nature of this design reflected the pragmatic choices of administrators
to channel participation away from new investments and toward areas of
governance such as health, which rely on external funding and for which
management of services is more important. The emphasis was on governance, broadly conceived. Participatory administration was understood as
a practical alternative to participatory budgeting.

Participation was high. But in a unique twist, delegates were elected to
four-year terms at the start of the process and played the role that government officials played in Gravataí—drawing participants, helping filter
demands, and negotiating scaled-up demands. A general election was held
and 120 delegates were elected (one for every thousand residents).
Associations—neighborhood associations and movements linked to health
and housing, among others—played important roles in the mediation of
interests, but they did so largely through this cadre of elected delegates,
which included many community leaders. The role of associations is evident, for example, in the privileged role that delegates (who tended to come
from movements) played. Camaragibe built a system that went beyond the
budget to encompass administration. Its participatory administration
resulted in a highly complex institutional design that combined forums
with a range of coordinating institutions.

Both cities reveal pragmatic adaptation to local conditions and heavy
reliance on earlier experiences with promoting participation. Both mechanisms highlight and help explain the extraordinary heterogeneity of actual
institutional design behind the idea of participatory budgeting. Differences
reflect pragmatic adaptations by participatory budgeting architects to local
realities, in particular the condition of local civil society, which was
perceived in both cities as unable to play a proactive role.

The iron cage of participation: Blueprintism in Ilo and Villa El Salvador, Peru

Two Peruvian municipalities (Ilo and Villa El Salvador) began to experiment with the idea of participatory budgeting in the late 1990s.[9] Both cities
had a tradition of local democracy and social movement militancy; both
were governed by the Izquierda Unida (IU) party.

In 1999 a representative of Porto Alegre toured Peru, introducing participatory budgeting. The visit was sponsored by the NGO Foro Ciudades por la Vida, a consultancy supported by the European Union (Hordjik 2005) which stepped in to address the perceived weakness of the association of Peruvian municipalities. Both Ilo and Villa El Salvador had achieved some renown as successful cases outside of Brazil when the UNDP exchange program (PGU-ALC) sponsored an international seminar on participatory budgeting in Vila El Salvador in 2001. Civil society activists, politicians, and university researchers attended the exchange (Hordjik 2009).

With the election of Alejandro Toledo in 2001 and the end of the Fujimori *demodictatura*, a number of national spaces of dialogue and consultation (*mesas de concertación*) were inaugurated. The most notable was the one on poverty alleviation. The National Agreement of 2002 followed. This document of *concertación,* drawn up by civil society, political actors, and private sector representatives, listed 30 policy objectives for Peru to achieve by 2020, including decentralization and the strengthening of democratic institutions.

In 2002, two relevant laws were passed. The law on regional government forced the publication of budgetary data. The law on decentralization increased transfers to local government and mandated participatory budgeting in the creation of local development plans.

Actors on the national stage were divided on the value of participatory budgeting, but a law project was introduced in 2002. The ruling coalition included several progressive parties and groups. Left-wing politicians, such as the former mayor of Ilo, were prominent in the introduction of the law. The Budget Office of the Economic and Finance Ministry was an "unexpected and unusual promoter" of participatory budgeting, drafting the participatory budgeting law. The ministry also launched pilot participatory budgeting processes in several states in 2002 ahead of passage of the law.

The law faced difficulties in Congress. Its final versions reflected compromises that ensured that participatory budgeting would not threaten representative democracy (Chirinos 2004). They included several aspects that weakened elements of direct democracy. For example, the law established that 60 percent of participants in the local councils that make final decisions over participatory budgeting processes be government officials. It also introduced language about official "participating agents," who had to be representative of a legally registered civil society organization that had been in existence for at least three years. This rule violated the guidelines originally proposed by the Ministry of Economy, which deemphasized councils and emphasized more direct participation (Goldfrank 2007). The language of the law itself changed, moving away from "social justice" and "social transformation," as participatory budgeting became "a mechanism to assign public resources in a just, rational, efficient, effective, and transparent manner, which strengthens the relationship between state and civil society." The modified law passed in 2003.

To make the law less vague, the Ministry of Economy created more specific guidelines for implementation. It created a working group that included members of the poverty alleviation roundtable, several NGOs, and groups like the Association of Peruvian Municipalities. USAID, UNICEF, and the United Nations Development Fund for Women (UNIFEM) sponsored two related groups, Participa Peru and PRODES, which also participated in the working group. Members of the Decentralization Commission, the Ministry of Women and Social Development, and the Social Development Fund also joined. This working group became the principal place to debate the rules of and challenges to participatory budgeting. It has produced annual reports and documents yearly changes to the process, which it determines.

In 2003 eight municipalities in Peru started to develop participatory budgeting processes. They presented their experiences at a national congress that year. With assistance from USAID, municipalities held training exercises about how to implement participatory budgeting. Implementation and growth were quick: by 2007 there were 661 participatory budgeting processes in Peru, which were present in a third of regional governments and all major cities.

The process, based on an annual cycle, is identical throughout Peru. First, workshops of information delivery are held. They are followed by working groups, which make proposals. A committee then performs technical assessments of the proposals, after which agreements are reached with the local coordinating councils and implementation begins (Grompone 2005). This process does not involve direct participation (proceedings are not open to everyone); it is consultative. Government has two veto points: the technical committee can change or reject projects, and the coordinating council ultimately makes the final decisions. The coordinating council is composed of 60 percent government officials and 40 percent civil society organization representatives, 30 percent of whom are from the business sector. There are no clear guidelines on the election of participants to the council, but a 2004 study finds that most did not hold elections (Chirinos 2004).

Especially in the first years, municipalities in Peru were "not successful in promoting participation, transparency, effective planning, or improvements in public infrastructure or service provision" (Goldfrank 2007, 31). Even in the open information workshops, participation of civil society was low (both absolutely and relative to participation by government officials) and participants from outside of organized sectors were virtually absent, according to internal evaluations by the Economics and Finance Ministry. Arroyo and Irigoyen (2005) conclude that less than 10 percent of participatory budgeting processes in Peru are actually participatory. Grompone (2005) criticizes the fact that a city of 750,000 like Trujillo and a small town in the jungle should have the same institutions.

An evaluation of the participatory budgeting process as a whole by Red Participa Peru (a network of promoters of citizen participation) describes the results of a discussion of the balance of citizen participation in Peru in late 2007/08. It is quite negative, in sharp contrast to the evaluation by the working group within the ministry, which argued that state–civil society relations had improved and participatory budgeting had had "a positive influence on the quality of democracy and governability" (Grupo Propuesta Ciudadana 2008, 16). The list of complaints about participatory budgeting processes in Peru is long, including the "notorious low quality of proposals, and the lack of capacity by participants"; "the lack of representativity of participants, and the low quality of their participation"; the "little political will of authorities"; the "lack of connection between participatory budgeting and the local development councils"; and the disconnect between the great "social mobilization that a participatory budgeting process implies and its low capacity to solve problems" (Grupo Propuesta Ciudadana 2008, 17–18).

In later years the process underwent some loosening. The possibilities for "unorganized sectors of society" and "natural persons" to participate in the local assemblies (but not the coordinating council) increased, and the length of time an organization had to have existed before participating was reduced. There was growing ambiguity about the relationship between councils and participatory budgeting. There is now greater attention to local complaints; civil society dialogue on the formation of rules, such as the composition of technical committees; and increased funding for participatory budgeting projects.

The case of Peru clearly demonstrates translation at work. Two factors are worth mentioning. First, what arrived in Peru as "participatory budgeting" from USAID was already quite hollowed out: USAID blueprints deemphasized binding decision making and local adaptation. This version eventually overcame more empowered and experimentalist versions that had come through political party networks. Second, the meaning of the process was slowly eroded. The language of citizen participation remained, but its meaning changed through each iteration, emptying its empowering potential while moving toward a rigid blueprinting process of transmission.

Reformers versus civil society: Participatory budgeting in Cordoba, Spain

The participatory budgeting process in Cordoba is emblematic for Europe for two reasons. First, Cordoba is sometimes described as the Porto Alegre of Europe because of its strong leftist tradition and the fact that the rules of and justification for participatory budgeting were closest to those in Porto Alegre. Second, its failure was both spectacular and unexpected. "The experience collapsed due to the opposition of the local civil society— mainly the *movimiento vecinal* [neighborhood movement]—that felt excluded from the process and as such to be the main victim of the institu-tionalization of participatory democracy" (Talpin 2012, 48). The inclusion of "average" citizens threatened the privileged role of associations of inter-locution with local government, "stopping a tradition of associative democracy and of large involvement of associations in the municipal deci-sions" (Talpin 2012, 49).

Local democracy has been an important part of political life in Spain since its transition to democracy. Demands for democratic decision making around urban issues had been part of the political landscape of movements in Spain since the mid-1970s in cities like Madrid, Barcelona, and Seville, where active neighborhood movements were important players in the pro-cess of transition and challenged the highly centralized nature of the Franco regime (Castells 1983).

Spain held its first free municipal elections in 1979. In 1985 it adopted the Local Government Act (LRBRL), under the first national government of the Socialist Workers' Party of Spain (Partido Socialista Obrero Español [PSOE]), which won the elections in several municipalities in 1983. Under pressure from its bases of support, such as the well-organized citizens' associations (*vecinales*), it devolved significant decision making to munici-palities (Navarro Yáñez 2004).

Spain is home to various forms of citizen participation, particularly in local government (Goma and Brugue 1998; Botella 1999; Pindado 2000; Blanco and Gomà 2006; Font 2001). A survey of Catalan municipalities found about a dozen forms of participatory budgeting, with varying degrees of inclusivity and decision-making power (Font 2002). These mechanisms range from citizen forums to participation in the development of strategic plans to environmental participatory planning. The fundamen-tal feature of these experiments is that they "went beyond the usual process of giving voice to an organized groups" to actively and directly engage citi-zens in policy formulation (Font 2002, 26). Much of this effort has been an attempt to recapture the quality of democratic engagement from the early years of the transition and to shift the focus away from the increas-ingly fractious and prominent regional politics (Navarro Yáñez 2004). What is distinctive about all of these experiments in citizen participation is that they often do not emerge from civil society demands. Indeed, neigh-borhood associations seem to be losing in organizational power (Garcia 1995; Goma and Brugue 1998).

Cordoba is a municipality of 300,000 people in the south of Spain, with a tradition of oppositional politics. It is ruled by a coalition of the United Left (IU) and the PSOE. In the early years of the democratic transition, local political party activists set up coalitions in places like Cordoba, and community activists demanded participation (Balfour 1989).

In 1999 activists from the Federation of Neighborhood Associations proposed the idea of participatory budgeting after a visit from the then-mayor of Porto Alegre. The process was implemented as a pilot project in 2001 and as a regular process in 2002. The participatory budget was introduced as an "attractive new way of government for the left" (Ganuza 2005, 515) and a way of addressing the concern that the PSOE was disconnected from the population.

Participatory budgeting was also introduced as a mechanism for modernizing the municipal administration. Supported by researchers linked to the graduate program in planning at the University of Madrid and with affinities to the antiglobalization movement, modernizers within government developed a process that adapted several of the Porto Alegre principles, including a yearly cycle with open district assemblies that elect representatives (*agentes*), who would be responsible for the next stages of the process and ultimately make binding decisions on projects to be carried out by the municipal administration. The *agentes* elected at the end of the first information assemblies received training in municipal government issues and debated the rules of the process, which changed yearly. They decided on the dates of meetings for the next stage of neighborhood meetings, where citizens were to bring forward and prioritize project ideas. *Agentes* worked on these proposals and returned them to a subsequent district assembly to ratify what would become the proposal for each district. A second group of *agentes* was then elected to decide on the overall city priorities and approve the budget (Ganuza 2005).

What the process did not include was a privileged role for the neighborhood associations. Early on, representatives of the Association of Neigborhood Associations of Cordoba approached the administration demanding that participation be organized along associational lines. A city with a history of active associations, Cordoba has more than 2,000 registered civil society organizations, more than 100 of which are neighborhood associations. The Association argued that each *vecinale* should have one or more of the seats of the representatives who choose projects and should be allowed to organize the process in all neighborhoods under their "jurisdiction." This demand was not met, and neighborhood associations began to criticize the process more actively.

Participation in the neighborhood assembly stage, which had numbered about 1,500 in the first year, nonetheless remained at the same level the following year, albeit with the absence of people linked to the leadership of the *vecinales*. In 2004 this leadership began a more active campaign against participatory budgeting, claiming that the process was antidemocratic, inconsistent with grassroots democracy, and part of a state strategy to co-opt and undermine neigborhood associations (Ganuza 2005).

The participatory budgeting process came to a halt in 2004, amid growing controversies in the local newspapers. A committee of *agentes* quickly started a counter-mobilization, demanding the continuance of the process. *Agentes* came from a cross-section of Cordoba society but included a number of activists in NGOs and alter-globalization movements, members of *vecinales*, and some members of the Communist Party, who understood participatory budgeting to be part of a "move to transcend bourgeois democracy."

As a compromise position, the process was changed from an individual citizen model to a mixed model that included both individual citizens and associations. In the new model, the *vecinales* got to organize and facilitate meetings throughout the city, and the role of *agentes* was abolished in favor of representatives. Representatives to a "city council" that would ultimately decide on spending priorities were to be elected from among participants, but a number of representative seats were reserved for *vecinales*.

The process continued for two years before being discontinued altogether under pressure from the *vecinales*, which mistrusted it. Still in contention were several of the rules of the process, such as the "social" criteria for the distribution of resources, the granting of higher scores to proposals that positively discriminate in favor of the weakest groups (Allegretti 2004).

As the Cordoba case floundered, other cities in Spain adopted their own participatory budgeting processes. All of these municipalities—Seville, Puente Genil, the outskirts of Madrid—abandoned "individual participation" in favor of mixed participation. In various cities "the associations, especially neighborhood associations, are indeed the only legal participants in the processes" (Talpin 2012, 48).

The fundamental issues for Cordoba are why associations felt so threatened that they undermined the project and eventually rendered it unviable and why they have come to play such an important role in these processes in Spain. These associations are not necessarily clientelistic, but they have a privileged relationship with city government. Associational democracy has been at the heart of the transition in Spain; it is a successful arrangement on its own terms. The demands of associations are often met; they have an institutionalized channel of communication with administrations. To leaders of associations, participatory budgeting represented a threat, in that it dislodged their position as an obligatory passage point, potentially rendering them irrelevant.

Conclusions

Participatory budgeting appeared on the world stage as a best practice at a time of great interest in participatory approaches to development. Originally introduced in Porto Alegre, Brazil, it spread rapidly, first in Latin America and later throughout the world. Local implementation of the practice shaped the form it took in different contexts. It is key—what I call the politics of instrumentation—as it decisively shaped the translation of the concept in different contexts. The array of actors and interests mobilized in a particular project helped account for the design of the institution, its justification, as well as whether the idea landed as a monocropped blueprint or material for democratic experimentation.

The case studies examined in this chapter yield several lessons. First, "participatory budgeting" refers to very different ideas and actions in different settings. The institutions implemented in Peru, for example, evoke the name and the yearly cycle from Porto Alegre, but they are different in nearly every other way.

Second, geographic distance from Porto Alegre does not account for divergence from the original formula. The cases in Brazil deviated most from the original participatory budgeting story. The Peruvian case first deviated but then returned to the original model. The Spanish case, which ultimately failed, started as a close copy.

Third, the role of civil society—who speaks for it, who is authorized to represent "the people"—is the most fragile part of the coalition that supports participatory budgeting. This issue represented the central worry for administrators in Brazil. In Peru it was the basis of opposition from conservative parties and was critical in defining the process that was ultimately adopted. In Spain it ended the effort altogether.

The three cases show a transformation of participatory budgeting as a result of the processes of local negotiation. This translation took many forms. The more politicized networks in Brazil and Spain maintained the element of social justice more than did adopters in Peru, where more politicized networks were present at first but were ultimately not able to exercise influence.

The experiences in the three countries give reason for both hope and caution. The hopeful part of the story concerns the democratic experimentalism in the two Brazilian cities, where the "right" conditions for participatory budgeting were not in place. Local agency was critical in both cities.

The Peruvian story is a cautionary tale of monocropping. Adoption of participatory budgeting was faster than in Brazil, but negotiation of the process produced an institution with little space for deliberation, no room for popular input, and no opportunities for local communities to determine how participatory budgeting worked in their city. Deliberative development and self-determination were transformed into a new, hybrid form of high modernism (Scott 1998).

The experience of Spain, where participatory budgeting was ultimately abandoned, also provides reason for concern. It shows that even in the presence of what appear to be promising factors—a leftist administration, sufficient resources, an active civil society—translation can fail.

Notes

1. The Porto Alegre story is well-known and well-documented. For one version of events in English, see Baiocchi (2005).

2. Giovanni Allegretti (2004) refers to this process as the "return of the Caravels."
3. For accounts of the global phenomenon, see Allegretti and Herzberg (2004) and Cabannes (2004).
4. The definition notes: "It is a particular type of institution, a technical device with the generic purpose of carrying a concrete concept of the politics/society relationship and sustained by a concept of regulation" (Lascoumes and Le Gales 2007, 4).
5. Scholars of diffusion argue that a program that seems appealing on the surface "attracts disproportionate attention" and is embraced because of "its apparent promise, not its demonstrated effects" (Weyland 1996).
6. These objects include ideas and ideologies, people and goods, images and messages, and technologies and techniques. This world is one of flows (Appadurai 2000).
7. Although Porto Alegre had high indicators to begin with, the PT administration significantly improved service delivery, particularly in basic sewerage and water, primary public schooling, and public transportation. There is also evidence of increased civic mobilization around participatory budgeting meetings and a decrease in protests and petitions (Baiocchi 2005).
8. Administrators also developed partnerships with the Brazilian Development Bank, the State Planning Department, and (once) UNDP.
9. This section draws on the work of several scholars, particularly Michaela Hordijk (2005, 2009) and McNulty (2012).

References

Allegretti, Giovanni. 2004. "The Return of the Caravels. Participatory Budgets from South America to Europe." University of Florence, Faculty of Architecture, Department of Town Planning.
———. 2005. *Participatory Budgets in Europe: Between Efficiency and Growing Local Democracy.* TNI Briefing Series 2004/5, Transnational Institute and the Centre for Democratic Policy-Making, Amsterdam.
Allegretti, Giovanni, and Carsten Herzberg. 2004. *Participatory Budgets in Europe: Between Efficiency and Growing Local Democracy.* TNI Briefing Series 2004/5, Transnational Institute and the Centre for Democratic Policy-Making, Amsterdam.
Appadurai, Arjun. 2000. "Grassroots Globalization and the Research Imagination." *Public Culture* 12 (1): 1–19.
Arroyo, Juan, and Marina Irigoyen. 2005. *Desafíos de la democracia participativa local en la descentralización.* CARE Perú, Lima.
Baiocchi, Gianpaolo. 2005. *Militants and Citizens: The Politics of Participatory Democracy in Porto Alegre.* Stanford, CA: Stanford University Press.
Baiocchi, Gianpaolo, Patrick Heller, and Marcelo K. Silva. 2011. *Bootstrapping Democracy: Transforming Local Governance and Civil Society in Brazil.* Stanford, CA: Stanford University Press.

Balfour, Sebastian. 1989. *Dictatorship, Workers, and the City*. London: Oxford.

Blanco, Ismael, and Ricard Gomà. 2006. "Del gobierno a la gobernanza: oportun-
idades y retos de un nuevo paradigma." *Politika, Revista de Ciencias Sociales*
2 (1): 11–27.

Borraz, Olivier, and Peter John. 2004. "Symposium: The Transformation of Urban
Political Leadership in Western Europe." *International Journal of Urban and
Regional Research* 28 (1): 107–20.

Botella, Juan. 1999. *La ciudad democrática*. Barcelona: Ediciones del Serbal.

Cabannes, Yves. 2004. "Participatory Budgeting: A Significant Contribution to
Participatory Democracy." *Environment and Urbanization* 16 (1): 27–46.

Callon, M. 1987. "Some Elements in the Sociology of Translation: Domestication
of the Scallops and the Fishermen of St. Brieuc Bay." In *Power, Action and
Belief: A New Sociology of Knowledge*, ed. John Law, 196–223. London:
Routledge Kegan & Paul.

Castells, Manuel. 1983. "The Making of an Urban Social Movement: The Citizen
Movement in Madrid." In *The City and the Grassroots A Cross-Cultural
Theory of Urban Social Movements*, ed. Manuel Castells. Berkeley: University
of California Press.

Chirinos Segura, Luis. 2004. "Participación ciudadana en gobiernos regionales:
El caso de los consejos de coordinación regional." In *La participación ciudadana
y la construcción de la democracia en América Latina*, ed. Grupo Propuesta
Ciudadana. Lima: Ser, Consode, Oxfam, Grupo Propuesta Ciudadana, Participa
Peru, DFID, EED, and USAID-Peru.

Cleaver, Frances. 1999. "Paradoxes of Participation: Questioning Participatory
Approaches to Development." *Journal of International Development* 11 (4):
597–612.

Dezalay, Yves, and Bryant G. Garth. 2002. *The Internationalization of Palace
Wars: Lawyers, Economists, and the Contest to Transform Latin American
States*. Chicago: University of Chicago Press.

Dorf, Michael C., and Charles F. Sabel. 1998. "A Constitution of Democratic
Experimentalism." *Columbia Law Review* 98 (267).

Evans, Peter. 2004. "Development as Institutional Change: The Pitfalls of
Monocropping and the Potentials of Deliberation." *Studies in Comparative
International Development* 38 (4): 30–52.

Ferguson, James. 1994. *The Anti-Politics Machine: Development, Depoliticization,
and Bureaucratic Power in Lesotho*. Minneapolis: University of Minnesota
Press.

FNPP (Forum Nacional da Participação Popular). 1996. *Poder Local Participação
Popular e Construção da Cidadania*. São Paulo.

Font, Joan. 2001. *Ciudadanos y decisiones públicas*. Barcelona: Ariel.

———. 2002. "Local Participation in Spain: Beyond Associative Democracy."
Working Paper, Del Institut de Ciences Politiques I Sociales 210, Barcelona.

Ganuza, E. 2005. "Cordoba." In *Participatory Budgets in a European Comparative
Approach Perspectives and Chances of the Cooperative State at the Municipal*

Level in Germany and Europe, vol. II (Final Report), ed. Y. Sintomer, C. Herzberg, and A. Rocke, 530–42. Berlin: Center Marc Bloch.

Garcia, Soledad. 1995. "Urban Communities and Local Political Participation in Spain." *Annals of the American Academy of Political and Social Sciences* (July): 63–76.

Gaventa, John, and Camilo Valderrama. 1999. "Participation, Citizenship and Local Governance." Background note prepared for the workshop on "Strengthening Participation in Local Governance," University of Sussex, Institute of Development Studies, June 21–23.

Goldfrank, Benjamin. 2007. "The Politics of Deepening Local Democracy: Decentralization, Party Institutionalization, and Participation." *Comparative Politics* 39 (2): 147–68.

Goldman, Michael. 2005. *Imperial Nature: The World Bank and Struggles for Social Justice in the Age of Globalization*. New Haven, CT: Yale University Press.

Goma, Ricard, and Joaquim Brugue. 1998. "Gobierno local: De nacionalizacion al localismo y de lad gerencializacion a la repolitizacion." Working Paper, Universitat Autonoma de Barcelona.

Grindle, Merilee S. 2007. *Going Local: Decentralization and the Promise of Good Governance*. Princeton, NJ: Princeton University Press.

Grompone, R. 2005. *La escisión inevitable: Partidos y movimientos en el Perú actual*. Instituto de Estudios Peruanos, Lima.

Grupo Propuesta Ciudadana. 2008. *Foros de debate: Red Participa Peru*. Lima.

Habermas, J. 2001. *On the Pragmatics of Social Interaction: Preliminary Studies in the Theory of Communicative Action*. Cambridge, MA: MIT Press.

Held, David. 1999. *Global Transformations: Politics, Economics and Culture*. Palo Alto: Stanford University Press.

Hordijk, Michaela. 2005. "Participatory Governance in Peru: Exercising Citizenship." *Environment and Urbanization* 17 (1): 219–36.

———. 2009. "Peru's Participatory Budgeting: Configurations of Power, Opportunities for Change." *Open Urban Studies Journal* 2: 43–55.

Jessop, Bob. 2000. "The Crisis of the National Spatio-Temporal Fix and the Tendential Ecological Dominance of Globalizing Capitalism." *International Journal of Urban and Regional Research* 24 (2): 323–60.

Keck, Margaret E., and Kathryn Sikkink. 1998. *Activists beyond Borders: Advocacy Networks in International Politics*. Ithaca, NY: Cornell University Press.

Lascoumes, Pierre, and Patrick Le Gales. 2007. "Introduction: Understanding Public Policy through Its Instruments? From the Nature of Instruments to the Sociology of Public Policy Instrumentation." *Governance* 20 (1): 1–21.

Latour, Bruno. 1987. *Science in Action: How to Follow Scientists and Engineers through Society*. Cambridge, MA: Harvard University Press.

Leal, Pablo Alejandro. 2007. "Participation: The Ascendancy of a Buzzword in the Neo-Liberal Era." *Development in Practice* 17 (4): 539–48.

Li, Tania Murray. 2007. *The Will to Improve: Governmentality, Development, and the Practice of Politics*. Durham, NC: Duke University Press.

McNulty, Stephanie. 2012. "An Unlikely Success: Peru's Top-Down Participatory Budgeting Experience." *Journal of Public Deliberation*: 8 (2).

Melo, Marcus, and Gianpaolo Baiocchi. 2006. "Deliberative Democracy and Local Governance: Towards a New Agenda." *International Journal of Urban and Regional Research* 30 (3): 587–600.

Navarro Yáñez, Clemente. 2004. "Participatory Democracy and Political Opportunism." *International Journal of Urban and Regional Research* 28 (4): 819–38.

Pindado, F. 2000. *La participación ciudadana en la vida de las ciudades*. Barcelona: Ediciones del Serbal.

Sabel, Charles. 2004. "Bootstrapping Development: Rethinking the Role of Public Intervention in Promoting Growth." Paper presented at the conference on "The Protestant Ethic and the Spirit of Capitalism," Cornell University, Ithaca, NY.

Scott, James C. 1998. *Seeing Like a State: How Certain Schemes to Improve the Human Condition Have Failed*. New Haven, CT: Yale University Press.

Talpin, Julien. 2012. "Schools of Democracy: How Ordinary Citizens (Sometimes) Become Competent in Participatory Budgeting Institutions." *Revista Internacional de Sociología* 70 (extra 2): 211–29.

Teixeira, Ana Claudia Chaves. 2002. "O OP em pequenos municípios rurais: contextos, condições, e formatos de experiência." In *A Inovação Democrática no Brasil*, ed. L. Avritzer and Z. Navarro. São Paulo: Cortez.

Tendler, Judith. 1998. *Good Governance in the Tropics*. Baltimore, MD: Johns Hopkins University Press.

UN-Habitat (United Nations Human Settlements Programme). 2008. *Participatory Budgeting in Africa: A Training Companion*. Nairobi.

URB-AL. 2006. *Datos generales de la actividad: Cordoba*. European Commission, Brussels. http://mezquita.ayuncordoba.es/participacionciudadana/urbal.nsf /de345f44544ead03c1256c5a005eb336/d19ba6899973c7b9c1256d030031b 424?OpenDocument.

Van Cott, Donna. 2008. *Radical Democracy in the Andes*. Cambridge: Cambridge University Press.

Wampler, Brian. 2007. "A Guide to Participatory Budgeting." In *Participatory Budgeting*, ed. Anwar Shan. Washington, DC: World Bank.

Weyland, Kurt Gerhard. 1996. *Democracy without Equity: Failures of Reform in Brazil*. Pittsburgh, PA: University of Pittsburgh Press.

World Bank. 1997. *The World Development Report: The State in a Changing World*. Washington, DC: World Bank.

———. 2007. "Africa Good Governance Program on the Radio Waves: Municipal Finance/Participatory Budgeting (Part I)." Washington, DC. http://web.worldbank .org/WBSITE/EXTERNAL/WBI/WBIPROGRAMS/CMUDLP/0,,contentMDK: 21344171~pagePK:64156158~piPK:64152884~theSitePK:461754,00.html.

———. n.d. "Participatory Budget Formulation." http://web.worldbank.org /WBSITE/EXTERNAL/TOPICS/EXTSOCIALDEVELOPMENT/EXTPCENG /0,,contentMDK:20509380~pagePK:148956~piPK:216618~theSit ePK:410306,00.html.

CHAPTER 7

Practices of Deliberation in Rural Malawi

Ann Swidler and Susan Cotts Watkins

In *The Making of the English Working Class* (1963), E. P. Thompson describes the historical legacy of embedded social practices that made "class" and class consciousness possible in 19th century England. This chapter describes deeply embedded practices of group talk (Eliasoph and Lichterman 2003) in Malawi, "styles of political discourse" (Rao and Sanyal 2010, 150) that both constrain and enable the ways people engage in collective deliberation. It examines what Malawians themselves see as deliberation—where and how they practice it and how various contexts define what is appropriate and inappropriate: who can talk, about what, and how. The chapter also tries to identify the historical resonances of these deliberative practices. Understanding these embedded practices will suggest both what difficulties formal attempts to promote deliberation might encounter and whether, where, and how violating existing practices might challenge existing inequalities.

We are grateful to colleagues, graduate students, and former graduate students for permitting us to draw on data they collected in rural Malawi. Particularly valuable were Kim Yi Dionne's interviews on the practices of chiefs, as well as information (and interpretations of that information) on schools provided by Maggie Frye, Monica Grant, and Nancy Kendall. We also benefited greatly from the thoughtful comments of Biju Rao and Patrick Heller on the first draft of this chapter, as well as the stimulating responses by other participants at the conference on Deliberation for Development: New Directions, held in Washington, DC, November 12–13, 2011, especially Jane Mansbridge. We also thank Jane Collier, Louise Lamphere, Kristin Mann, and Daniel Mpeleka for valuable advice and Margaret Frye for calculations of school completion rates.

Much of the evidence presented comes from a set of ethnographic journals that capture conversations overheard in rural Malawi. About 1,100 ethnographic journals were written in conjunction with a study of the role of social networks in rural responses to the AIDS epidemic. The journals, written by field assistants who live in the villages, cover the period between 1999 and 2010. The field assistants (referred to here as journalists or diarists) were asked to pay attention to any conversations they heard about AIDS during the course of their daily lives and then to write them down in as much detail as possible (see Watkins and Swidler 2009).

These texts are supplemented by interviews that we, colleagues, and graduate students conducted in similar villages; evidence from documents; and our own field observations. Together these data allow us to identify the background of practices of collective discussion and debate that define what deliberation might mean in places like rural Malawi.

The vast majority of Malawi's population lives in villages in which families depend primarily on subsistence agriculture, supplemented by small-scale income-generating activities. Roads are poor, the villages are not connected to the electric grid, and homes lack piped water. Among children who begin primary school, only 54 percent complete it and only 5 percent complete secondary school.[1] It is thus not surprising that Malawi has received a great deal of external funding to support a variety of rural development initiatives, as well as humanitarian aid to deal with problems such as AIDS and drought. Much of this aid goes to nongovernmental organizations (NGOs).

Rural Malawi differs in important ways from the village in India that Rao and Sanyal (2010) describe, but there are also important similarities. The most important differences are that the Malawian state penetrates local life much less thoroughly and impinges on the daily life of villagers much less than the Indian state does. Various government or NGO initiatives (sometimes not clearly differentiated in villagers' understanding) occasionally bestow small benefits on a particular village. A community-based organization might provide blankets for a dozen orphans or a church group might provide a few bags of fertilizer or some enriched porridge for village children; a clinic might be promised, or occasionally even materialize, in a nearby village; the government occasionally offers short-term road repair work to poor villagers and is supposed to provide free primary schooling (assuming there is a school nearby) and free access to government hospitals in district capitals. In the day-to-day life of most rural villagers, however, such benefits are capricious windfalls, not rights, which do little to mitigate the constant insecurity of subsistence farming (Swidler and Watkins 2009).[2] Thus Malawians rarely focus on government benefits and are more likely to pursue grievances and assert claims in more immediate and informal contexts, with neighbors, spouses, or local authorities such as school teachers or religious leaders.[3]

Malawian villages also lack the sharp inequalities of Indian villages. There are no castes; everyone is poor. Although the village's structure is formally hierarchical—each village has a village headman, who is subordinate to a Group Village Headman, who is, in turn, subordinate to a Traditional Authority—these local chiefs are often as poor as other villagers, and, concerned to maintain village harmony, feel obliged to consult with villagers on most matters. Nonetheless, the village headman, like the *gram sabha* Rao and Sanyal describe, allocates what government benefits do come along—subsidized fertilizer coupons or opportunities for road repair work, intended for the poorest villagers. Chiefs often use their discretion to allocate benefits to emphasize their "love" for their people, by, for example, asking households to share fertilizer coupons or dividing opportunities for public works employment so that more can benefit. Alternatively, chiefs distribute such benefits to reward people who have cooperated in village endeavors or sometimes simply keep them for their own kin.

Everyday deliberation

Gerry Mackie defines deliberation as "the reciprocal exchange of public reasons" (see chapter 5 of this volume). Malawians rarely offer "public reasons" for their claims, if public reasons include only those that refer to some form of public good. They do assert all sorts of claims in public, and they frequently offer what they see as general moral principles to back their claims.

By this standard, rural Malawians practice deliberation frequently, energetically, sometimes vociferously, in several everyday settings. These settings range from brawls in the marketplace, where bystanders debate the rights and wrongs of combatants, to the more decorous settings of a chief's court or a village association. In these settings, villagers have no trouble voicing claims and providing public reasons. Even in settings that emphasize status inequalities, such as those involving village chiefs, the chiefs' traditional concern to forestall envy and restore harmony gives villagers at least some opportunity for redress of their grievances.

At the end of this chapter, we consider "modern" contexts in which the sort of participation and deliberation that the World Bank hopes to foster might occur. These are also the contexts in which NGOs implementing Western donor–funded programs attempt to inculcate Malawians in formal practices of deliberation and from which Malawian understandings of modern, participatory deliberation are generated (Englund 2006). We show that despite what their promoters envision, such settings inevitably invoke the hierarchical template of school, with its colonial remnants and deference to the prestige of modern learning (Frye 2010; 2012).

Malawians argue their claims in public in a wide variety of situations. Two principles structure many of these collective contexts, from churches and community organizations to the very consequential decisions made by chiefs and village elders. The first is that matters should ideally be first discussed by an inner circle of knowledgeable or important people, such as the board or executive committee of an organization or elders of a community, before being announced to the general membership. The second, and probably related, principle is that priority should be given to preserving harmony and preventing disruptive conflicts. This principle may derive from the fragile nature of village society in Malawi.[4] Thus, for example, although chiefs are likely to consult largely with their relatives or influential people in a village, they use their power to seek resolution of conflicts behind the scenes and, as much as possible, meet their people's expectations.[5]

Spontaneous and unremarked deliberation

Rural Malawians have no difficulty asserting themselves in public—vividly, energetically, and sometimes strategically. Claims are usually made by individuals, but they appeal to public standards of justice and morality. In public quarrels and fights, participants hurl insults—and sometimes blows—at one another, asserting the justness of their case to the audience of neighbors that quickly gathers to watch the action. The audience joins in to debate the morality of rights and claims.

In the more than 1,000 ethnographic journals we collected in rural Malawi, by far the most common form of violence is between a wife and a girlfriend. Typically, the wife attacks the girlfriend in order to defend her property (that is, her husband and the resources he provides for her and her children).[6] As rural women have far less access to cash than men, the monetary support provided by a husband—however small it may be—is valuable and evidently worth fighting to protect.

In one typical journal excerpt describing such a fight, the husband skedaddles (as is typical in these incidents). [7]

> This morning I went to Mangochi Turn off where I found women fighting and after investigation, I heard that the fighting was between three people. A certain business man is married and has got four children but he has also a sexual partner who is well known for having sex with married men. Today the man went to chat with the girlfriend who has spent the night at Isha Allah Rest House. . . . [T]he friend of his wife who was going to the market saw him and wondered why the man was going that path and what he was going to do there so she followed him at far distance so that the man should not see and recognize her. She saw the man entering the rest house and she rushed to her friend and tell her the whole story that her husband has entered the rest house. (Patuma Nagalande, July 17, 2004)

The wife and her friend wait in the market until they see the husband and his girlfriend coming out of the rest house "holding hands," "talking lovely," laughing and kissing. They start after the girlfriend, and the husband runs away. In this case there is no moral consensus: some in the audience claim that the husband was wrong, while others maintain that the girlfriend was wrong.

> Many people come to witness the fighting and encourage the women to beat the girl because it is her behavior of having sex with other women's husband and that always she said that she is queen of the town and that every man in the market has sex with her and that she used to tell people that women around the market were not clever ladies for they let their husbands have sex with her without jealousy with them. . . .
> Many people rushed to the scene of the incident and supported the two women. The two women beat the girl seriously and tore her clothes. The girl cried with pain for she had several wounds on the face and she managed to cut the finger of the wife of her boyfriend leaving it about to fall down and the wife cried with pain then she touches the breast of the girlfriend and cut it with her mouth.
> Then the girl cried for help saying that she is going to die then certain young men come and stop the fighting but the girl lies down, she failed even to sit or stand up, then other men come and took her to a certain shade under a tree other people tied her wounds and a certain woman takes her *chitenje* [wrap skirt] and covers the girl, for she was half naked because her clothes were torn to pieces and she left with only underwears. . . .
> Several people were still at the place of incident talking to each other. Other people said the women were wrong, for they have beaten an innocent person because the girl did not propose the man but [it] is the man who had proposed her and the woman should have beat the husband. Others said that the girl is a wrong person because she knows that the person who is proposing her has got a family and she did not refuse him so she must receive the reward from her behavior.

Fights like this seem to be a recognized form of "rough justice" (Davis 1973), although they are not always so violent. Most of the fights described in the journals are about infidelity, possibly because the journals focus on AIDS. Wives, girlfriends, and their neighbors understand that a fight over who should be having sex with whom is a fight about how a man's resources should be distributed. Each combatant articulates her reasons for taking action, and members of the audience shout out their reasons for supporting one side over the other.

The contestation may be more decorous than the one described above. In the following example, the conversation begins when two women visit a neighbor to inform her of the death of their mutual friend Mrs. Jalani. The neighbor is the mother of one of the diarists, who lives next door and overhears the conversation.

They begin by agreeing that Mrs. Jalani was innocent: she had had only one previous husband and no other sexual partners, but her husband had had many. Then they generalize from the particulars of the case:

> My mother said that indeed if there is high prevalence of AIDS in the world its because of men. Men are discontent and most of them are unfaithful ones and they don't go after one sexual partner but several of them to be theirs. She said that but women are most of them the faithful ones and they just accept whatever her husband brings to them. Then another woman (a neighbor) agreed and said my mother was saying the truth that men are very unfaithful ones and . . . that them being women they were given a very unique heart that is forgiving and as well as that of silly nature and they were laughing and I was just listening. The friend of mother continued saying that she was saying that they were born rather given the silly heart because most of the times it happens that you really know that your husband is running a love affair with such a woman but you just keep on doing jealousy and be frowning over him or keep on fighting with the woman which doesn't help at all instead of divorcing the husband bearing in mind that there is Aids and the only way to prevent it is acting against it, that's when a woman noting that her husband is movious [promiscuous] she should just, without hesitating, divorce him without mercy because this disease Aids is the incurable one and mercy or lenient can't help at all. Mother plus/ together with her friend (neighbor) agreed and her friend continued saying that the same should be applied to men that when the man has come to discover that his wife is movious its better to drop/ divorce her. (Simon Bato, December 18, 2003)

In the discussion of Mrs. Jalani, generalizations do not extend to taking public action.

In the following excerpt, the personal becomes political, as villagers debate what public action might reduce the dangers of AIDS. Several men and women are talking at the minimart at a trading center. The excerpt begins with two men talking about a particular prostitute. One says that because of behavior, HIV will not go away. The second generalizes, saying:

> We men are stupid when we see a woman prostitute even if she demands a lot of money we still have to pay forgetting that we have left our homes without household needs we can pay a lady MK 100

or MK 200 while our family is starving this is common. (Daniel Haji, July 1, 2005)

After a bit more discussion of this prostitute, a woman enters the conversation, commenting, "we will be dying in the families because of these prostitutes." A second woman suggests public action:

> What I think is that when a man and woman are caught doing sex they should be locked up in prisons for life and all prostitutes also must be locked up so that the Aids can get finished failing which Aids shall not end.
>
> All the men laughed and shouted "Aaaa getting arrested because of that!"

The woman disagrees:

> Yes, why not? AIDS is killing it is a deadly diseases you think I am joking! And some women are stupid. In most of the households they know their husband have a sexual partner but they do not even asks they just keep quiet, they say and believe that once they ask their couples [husbands] they will get divorced [but] that was long time beliefs and traditional customs.
>
> Not now AIDS is not a thing to play with most of the women are fearing to be divorced if they criticize their husband, so it is better and the Government must implement this once a couple is found making sex of outside marriages and are found in rest houses or in the bush wherever once found they should be locked up in prison!
>
> All the people at the minimart laughed. Then the lady said yes I have talked, what pains me nowadays we have a freedom of speech which [former president] Dr. Bakili Muluzi brought in Malawi in 1994 [the year the first multiparty elections were held in Malawi]. It is not time for fear, we have the freedom.

One of the men responded:

> Aaa [that lady] was targeting we men but if you can see properly these young adolescent girls of 14 to 21 they are looking nice and they are selling themselves as we greet them they show smiling teeth which is an attraction. [O]nce the men propose them they do not deny they accept and says that as long as you have cash there is no problem of doing sex so it is the women and girls who cause [the problem]. . . .

The woman responds to his argument:

> People should be locked up once found doing sex [because] it can minimize these cases but if possible the NGOs and the government must introduce loan schemes for the girls and women so that they

can totally stop being money hungry and get themselves busy with the small businesses they can be doing.

Then an old man says:

I have been listening to what you have been chatting and discussing all that time, nothing have convinced me, you should know that even somewhere in the Bible it is written that miracles and outbreak of disease shall occur. So the *kachilombo* [the virus] is *Mluli* [a plague of Biblical proportions]. It is time! And time has come it is a punishment from God people are enjoying and have enjoyed too much God wants his people to take a lesson and repent about all the sins.

The old man goes on at length, and the audience disperses.

Structured contexts in which deliberation occurs

Many organizational settings in Africa are, at least on paper, elaborately structured voluntary organizations, with officers, boards of directors, and all the apparatus—sometimes taken to what seem fanciful extremes—of an American (or more likely British colonial) church or garden club. A local NGO or community-based organizations (CBO), like any African church, will have a board of directors, committee chairs, and many other officers.[8] Such organizations appear to have a dual aspect, at least from the point of view of deliberation. On the one hand, their formalized hierarchy implies that ordinary members of the organization are different in status and have different rights from the inner circle that runs the organization.[9] On the other hand, in many organizations, the "inner circle" of officers and board members may be virtually the entire organization. The funding applications and constitutions of many CBOs, with their elaborate lists of committee members, boards, officers, and so forth, reveal that many of the same names reappear on each committee and that the major function of the organization is to seek donor money to fund "trainings" and other activities for those board and committee members. Our previous work (Swidler and Watkins 2009) suggests that unlike churches, NGOs and CBOs tend to have no wider membership outside the "inner circle."

The CBOs we studied often have little purpose except to access outside funding. Their members thus have little to discuss once the negotiations about who will be on the board, who will be on the various committees, and so forth, have occurred. Access to outside funding is a valuable good in rural Malawi, and inequalities in access to such opportunities are a major issue in poor communities. But as the chief and his counselors or relatives, along with people literate or skilled enough to help write a proposal, will inevitably be the ones constituting the organization, the CBO itself would not likely provide an arena for deliberation (Swidler and Watkins 2009).

Many local organizations do provide real benefits for their members. Although they are also set up on formally hierarchical lines, with ornate offices and boards, they sometimes provide contexts for vigorous debate.

One example is a village Seed Multiplication Group (SMAG). One of our journalists is the secretary of the group, probably because she is one of the few people in the village with secondary education (she is the secretary or treasurer of several groups). Within the inner circle (the executive committee) discussion is very robust. At one meeting members defied the wishes of their chairman in favor of local norms of shared responsibility for community members:

> It was on Saturday morning when I went to Ulongwe for the meeting about our Club of the Seed Multiplication. On that day, we had some new members who came to join our SMAG. (Alice Chawake, October 10, 2002)

Several new members were signing up to join the group, including a Mr. Dumani, who had clear symptoms of AIDS. "Mr. Dumani was looking very weak and unhealthy body therefore everyone knew that he was sick." After the meeting, "the Chairman asked me as the secretary, Mr. Lakuna the Treasurer and Miss Charles the Committee member to remain in the room to meet with the Chairman."

The chairman urged that Mr. Dumani not be allowed to join the group because he was unlikely to be able to repay what he borrowed and the group would be left with his debts:

> The chairman Mr Mvula asked the committee if it was good to allow Mr Dumani to join our farming club. He said that he asked that question because Mr Dumani looked very weak and sick as everyone seen him. He said that we have to discuss first and find the solution because farming is a hard labor and even if one have money, but it needs the owner to look after that job every time.

The chairman's suggestion was vigorously contested. "The Treasurer Mr Lakuna said that the Chairman was saying the truth that Mr Dumani was sick and in addition to that Mr Lakuna said he saw the sores on Mr Dumani's body. The sores were many and covered his whole body." The club's officers first debated the state of Mr. Dumani's health and the evidence that his symptoms were really from AIDS. They then discussed the practical problem of ending up with debts of someone who cannot repay them.

> [The chairman noted that] ours is a club and now if we allow him to borrow the bags of fertilizer from the Agora through our club, we should just know that it will be our problem because we will be forced to square that credit for him this year, the European Union will not provide us with anything and the Agora which have accepted

to lend us the bags of fertilizer is a company and if we shall fail to square their credit, they will come to our houses to carry all the properties that we have and sell them to square their money that we borrowed. What we should bear in mind is that Mr Dumani is sick and he cannot work in the garden even in the office.

After expanding further on the dangers of the club taking on obligations of someone who could never repay them, the chairman said,

If he would be a member of this club since some years ago we could have said nothing, but him as a new member and he comes to join the club while sick, that is very dangerous. The chairman stopped there, and he asked us to tell him our ideas about him.

The other members of the executive committee developed a different analysis. Mrs. Charles suggested that Mr. Dumani "should just join our club for him to have the right place for selling his crops, but he should buy the implements by himself." The diarist disagreed:

When Mrs. Charles finished speaking, I was asked to give out my suggestions, and I said to them that there is no need to refuse him joining the club because we don't know about the type of disease that he is suffering from. We can just say that he has AIDS yet it is not [true] and though it can be that he has AIDS, we don't know when he will die. He can maybe stay for two or three years alive and may be strong if he can get recovered very well. He has also his wife who can be working for him if he will find that he is sick and in addition to that, Mr. Dumani is a field assistant, he is receiving money every month end. He can employ people to work for him in his garden and he can even pay back the bags of fertilizer's money when he will fail to work in his garden. I can see nothing wrong there because he is not a young man, he knows what he is doing and if we refuse him, it will show that we have isolated him from our club because he is sick. Let him use his freedom of life. Nobody knows about his plan. It might be that he has enough money which he has kept for farming.

The Chairman, Mr. Mvula, was not happy with my speech. Therefore he said that the committee should think twice, because our club is for business and not that we are growing our crops for food.

In the end, "the committee told the chairman that he should ask [Mr. Dulani] if he is ready for his farming in terms of money but he should not be told that we have not allowed him to join our club."

This exchange is certainly deliberation. Indeed, there was a fuller airing of the issues—including an extended discussion of the man's health, the potential risks to the seed club, and possible alternative ways Mr. Dulani might repay his debt—than we can present here. After the parties aired their views, the chairman was overridden by the other members of the executive committee. This deliberation was robust, albeit not among all the members of the group. An inner circle—the office holders—debated and decided the issue as equals.

A second example is a conflict between parents and teachers that escalated when participants called on the authority of the headmaster and the chief. Although the parents ultimately apologized for their disrespectful behavior toward teachers, they were able to confront what they saw as injustices and have the merits of their case considered.

Catherine, a friend of the diarist, told her about a group of children who had been dismissed from school just before taking their Standard 8 Primary School Leaving Exams (PSLEs) because they had been found to have had sexual partners.[10] (Standard 8 is equivalent to the 8th grade in the United States, although many students would be well into their teens; the PSLE exams are important because they are a requirement for proceeding to secondary school.) Some students preparing for the exams had been allowed to spend their holidays at the school, so that they could concentrate on their studies.

> The teachers were saying that . . . this behavior is not allowed at that school. So they have decided to dismiss them. This behavior does encourage HIV to spread among the youth members. So to give a lesson to other children who have not yet started this behavior it is better for them to leave school and take care of their marriages.
>
> Then the parents went to the chiefs to complain about their children's dismissal so that those chiefs should talk to the teachers instead of them. So that they must forgive the children so that they should write the examinations. (Anna Wiles, November 12, 2006)

The teachers argued that "before [the students] started school, there was a meeting between the teachers and the parents. The chiefs were also invited. The teachers told the parents that the children will be alone at school [during the school holidays, when some of them boarded at the school]. Nobody will not know what they will be doing there at school."

According to the teachers, parents and students had agreed to the rules prohibiting sexual partnerships. But the parents

> were angry to see that their children have been dismissed. So the chiefs went to the headmaster to complain what the parents have told them. The headmaster told the chiefs that they cannot do otherwise because they have already agreed about the school rules before they start boarding [at the] school. If they have seen that the teachers

are wrong, the chiefs should go and tell the parents that they should meet with the teachers and discuss about the case, Catherine said. "Did the chiefs tell the parents to meet with the teachers?" I asked. Yes they all replied. But they were angry when they were going to school. On the way they were saying that the teacher did not have an authority of dismissing a child, because a school is for the community. The parents were the ones who have molded the brick and built that school. They were working on development.

Then the teachers were also saying that the parents were not the ones who have employed them. They don't make any contribution to make their salaries. They are following the Ministry rules. If the parents will choose they can go to another school and work there. The school can be closed until other teachers came. Do they advise their children to make marriages at school or advise them to be concentrate at lessons? So it seems that the parents do encourage their children to make partnerships when they are at primary school, which is not good.

So the chiefs failed to calm their tempers. The parents told the headmaster that he is a stupid person because he has dismissed their children without telling their parents about the behavior.

Then the teachers saw that the parents have got much intelligence, so they told them that they [the teachers] are going home. [The parents] must come every day and teach their children. Then they [the teachers] left the parents and the chiefs there.

So the chiefs talked to the parents that they were wrong because they have shown arrogance to the teachers which means that they tell their children to be arrogant to their teachers because they are not their relatives. Can they manage to teach their children like how the teachers do? the chiefs asked.

So the parents started to apologize that they were wrong. And the chiefs should go and tell the teachers that they must come and teach the remaining children because their children were on punishment. They are going to tell their children that they must study very hard at home so that they should pass the exams.

So the chiefs went to the headmaster's house and told him what the parents had said. Then the headmaster told the chiefs that they should tell the parents that they should come any day to finish their discussions because he cannot manage to go to every teacher's house.

So the chiefs said they wanted the discussions to be the next day so that the teachers wouldn't miss many days of teaching their children.

So the following day they finished their discussions. The parents apologized that they cannot manage to teach their children because they don't have an experience of it. They were just talking that time when they were challenging.

This story was relayed to the diarist as gossip. It is likely to have circulated widely among all the parents, not just the parents of the dismissed children. It thus contributed to the fund of stories of protest that are available when similar occasions occur.

In a second incident, the aggrieved parents were successful:

> Wiless Yuda [one of the drivers of the University of Pennsylvania research team] told a dramatic story of how the sheikh of his mosque was caught having sex with a school girl. He had been warned about this behavior a week earlier, so the people were very angry. They had a big meeting in the mosque, everyone spoke, including the women who were very angry, shouting, and the village decided to fire the sheikh. (Watkins field notes, July 1, 2010)

Although the sheikh had apparently been a very good teacher, everyone agreed that he must be fired.

Structured village contexts with the potential for deliberation

This section examines another potential context of deliberation, one familiar to all villagers. These contexts of "community governance" are largely in the village, organized by lineage and clan imagery in the person of chiefs (also called village headmen); superior chiefs (Group Village Headmen [GVH]); and above them, Traditional Authorities (TAs and sometimes sub-TAs). Much of the material in this section comes from interviews with chiefs and with villagers about chiefs, in an area where some chiefs are women. We conducted some; a colleague, Kim Dionne (Dionne 2010), conducted others.

The chief, as "owner" of the village, has considerable powers in rural Malawi; in extreme cases, he can expel people from the village and thus from their land. But he also has obligations, the most important of which is to be a "good chief." A good chief is one who maintains harmony by resolving disputes equitably (either in the chief's court or informally); organizes the production of collective goods like village paths or school buildings; and, increasingly, brings "development" to his community (on the role of the chief, see Collier 2004; Cammack and Kanyongolo 2010; Swidler 2013). A chief who violates his obligations—a "bad chief"—can be deposed.

The most common settings of community governance are chief's meetings and court hearings, both usually held at the chief's compound. Much is at stake: if deliberation happens, it deals with consequential issues. The interdependent village community has resources to distribute (fertilizer coupons, seeds, opportunity for income from public works, and charitable donations like blankets, medicines, and food for orphans). It is also in villages where inequalities in resources, access to land, and inequalities in power and influence are keenly felt. Decisions have to be made. Who should govern (choosing and deposing chiefs)? Which community investments should be made (repairing bore-holes, attracting donor projects, repairing paths), and who should make them? And, most important of all, who has the right to what piece of land, the basis of subsistence for most villagers?

We begin with a case (Alice Chawake July 20, 2007) in which a chief exerted the ultimate punishment on an unruly villager: he expelled her. As such cases would be known to everyone, they demonstrate to all the power of the chief, the price of directly confronting him or her. But this case also demonstrates that a chief's decisions are subject to public discussion, moral evaluation, and ferocious argument, in which people assert their claims and defend their interests.

The issue here concerns mutual obligations of villagers to a cooperative established by the Catholic Development Commission (CADECOM), a body of the Episcopal Conference of Malawi.

> I have my neighbor Miss Dymon, she is very talkative and rude. She does not chat with anybody else here because of her Behavior. She likes quarreling with other people always.
>
> Last year the CADECOM club went to our village headman to tell him that he should tell his people to join that club, where they will be given crops and livestock by credit. In addition to that, they will be asked to have another garden, a club garden, where people will be asked to work and plant the club crops.
>
> Our village headman, Mwamula, told all other people in his village to join that group except my neighbor. He did not send her message for her to join that club. But Miss Dymon heard from people about the club, then she just gone alone to join it. The headman saw her but he did not say anything he just looked at her since he is a headman and all the people who are in his village are for him. But he was not happy to see her.

Despite receiving seeds and fertilizer from the club, Miss Dymon refused to work in the club garden. When it was time to repay the seeds from her current crop, she refused, even when the headman

> told the chairpersons of the club to go to Miss Dymon and her son in-law to ask them to give back the credits. The chairpersons went back to tell the headman, Mwamula, and other members of club on what Miss Dymon answered and what her son in-law has answered as well. The headman Mwamula got bored [irritated]. Therefore he went to the police to report on what Miss Dymon said. The policemen gave him a letter to ask Miss Dymon and her son in-law to go to the police in the following day.

When he went there with a letter, they began quarreling with Miss Dymon's husband. "What has my wife done to you? why calling her to the police before I am told about that mistakes as a husband of her? I can tell her not to go there because I know nothing if she is wrong to anyone else. If you hate her with something, we shall see" her husband said.

The police eventually "forced" Miss Dymon and her son-in-law to repay the crops they owed. But then another conflict erupted, when the son-in-law refused to pay back 10 chickens he "took by credit." Again the issue was taken to the police.

When they came back from police, Miss Dymon went to the [group] village headman Kawinga to summon [the village headman] Mr. Mwamula that he has told her that she is no longer in Mwamula village because she is rude. Now she would like him to tell her what she did to him?

Mr. Mwamula told group of people that Miss Dymon is rude to me. She always refuses working in the village. She talks the bad words to my people if they have gone to her house to tell her what is supposed to be done in the village. Many people in this village are complaining about her.

The counselor asked him, is there any day which you asked her to come to your house and advised her on the Behavior that she is showing to you?

Yes. I have been advising her but she does not want to listen to me. I am now tired with her and I am no longer her village headman. If something will happen to her home like the funeral, she should better take that funeral to her home at Ulongwe, not in my village.

Miss Dymon became furious with that word. She went to summon the headman to the Group Village Headman, where her husband told the [Group Village Headman] that Mr. Mwamula told [the husband] that he will just . . . give [the husband] his position of being a headman. . . . [Note: The headman has insulted the husband by saying "if you don't like the way I do my job, you do it."]

The counselor at Kawinga said that the headman Mwamula was wrong if his people are rude or wrong, he must call them and talk properly with them because these are his own people. In addition to that, the headman [Mwamula] was told to pay Mr. Blantyre [Miss Dymon's son-in-law?] the chicken. The village headman Mwamula was told to take a chicken and give it to Mr. Blantyre as a fine on what he talked to him.

Despite her defiant attitude, Miss Dymon asks the Group Village Headman to find a new village for her:

> She also told the [group] village headman Kawinga that I would like to come out from Mwamula village. Tell me where I should go from now, which village headman should I be found.
> Mr. Kawinga told her to wait. "I will answer you next time, but as of now I have nothing to answer."
> They were coming back and the village headman Mwamula does not speak to her and her whole family. She is out of Mwamula but nobody knows about the village which she has joined, since the headman Kawinga did not answer her anything.

In this case, a difficult villager is finally expelled, but not before she hauls her headman to his superior and demands justice and the superior tries to suggest fairness by chastising and fining the headman.

Chiefs' meetings

Chiefs in Malawi regularly summon their people to "meetings." The meetings, however, are not sites for deliberation. Rather, village meetings are where the chief relays information from the government, announces that a survey or an NGO is coming to the village, or calls on community members to contribute to the village's development by repairing a road or bridge. The chief may have discussed these issues in advance with at least some of his or her counselors, but the general membership of the village is informed rather than consulted. The situation appears to be similar in court cases: after both sides present their arguments, the chief and his or her counselors deliberate. The chief then announces the decision.

In both settings, however, villagers can make their opinions known in more subtle but publicly recognizable ways. One is simply not attending the meeting called by the chief; another is not turning up for, say, bridge repair detail. When the audience approves, it may respond by clapping enthusiastically and ululating; when the audience disapproves, it may engage in *sotto voce* murmuring.

The absence of community deliberation in these formal settings does not mean that grievances cannot be recognized and injustices righted in other ways. In July 2010 one villager, Anna, told us a story about her chief, who both she and we think is a "bad chief." Her village is relatively large, about 700 families, mixed Moslem and Christian, located next to a large trading center. Many of the villagers, including Anna's parents, do not belong to the chief's clan; they are migrants to the village.

> When a woman has a child without a partner/husband, the chiefs tell them to pay a fine. So villagers complained to the Group Village Headman [GVH]. It started first in another village and our village

headman copied it. He did it to make money from the fines. And also he told people to pay MK 200 per household for a house for his grandfather, the real chief who had appointed him as the acting village headman. But the acting headman used the money to go to South Africa to work. He stayed there for one month, came back. In May the GVH met with the people and said he will be looking, so now both the real headman, who is weak, and the acting village headman, who is stronger, are suspended. (Watkins field notes, July 15, 2010)

There was also an issue about bricks:

The chief made every family produce 300 fired bricks, saying he needed them for a courthouse for the GVH. If they didn't, he would "chase them" [expel them from the village]. But then the GVH said that isn't right. The GVH has a court under a tree, and if the TA [Traditional Authority], who does have court in a building, needs a building he'll take care of that himself. Anna said that the headman was probably going to use the bricks for his grandfather's house. But then the GVH suspended the acting headman and his grandfather.

Anna said that currently they go to the GVH for problems. If anyone goes to the suspended headman, he will be punished. The GVH told the relatives they should choose a new chief. The relatives were also complaining. At first the relatives went to the GVH. Then he came to the village and acted as if he were researching. He talked with the "intelligent people" in the village. He didn't call a meeting at first, and then called a meeting to explain what he had done. He announced that he had suspended the two and the village headman had accepted. The people clapped, ululated, cheered they were so happy.

We asked Anna if the chief had consulted her, as she is certainly "intelligent" and, with a high school degree, well educated compared with most villagers. She laughed at the idea, and then said that he would not have consulted her, perhaps because she is too young.

In this case, there was no public confrontation. The complaint of the villagers could not be brought to the headmen themselves, of course, but to the chief's superior, the GVH, by the "relatives" (either of the headman or the GVH; some villagers would be relatives of both). The GVH then consults with "intelligent people," perhaps knowledgeable village elites, which could include village elders and religious leaders. The villagers' role was to express approval, which they did by clapping and ululating. In the end, there was public affirmation of village solidarity.

Chief's court

The issues most likely to be brought to the chief for adjudication are marital disputes and disputes over land; they may also include cases of theft and accusations of witchcraft. Our impression from these journals written by a chief for Kim Dionne, our other journals, and interviews is that the chief always aims at harmony in the village and thus first tries to settle these issues out of court.

Arguments before the chief's court may allow claimants to assert their rights in vivid, public ways. The case of "property grabbing" by a deceased husband's family presented here (Trueman Uyezani, February 6, 2005) is complicated, because the deceased husband's relatives, who took his property away, are from the northern region of Malawi, which is patrilineal. In this part of the country, a man's family pays a brideprice for the wife. The wife in this case is from the (matrilineal) south, where there is no brideprice.

Although in some cases claims are made by elders on behalf of the individual, in this case the wife presents her own claims to the court—and, importantly, to the audience attending the hearing. The report of the case is unusually detailed, probably because the journalist, himself a chief and thus a counselor to the TA, was present throughout. After many formalities, the plaintiff told her story:

> I was married in 1991 by Mr. Gift Mponda, we have been together for about 14 years and we have got three children early of 1993 my husband started suffering he has been on and off of hospital for quite a long time up to June in 2004 when he announced death. During the days of his life, he has been working at Zomba state house as a flower attendant and we managed to build a house for rent at Songani trading center and the other house is not finished. Your Honorable our chiefs ladies and gentlemen after the death of my husband, it only took five months and it's when Mr. Apollo Mponda came with his uncle Mr. Chilumpha. I thought that they only came to see me and the children but after welcoming them it's when they started telling me why they have come. It was Mr. Chilumpha who was on the forefront telling me the agenda of their journey. In his statement Mr. Chilumpha informed me that, he and his relatives after discussion they have decided that I should get married to [Mr. Apollo Mponda] the brother of [my late husband] that he should take care of the children of his late brother and me. I openly told them that this is impossible because my clan and culture doesn't allow that to happen and that we are living in the world of AIDS, which is claiming a lot of life of people; "You don't know my blood status and Mr. Apollo Mponda's blood status, and this habit is being discouraged."
>
> But still these men could not take what I was speaking they still insisted on their ideas [so] I decided to call my uncle Mr. Makelele and my mother who tried their best to reason with them but still they could not [convince them].

And at the end, they gave an option that if I don't get married to Mr. Apollo Mponda, then they will take the children and that property of their relative. After that it didn't take long that they came with a pick up car. It was on the 11th of January 2005, that these two people together with other two men that took almost everything in my house, two bicycles, a big radio, our small video, chairs and they said that they have also taken my house at Songani trading center.

Honorable our T/A, with this situation, I'm desperate and I don't know what to do that's why I decided to come here to seek an assistance from you. With these words honorable our chiefs, ladies and gentlemen I stop there, thank you very much.

After the widow presented her case:

There was a lot of murmuring and noise among the people who were listening to the case, "*Kodi zimenezi zikuchitikabe* (Is this still happening)" asked one of the listeners in a low tone, "*Koma ndiye zachikaletu* (This is old fashioned)" commented a certain woman among the listeners.

Each party was allowed to question the other. The Northerners insisted that they had proceeded according to their culture and that they had taken only the property to which they were entitled. The widow asked why she should have to obey their culture. When the husband's relatives insisted that they had a right to the property because the widow had never bought any of it herself, the crowd again made its views known.

Many listeners murmured at this point. Some were laughing at what the man was saying. "And we only took those which belonged to a man not to the woman; all that belong to her we didn't take and what we was doing is what our culture says."

The relatives claimed that the younger brother needed to marry the widow in order to take care of the children. The widow replied by asking what taking her property had to do with caring for her children. The audience again expressed its views:

"That's true" shouted one of the women who sat near where the woman was speaking and a lot of people clapped their hands in agreement to what Mrs. Mponda was saying. . . . And she sat down, leaving people clapping their hands and some murmuring a lot of things, condemning Mr. Chilumpha and his relatives.

After several more challenges and responses from the parties to the dispute, the chiefs delivered their verdict. The crowd clapped in approval:

"We found you Mr. Chilumpha and Mr. Apollo Mponda guilty for your ill intentions and for property grabbing. We are coming up with this judgment upon looking to the fact that, this is an old fashion behavior, as we are looking at *Chokolo* [the system of marrying the wife of one's deceased relative] as one of the factors which is spreading AIDS, and this is not encouraged any more. Let us not beat about the bush and I agree with Mrs. Mponda's statements that you don't know her blood status and she too doesn't know your blood status [or] know more exactly what killed her husband so let us not behave in an abnormal way, this kind of culture is being condemned throughout the country and this kind of culture will never be given a space at all in this country."

People clapped their hands as the chief was speaking with serious face and a strong emphasis to his words. "Talking of the property which Mr. Chilumpha and your relatives took, this is very sad and pity."

After inquiring about the property the Northerners had taken from the widow, the chief continued:

"You can see now, these things are being done without any true purpose, only for greedy."

A lot of people clapped their hands in agreement to what the chief was saying. "And you Mr. Apollo Mponda, your uncle Mr. Chilumpha has said that you are a younger brother to the late, so why don't you just marry another woman than of your late brother?"

A lot of women shouted "*Zoona*" (that's true).

The chief continues "I've already heard that you have got a wife, so you mean you want another one?! So me and my fellow chiefs we have agreed that the property you took must be returned to the owner who is Mrs. Mponda, and that should be done by the end of this month. The real owners of the late's property are his wife and the children."

The crowd gives a cheers to the chief's statement and he continues, "I don't want this to happen again in T/A Malemia, and as long as I'm a T/A hence, I will never tolerate this okay! Lastly, I have to emphasize here that me and my fellow chiefs, Chief Nkwanda and Chief Malonje we will make sure that what has been said here is being done accordingly and in time without any problem. And I have to warn here that if this will not be followed, the matter will be taken to another authorities and you, Mr. Chilumpha, you have to follow all what has been said here."

In this chief's court, as in others, people have a chance to debate claims and counterclaims. But the real spur to righting perceived injustices is not confrontation and the public airing of grievances but the chief's need to maintain harmony and prevent envy and witchcraft. In courts people can express grievances, not against the chief but against one another. The guiding principle is deference, not to education but to the status of chiefs, who in turn maintain their status by preserving public harmony (Swidler 2013). People do assert claims and rights and sometimes do get justice, but, as in the case of the corrupt chief who was eventually removed, they often do so through informal channels that reinforce the prerogatives of chiefs and their relatives. Far from fostering debate and deliberation, chiefs try to defuse potential conflicts, to encourage people who have resources to redistribute them, and to get people to share limited resources (such as fertilizer). Even the case above, in which a chief expelled a woman from the village, seemed to rest primarily on the fact that the woman and her family were causing conflict.

Modern contexts with the potential for deliberation

This section describes the practices that govern what Malawians themselves would regard as "participation" (or "deliberation," had NGOs begun to use this term) in relatively formal settings in which participants are, at least in theory, supposed to address issues of common concern. Despite the rhetoric of egalitarian participation, such contexts are invariably structured by practices derived from the contemporary Malawian classroom (and earlier missionary schooling), where the person with the requisite knowledge conveys it to the people who need to be "enlightened."

An excerpt from detailed notes on a classroom interaction reveals the emphasis on rote memorization and a pedagogical style that relies on a barrage of questions, each of which has a specific right answer, which the teacher communicates and reinforces (Kendall 2004, 178–82):[11]

> 10:53 a.m. Mr. Lwangu enters the standard 8 class to teach Agriculture. After a few minutes writing on the board, he turns around and addresses the students: Who can give me two diseases of cattle that do not have any treatment? James? [James does not answer, stares at desk and does not raise head to acknowledge question has been put to him.] After about four seconds, Mr. Lwangu: Charles?
>
> Student: East Coast Disease.
>
> Mr. Lwangu: I said two. [Teacher calls on boy seated in seat 5; he cannot name a second disease. Teacher calls on girl seated in seat 32, she does not answer. Teacher calls on girl in seat 15. She does not answer. Students examine their notebooks or appear to be studiously writing in them as they are targeted for responses.]
>
> Mr. Lwangu: What treatment for these diseases do you give? [Teacher calls on boys in seats 36 and 8, who give incorrect answers.] I'm saying what drug can you give for treatment for this disease?

It's what I told you yesterday. Not writing but listening will help you. [Teacher calls on boy in seat 3; he does not respond. Boy in seat nine responds "Salmonin," which is incorrect.] Open your books and see. [There is a scramble as students reposition themselves to be able to see one of the books. There are 26 books for the 48 students] That is very unfortunate. You are writing notes not to fill the shelf but to be used. [The textbooks are kept at the school; they are too precious a commodity to allow the students to take home. The notes that students write in class are thus expected to provide them with all of the information about the textbook unit that they are studying that they might need for the test.] Now, what disease does penicillin cure? [He points at seat 1]

Student: TB.

Mr. Lwangu: [Responds to this as an incorrect answer] I'm saying your exams are multiple choice, so take care. Just writing notes won't help you, but listen. Now close the books.

In a discussion of "agricultural markets," the teacher again peppers the students with questions, each of which has a single right answer:

Mr. Lwangu: Now, what is agriculture? [Calls on girl in seat 18.]

Student: [Gives exact definition from textbook, from memory. The phrasing seems odd enough to me that I look it up. Teacher calls on boy in seat 42, who gives the exact same memorized definition.]

The reason for this emphasis on memorization becomes clearer when Mr. Lwangu again stresses "Your tests come in multiple choice form. You have to know exactly what is sold in every market!"

One formal setting that aims to encourage participation and open deliberation is the focus group.[12] The following excerpt, typical of the many focus group transcripts we have read, comes from the transcript of a discussion with rural school girls age 12–19 conducted in 2003 by an international NGO, AGI, for its research on "Protecting the Next Generation." It is striking that the focus group, which is supposed to create open discussion, morphs into a school-like situation in which the moderator quizzes participants looking for correct answers or, as sometimes happens, lectures them, asking only for assent. The moderator's repeated assurances that everything said is confidential, that the researchers want to know what the young people think, that "there are no right or wrong answers" seem to emphasize the moderator's authority and to imply that the participants should produce correct "facts":

Moderator: We are chatting here. Don't say that one was saying this when you go out. Everything is confidential. Now we want you to tell us, be free because if you are not free minded, facts will not come out during our discussion. There's no right or wrong answer, those are the facts we want, everybody should be free to speak one after the other, but there should not be any side discussions. Be free to agree or disagree what your friend says, since during discussion some agree while others disagree. . . . So everybody should say according to how she knows/thinks when we give you a topic/fact or a question.

The entire discussion proceeds with the moderator asking questions and participants occasionally answering with a brief "fact" before the moderator moves on to the next question, which is most often met by silence. The goal of the questions seems to be teaching rather than asking. Here and elsewhere in the transcript, the young people never address one another, only the moderator:

Moderator: Mmm! So on this issue is there anything that can prevent the spread of infection? [Silence] Can having less sexual partners reduce the spread of infection? You said many have several sexual partners, four, three like that. So that they reduce the spread of infection, how many do they think they can have?

Participant: Only one.

Moderator: Only one? So what do boys think of about a girl who has unexpected pregnancy?

Participant: Sometimes they laugh at them.

Moderator: Others laugh, some do what? [Silence] When adolescents girls here have a problem with a sexual relationship or they have a reproductive health problem, whom do they ask?

Participant: Their grandmother/father

Moderator: Their grandmother/father? Who else?

Participant: Their friends

Moderator: Their friends, others? Do you discuss with teachers? What about church people? [Silence] concerning . . . who do they discuss with on what?

Participant: They discuss with fellow adolescents.

Moderator: Mmh!

Participant: They discuss problems they have.

Moderator: Problems like what? [Silence] So you've said that they discuss with their granny, what about parents? Don't they discuss with them?

The shared presumption of both moderator and participants that they are to "learn" from the focus group discussion is pervasive in settings where villagers are to be transformed into more "modern" people, even where that transformation is meant to empower them. Both moderators and participants assume not that villagers are to talk and be listened to but that they are to be "developed." Indeed, when the word *discussion* is used, it invariably refers to such situations.

Englund (2006) vividly describes the way a major civic education project in Malawi (the National Initiative for Civic Education [NICE]) sought to "empower" villagers by teaching them the skills they supposedly lacked. The only-slightly-more-educated trainers were eager to emphasize how backward and in need of enlightenment the villagers were:[13]

> The tacit teachings at the workshop, from personal cleanliness to language use, were crucial to the transmission of more explicit messages. The overt theme was to train the volunteers to acquire skills (*luso*) to be deployed in civic education. While issues such as cleanliness and language served to enhance volunteers' status and self-esteem, the issue of skills revealed in a more obvious way that the volunteers' recognized distinction between themselves and the grassroots was a precondition for civic education. A central item on the agenda was the "skill to teach elders" (*luso lophunzithsa anthu akuluakulu*). This item recognized the challenges of conducting civic education among adults, particularly elders, who were seen as the embodiments of wisdom and authority. The very idiom of "teaching" (*kuphunzitsa*), rather than, for instance, "discussing" (*kukhambirana*), betrayed NICE representatives as the ones with knowledge (93–94).
>
> The challenges of imparting this knowledge received somewhat ironic remarks from both the volunteers and the officers, often provoking laughter. A volunteer, reporting from a small-group discussion, observed that "elders do not make mistakes, they merely forget" (*akulukulu salakwa, amangiowala*). The district officer also stressed that "we do not disagree, we only add a little bit" (*sititsutsa, timangoonjezerapa*). The meaning of elders "forgetting" and NICE representatives "adding" something was immediately evident to the volunteers. Their "skills" included subtle ways of making the elders agree with civic education experts' indisputable knowledge.

Englund summarizes the civic educators' view of villagers: "The grassroots, also known as villages, existed as the audience of messages that only civic education officers fully understood" (95).

Given these hierarchical assumptions, words such as *discuss*, *chat*, and even *debate* do not have the resonance one might imagine. An invitation to participants to "chat" or "discuss" is based on the assumption that they will be mainly passive recipients of the leader's advice and information. Indeed, Malawians see "advising" (combining information with moral exhortation) as a major obligation of status superiors to their inferiors, part of the system of patron-client ties. Respectful appreciation of such advice is incumbent on the recipient. A common complaint of village elders is that "youth don't listen to our advice, that's why they will all die of AIDS."

Even the word *debate* has a different valence in Malawi. The wall around the football field in Balaka has a large hand-painted advertisement for the Balaka Debate Club, with its motto "Knowledge Is Power." But the picture and the legend underneath the motto tell a somewhat different story. The legend reads, "For civic sensitization and development." In the center, a small group of villagers, mostly women, sits on a mat under a tree, while a man seated facing them gestures as he expounds and they quietly listen. "Debate" is not the exchange of competing views but a setting where the knowledge and skills of participants can be improved, as participants are "enlightened," moved closer to some modern ideal. Knowledge is power only in the sense that access to knowledge uplifts and develops its recipients.

The extreme example of formal settings that invite "discussion" in the service of enlightenment of the unenlightened are the many "trainings" that litter the African NGO landscape. We have observed primarily AIDS trainings, but during long stays at low-budget rural motels we have become aware that "training" as a practice is pervasive in development activities of all sorts, from training in AIDS prevention, home-based care, and psychosocial support for orphans to training in early childhood education, democracy, and other development activities. Elsewhere we have written about why, from the point of view of both donors and participants, training is a way to address problems without actually committing resources for salaries or services that might make projects unsustainable (Swidler and Watkins 2009). We have noted that one of the reasons "training" is considered sustainable is that it is presumed to empower participants, to turn them from backward, passive, and helpless into empowered, knowledgeable, active subjects.

The structure of "training" reproduces exactly the hierarchical, mystified notion of modernity that animates many other contexts that might be thought to foster deliberation. With its apparatus of flipcharts, markers, and notebooks; use of trainers and facilitators to organize meetings; and frequent use of children's games and songs for adults, trainings replicate many of the inequalities of school. These sessions are empowering perhaps only in the sense that the people who are trained may feel raised a notch in status as a result of their initiation into the rhetoric of global modernity (Frank and Meyer 2007) and thus authorized to go back to their villages perhaps to "train" others, sharing the enlightened knowledge they have received.

NGO trainings are themselves vectors for exposure to this hierarchical notion of what participation means. NGOs in Malawi and other places that need to be "developed" do much of their work on the ground by conducting trainings, which, unlike the provision of actual services, are seen as participatory and sustainable (Swidler and Watkins 2009). The facilitator outlines the points on a flipchart; the discussion follows that outline, with participants often asked to provide examples of the points the facilitator suggests. Respondents are given notebooks in which to record what they have learned. In one training we observed, the students, one by one, were asked to practice conducting a session in which they would train their peers. The trainee stood in front of the rest of the group and spoke in the stern voice of a teacher.

These trainings reinforce a very asymmetrical version of participation. Yet the participants do not seem to feel that they are being mistreated or disrespected by participating in an obviously subordinate role in the proceedings. Rather, they themselves define the value of the event as allowing them to partake in what they see as a higher, more cosmopolitan arena of formal knowledge (Frank and Meyer 2007). They also appear eager to replicate the authority of the facilitator when they return to teach the people who were not fortunate enough to attend the training.

Trainings reproduce hierarchies of symbolic value in the very structure of their practices, as illustrated most forcefully by looking briefly at Malawian CBOs' applications for funding from the National AIDS Commission (NAC). The language of the NAC community mobilization project was one of participation: villagers knew the situation of their village best, recognizing both what was needed and how to mobilize their community; NAC would merely support their efforts.

But comparison of proposals written early in the project with those written in 2009 showed that over time, the CBOs learned that there was a small menu of requests that had a chance of being funded. Moreover, the process had been rationalized, so that every CBO had to have the same basic structure, with the same hierarchy of officers; the same committee structure; and the requisite constitution, bank account, and board of directors.

A typical budget for a CBO training (the major activity of CBOs) reveals the hierarchy. It includes substantially larger allowances for lunches of the elites (the trainers and facilitators) than for ordinary participants. We found this shocking, but we found no indication that any Malawian did: it appears to have been taken for granted that the elites deserved more than participants.

The way training mimics school applies not only to training to improve health or nutrition. In the summer of 2008, we stayed in the same motel as participants in a support group for people living with HIV/AIDS, who were being trained in "advocacy," a then-current development buzzword.

Over a shared breakfast table, we asked what they were advocating for. "Oh, our issues," was the reply. Were they going to protest at Parliament, make demands at the local District Commissioner's office, insist on access to antiretroviral drugs? No, they said, they were "advocating" about issues like "stigma and discrimination," which turned out to mean becoming educated about them. (One would expect that if people living with HIV/ AIDS in Malawi were stigmatized, the attendees would not need training to recognize it.) The purpose of the exercise was not to explore grievances, or to "train" participants to make demands on others but to "develop" them through "sensitization."

Many NGOs and other development organizations attempt to build participation and deliberative governance into the very structure of their development efforts. Typical of such efforts is the description by a staff member of such an organization, who sees himself as eliciting the villagers' own priorities, even as he enacts, once again, the didactic practices of school:

Before TABARD [a project that provides adult literacy training to villagers[14]] enters a Traditional Authority, we have to have an area meeting with chiefs, stakeholders who are doing other development things, we throw out the idea to do literacy. We explain that the problem of village development is ignorance and that the solution is read, write, enumerate.

When we start the meeting we ask them to mention their problems. [If] the main dominating problem is the shortage of food, [we] then find cross-cutting HIV, orphanhood issues, they really point out problems. Then we bring in a graphic with pairwise ranking, what is the most important problem? When that is figured out we get another graphic, a problem tree. If the problem is food insecurity, we ask "What do you see on the tree?" They say, "We see leaves, stem, roots." We say "Food security is the stem, but what are the roots?" They will say, "Maybe it's poverty, because we can't afford fertilizer, or the land has been overused or area is waterlogged." Then we go to the leaves. "It is hunger, malnutrition," they say. "Then what about the fruits, what are these?" Then they talk about people stealing the fruits, which may lead to fighting, even killing. . . . When we finish with the problems, then we look at action points, people select what they should do. They select literacy classes and IGAs [income-generating activities]. . . . They write a proposal of what they have agreed. I ask if they have help in writing proposals. Yes, each village circle has a facilitator. It's not me, but someone from the village has been trained in this. Facilitator gets MK 1,000 per month. [Interviewer: Is the facilitator a relative of the chief?] Not always. As an example, maybe the chief has somebody in mind, a man, but we want gender balance. The facilitator helps us to find new facilitators. [Interviewer: Are they relatives of the chiefs?] Yes, always, but we screen. Most of the communities don't understand what we are about. They think we are there to offer money. The chief want his relative to get the money. If his relative is turned down, then we go back and meet with the chief, we explain why. "The facilitator should have at least the lowest JC certificate, your son doesn't have this. How can we take him?" And we tell him that if he insists we will go to another village. (Interview with TABARD supervisor, June 16, 2007)

What if the villagers do not cite literacy? "That doesn't happen, because people are aware of what we do," noted the facilitator. "The Group Village Headman, who organizes the meeting, knows we are literacy people." What happens if the villagers think a different problem is more important? "UNDP wants to finish out its literacy project," he said. This facilitator of training in literacy concludes with his vision of what empowering villagers really means: "What we want is to uplift the community so that when the project phases out the community should be able to source more resources."

Conclusions

What is the potential for deliberation in rural Malawi? Only rarely does anything that could be termed "deliberation by the people" take place in the modern contexts that are meant to be participatory, such as focus group discussions or the executive committees of foreign-funded NGO projects. We therefore believe that project evaluations claiming that the "community" democratically decided how to allocate its resources are unlikely to be true. Just as the template established in the classroom shapes the interactions of both moderator and participants, so, too, does it shape the responses of villagers to the government and NGO staff who are sent out to rural villages to "mobilize the community." In part, villagers are likely to defer to these visitors because of their respect for a higher level of education. Villagers will also defer in the hope of material benefits.

The village committees mandated by the government (the Village Development Committee, the Village AIDS Committee, the CBOs funded by the National AIDS Commission) appear to be appointed; they do not have democratically elected officers as they are supposed to (Paz Soldan 2003; Swidler and Watkins 2009). Once they are appointed, however, there is evidence that they do deliberate and debate, albeit behind closed doors.

Indigenous structures offer more opportunities for participation, although they are predominantly opportunities to express individual rather than community claims to justice. Rural Malawians can use lineage channels to reach the chief or higher authorities; they can also vigorously argue their individual claims in the chief's court and before their peers. These efforts are likely to be taken seriously by chiefs—even bad chiefs—and their counselors, who have an obligation to maintain a harmonious community and are judged by their ability to do so. Malawi is not a feudal society in which an oppressed peasantry live in fear of an overweening landlord class. Despite slave-raiding and slave-trading before the colonial period and the acute inequalities of colonial rule, for most people, poverty is not directly attributable to oppression and exploitation by the people with whom they interact at close quarters.[15] Malawians did suffer for decades under a repressive dictatorship, however. And like the poor in many other places, they are aware that others expect bribes or steal public funds or use their contacts to advantage themselves (scandals fill the daily papers). They are certainly frustrated by unfairness.[16]

Malawians have a vibrant sense of their legitimate claims on others and of their right to pursue their interests aggressively and strategically. They usually assert themselves primarily as individuals, making their claims largely in terms of the interpersonal claims they have on others through the ties of "unequal interdependence" that permeate their society (Swidler and Watkins 2007). But they also defend the rights and claims of other individuals (as when the audience at a court case murmurs and claps, for example). Even the deference shown to chiefs gives people leverage to have legitimate grievances addressed, if only to avoid destructive conflict. It thus might seem like a short step to adapt existing practices of deliberation so that they could be used to assert a more generalized notion of the rights and claims of citizens in a formal and structured setting, such as the village councils Rao and Sanyal (2010) describe. Modern contexts inhibit deliberation, however, simply because of the expectations that both facilitators and participants bring to such settings.

These expectations derive from the extraordinary enthusiasm with which Malawians have embraced the value of education and its associated status hierarchy. Any program to introduce deliberation as a path to social justice will have to find a way to confront the longing Malawians have to be educated and modern and the way they turn virtually any modern context into an opportunity for what they have been taught to see as enlightenment. Although it may be that expanding claims-making beyond the individual to a group will be relatively easy, we see little potential for even the enunciation of group claims in a setting where people expect to listen and learn to become enlightened.

Notes

1. Margaret Frye conducted the cohort analysis of the UNESCO (2008) and Ministry of Education and UNESCO (2008) data.
2. Rao and Sanyal (2010, 154) write: "Overall, citizen-state relationships in rural India exist more in the matrix of a gift economy than in the realm of rights and responsibilities. Poor accountability mechanisms, lack of resources, and the identity-based nature of electoral politics result in a culture of supplication and

benefaction." The decision-making powers of the *gram sabha* are not totally dissimilar from those of a Malawian chief, except that Malawi's government provides far fewer public benefits and ethnic or tribal divisions play almost no role at the local level. A village headman in Malawi can make allocation decisions when government benefits are available, with the constraint that benefits are few and almost all are supposed to be targeted to the poorest villagers. Most collective goods, however, come from the villagers' own efforts; the chief oversees and enforces such collective obligations. Nonetheless, what Rao and Sanyal observe about *gram sabhas* also applies to at least some Malawian village disputes: "Most discussions in the *gram sabha*, therefore, arise in the form of a demand or supplication. Villagers ask the GP to provide a public good in a particular location or to recognize someone as poor enough to deserve private benefits" (154).

3. The closest thing to monetary aid provided by the government is access by targeted groups to subsidized coupons for fertilizer and to opportunities for a few days of paid work on public works projects. The chief controls access to both benefits. In 2006 a social cash transfer scheme targeted to ultrapoor households with high dependency ratios was introduced, financed primarily by UNICEF and the Global Fund, first in the Mchinji district in central Malawi (Miller, Tsoka, and Reichert 2008) and later in 6 of Malawi's 28 districts (Chinyama and Siu 2010).

4. Colson (2002) and Collier (2004) make similar points about the need of chiefs to prevent disruptive conflict.

5. Karlström (1996) notes that local understandings of "democracy" among Baganda are grounded in ideals of civility and the concern of leaders for their followers, which they see as inherent in the clan system. Even Mamdani (1996), who makes a strong case that the traditional chief's role was corrupted by colonial law, offers a wonderful example of a chief's insistence, in the face of colonial incomprehension, that he has the power to make decisions, but only in consultation with his headmen.

6. In rural Malawi, fights about sexual relationships are fights about the distribution of resources. Both wives and girlfriends depend on men's money for an important part of their livelihood: both defend their right to his money. In one spectacular fight between a wife and several bar girls, the wife, by then bleeding, said defiantly that she got the man's salary but his girlfriends got much less. A bar girl answered, "You have the big problem, big mum, your husband is not for you alone! He was born not for you special, and indeed he will be sleeping with all of us here, because we also need what he has, we need the penis as well, for once it enters on us, we just know that we are to eat that day. No penis, no money!" (Simon Bato, February 15, 2004). We have not yet read about or heard of a quarrel or fight between a wife and a girlfriend where the wife was blamed. In a particularly scandalous case enthusiastically covered by the media, in 2007 Malawi's Minister of Information and Civic Education, Patricia Kaliati, badly beat the maid of an acquaintance, whom she believed was having an affair with her husband. The case did not come to trial.

7. We retain most of the journalists' idiosyncrasies in grammar and spelling, although on occasion we make minor grammatical changes to improve readability. We identify the journal extracts by the journalist's pseudonym and the date of the journal.

8. Smith (2003) describes how workshops and trainings that NGOs sponsor bolster the local system of patron-client ties in Nigeria.

9. Formality seems to suppress participation. Even in the middle of a vibrantly participatory church service, the secretary, dressed neatly in a suit and wearing the requisite spectacles, will read out a lengthy report on a recent meeting or the budget, sometimes droning on with a list of figures while the members of the congregation sit in silence.

10. Although there is a formal rule, dating from 1993, that students expelled from school because of pregnancy may return after the baby is born, schools also have rules that forbid sexual partnerships. Students can be suspended for kissing and expelled for "immoral behavior." Teachers complain that democracy and human rights organizations have interfered with their authority to discipline students who have sexual partnerships. In interviews Maggie Frye conducted with secondary school teachers in Malawi in 2009, teachers lamented the coming of human rights: "You know, democracy, there were a lot of human rights organizations. So it was like, the authority of the teachers was declining. Because even the teachers are also afraid that the human rights organizations were accusing them of how they teach their students. Because previously the teachers were the authority over the students. They could control the students. . . . If a student has done something wrong, I will give [her] a severe punishment. . . . But once that happens, the student will say, my rights have not been respected. So the teacher says, okay, if this girl recognizes that [her] rights are not respected, definitely this issue will go beyond the school. It will even go beyond the parent, and the parent may be a member of one of the human rights organizations."

11. Kendall added in brackets notes on what she observed. We have abbreviated some of these notes and labeled speakers for clarity.

12. A critical review of the history and uses of focus groups speaks to their fit with ideologies of participation: "The ideal these focus group guidelines and assumptions seek to achieve is a kind of communicative democracy in which all participants can and should speak equally and the topic at hand is open for all to discuss, neutralizing constraints of power, status, or propriety" (Kratz 2010, 811).

13. Many observers report witnessing similar scenes. See, for example, Marsland's (2006, 71–72) report of a training in which she participated in Tanzania: "Throughout the training seminar, I was aware that the methods did not fit my understanding of participatory work: the atmosphere was educational. For example, there was group work, in which we had to divide up and discuss what *maendeleo* (development), health and the 'characteristics of an adult' meant to us. One person from each group wrote up their conclusions on the

blackboard, and then the trainers wrote up their definition of *maendeleo*, which we all had to write in our notebooks. An attempt was made at a transect walk—we had to walk around the hospital grounds and report back three things that we had seen. The participants seemed to know what was expected of them, and received approval from the facilitators for noting items of interest to public health, such as the use of mosquito nets, the rubbish dump, and the tidily tended gardens (reducing resting places for mosquitoes after their blood meals)."

14. The program, aimed at "bringing in development," is called REFLECT (Regenerated Freirian Community Techniques).

15. J. Clyde Mitchell (1956, 38), who studied the Yao of southern Malawi (then Nyasaland), describes the parallels between the way the Yao experienced their submission to the British and the earlier submission of refugee groups accepted as slaves: "It is clear that they looked upon their submission to the Whites in much the same way as they looked upon the submission of refugees to themselves. To submit to a man was to accept slave or near-slave status. . . . A chief with whom I was once discussing slavery expressed neatly the attitude of the Yao chiefs to their subjugation. He said: 'There is no slavery today—we are the salves of the government.' The chiefs who returned to the Protectorate, therefore, returned as subjects, and were fully aware of this. In the new regime, the former chiefs had to recognize a superior authority and the British Administration provided the framework within which the old rivalries had to be rephrased."

16. In July 2011, demonstrations erupted in Malawi's three largest cities, protesting government corruption, fuel shortages, and a foreign exchange crisis. Twenty protesters were killed (see Cammack 2011 for a detailed analysis).

References

Cammack, Diana. 2011. "Malawi's Political Settlement in Crisis, 2011." *Africa Power and Politics Background Paper 4*, Overseas Development Institute, London.

Cammack, Diana, and Edge Kanyongolo. 2010. "Local Governance and Public Goods in Malawi." In *Africa Power and Politics Series*. London: Overseas Development Institute.

Chinyama, Victor, and Vivian Siu. 2010. "UNICEF Executive Director Spotlights Malawi's Social Cash-Transfer Programme." http://www.reliefweb.int/rw/rwb.nsf/db900sid/MMAH-8AP3WS?OpenDocument.

Collier, Jane Fishburne. 2004. "A Chief Does Not Rule Land; He Rules People (Luganda Proverb)." In *Law and Empire in the Pacific: Fiji and Hawaii*, ed. Sally Engle Merry and Donald Brenneis, 35–60. Santa Fe, NM: School of American Research Press.

Colson, Elizabeth. 2002. *Tradition and Contract: The Problem of Order*, 2nd ed. Chicago: Aldine Transaction Books.

Davis, Natalie Zemon. 1973. "The Rites of Violence: Religious Riots in Sixteenth Century France." *Past and Present* 59: 51–91. Available at http://www.itc. csmd.edu/fin/janete/HST1012/RitesViolence.pdf.

Dionne, Kim Yi. 2010. "Seeing Like a Village: Village Headmen and AIDS Intervention." Working paper, Department of Political Science, Texas A&M, College Station, TX.

Eliasoph, Nina, and Paul Lichterman. 2003. "Culture in Interaction." *American Journal of Sociology* 108 (4): 735–94.

Englund, Harri. 2006. *Prisoners of Freedom: Human Rights and the African Poor.* Berkeley: University of California Press.

Frank, David John, and John W. Meyer. 2007. "University Expansion and the Knowledge Society." *Theory and Society* 36 (4): 287–311.

———. 2010. "Education as Devotion." Departments of Demography and Sociology, University of California, Berkeley.

Frye, Margaret. 2012. "Bright Futures in Malawi's New Dawn: Educational Aspirations as Assertions of Identity." *American Journal of Sociology* 117 (6): 1565–624.

Karlström, Mikael. 1996. "Imagining Democracy: The Political Culture and Democratisation in Buganda." *Africa* 66 (4): 485–506.

Kendall, Nancy O'Gara. 2004. *Global Policy in Practice: The 'Successful Failure' of Free Primary Education in Malawi.* PhD diss., School of Education and Committee on Graduate Studies, Stanford University, Stanford, CA.

Kratz, Corinne. 2010. "In and Out of Focus." *American Ethnologist* 37 (4): 805–26.

Mamdani, Mahmood. 1996. *Citizen and Subject: Contemporary Africa and the Legacy of Late Colonialism.* Princeton, NJ: Princeton University Press.

Marsland, Rebecca. 2006. "Community Participation the Tanzanian Way: Conceptual Contiguity or Power Struggle?" *Oxford Development Studies* 34 (1): 65–79.

Miller, Candace, Maxton Tsoka, and Kathryn Reichert. 2008. "Impact Evaluation Report External Evaluation of the Mchinji Social Cash Transfer Pilot." U.S. Agency for International Development, Boston University, and UNICEF.

Ministry of Education, and UNESCO (United Nations Educational, Scientific and Cultural Organization). 2008. *National Report of Malawi 2008.* Available at www.ibe.unesco.org/National_Reports/ICE_2008/malawi_NR08.pdf.

Mitchell, J. Clyde. 1956. *The Yao Village: A Study in the Social Structure of a Nyasaland Tribe.* Manchester: Manchester University Press.

Paz Soldan, Valerie A. 2003. "Diffusion of Contraceptive Intentions and Practices in Social Groups in Rural Malawi." Department of Maternal and Child Health, School of Public Health, University of North Carolina, Chapel Hill.

Rao, Vijayendra, and Paromita Sanyal. 2010. "Dignity through Discourse: Poverty and the Culture of Deliberation in Indian Village Democracies." *Annals of the American Academy of Political and Social Science* 629: 146–72.

Smith, Daniel Jordan. 2003. "Patronage, Per Diems and 'the Workshop Mentality': The Practice of Family Planning Programs in Southeastern Nigeria." *World Development* 31 (4): 703–15.

Swidler, Ann. 2013. "Cultural Sources of Institutional Resilience: Lessons from Chieftaincy in Rural Malawi." In *Social Resilience in the Neoliberal Era*, ed. Peter A. Hall and Michèle Lamont, 319–45. New York: Cambridge University Press.

Swidler, Ann, and Susan Cotts Watkins. 2007. "Ties of Dependence: AIDS and Transactional Sex in Rural Malawi." *Studies in Family Planning* 38 (3): 147–62.

———. 2009. "'Teach a Man to Fish': The Sustainability Doctrine and Its Social Consequences." *World Development* 37 (7): 1182–96.

Thompson, E. P. 1963. *The Making of the English Working Class*. New York: Random House.

UNESCO (United Nations Education, Scientific and Cultural Organization). 2008. *UNESCO Institute for Statistics in Brief for Malawi 2007*. Available at http://stats.uis.unesco.org/unesco/TableViewer/document.aspx?ReportId=121&IF_Language=eng&BR_Country=4540.

Watkins, Susan Cotts, and Ann Swidler. 2009. "Hearsay Ethnography: Conversational Journals as a Method for Studying Culture in Action." *Poetics* 37 (2): 162–84.

CHAPTER 8

The Role of Emotions in Deliberative Development

Paromita Sanyal

Since the 1980s, sentiments—emotions, feelings, and passions—have been recognized as playing a strategic role in directing human actions (Frank 1988; Frijda 1986; Hirshleifer 1987; Elster 1996; Calhoun 2001; Barbalet 2002).[1] As a force that directs human action, emotions have some distinctive characteristics.[2] They have a "component of arousal" (Elster 1994, 25), the heightening or amplifying of feelings that stimulates or provokes individuals into actions. Emotions are also characterized by their "indeterminacy" (Berezin 2002, 39), which makes them salient in the political realm. Emotions also have "reflexive, meaning-making," "communicative," and occasionally "tactical" functions (Ng and Kidder 2010, 193–94). Views on how emotions surface vary in these perspectives from arousal (the intensification of feelings and their spontaneous release) to performance and enactment (feelings conveyed through a performance that draws on the cultural repertoire of interpretive frameworks and dominant narratives) (Polletta 2001; Ng and Kidder 2010; Xu 2012).

This chapter draws on first-hand field-level data (transcripts of village meetings [*gram sabha*]) from India to theorize about the role of emotions in the realm of development deliberations. Inspired by the ideals of deliberative democracy, this realm encompasses participatory forums of decision making, such as civic settings and "invited spaces" (Cornwall 2004). In these forums the publics, sometimes in conjunction with public officials, deliberate on issues related to community development, engaging in discursive exchanges of ideas, arguments, and justifications on issues of public need and interest. This realm has been enlivened by the effort of governments around the world to translate into practice liberal political theory and alternative populist models of development, with the aim of making community and village development decisions representative and participatory, more democratic with a public input, and more moral and consensual. In development deliberations, public discussions usually center on the allocation of public finances to community infrastructure and resource building, the allocation of state subsidies and benefits to groups and individuals, or decisions that affect the entire community and in which different groups in a community have stakes. This realm is expanding globally, with a slowly growing number of countries adopting some degree of public deliberation into development planning.

This chapter highlights the role of emotions in spheres of development deliberations. To the extent that development deliberations represent deliberative democracy in practice, the role of emotions is relevant for deliberative democracy in general. However, these roles are not all-encompassing, as emotions may play different roles and have different effects in different settings of deliberative democracy.

Just as cases of deliberative democracy vary in form and function, models of development vary with respect to whether or not they incorporate public deliberations in their planning methodology. There are two distinct models of development. The first, which has a longer history, represents the top-down mode of development—development that is designed and directed by political leaders, government bureaucrats, and technocrats. This model does not include public participation or deliberations in its decision-making methodology.

The second model, of more recent origin, is decentralized development. It incorporates public participation and deliberative decision making on issues of community development and often involves the allocation of public finances to meet the development needs of localities. For example, municipal-level participatory budgeting exercises in Brazil incorporate citizens' deliberation on allocating monies to public resources and infrastructure (Baiocchi 2005; Baiocchi, Heller, and Silva 2011).

One form of decentralized development is community-driven development (CDD), the preferred technique among governments and international aid and development agencies (including the World Bank) when implementing development interventions in the global South. CDD institutes community-based public deliberations that try to arrive at solutions to locally relevant problems and make corresponding decisions about economic allocations for resource and infrastructure development (Mansuri and Rao 2004, 2012; Gibson and Woolcock 2008). These community-based deliberations may be institutionalized in the form of community groups and neighborhood associations. Recently, such deliberative forums have begun to be used even in the developed countries of the global North for civic and administrative purposes. Innovative experiments that incorporate deliberation on matters of community development have been pioneered by states and provinces such as Vermont, Oregon, and British Columbia (Fung, Wright, and Abers 2003; Delli Carpini, Cook, and Jacobs 2004; Gastil and Levine 2010).

Some democratic states have established institutionalized mechanisms of public deliberation and constitutionally built them into the political system, giving them a countrywide presence. These attempts and institutions are often referred to as ushering in "deliberative democracy."

The most extreme and significant example of deliberative democracy is the Indian *gram sabha*. These village-based public forums are held two to four times a year as a part of the nationwide decentralized governance system. They concern the development outcomes and aspirations of millions of India's rural citizens. These public meetings were mandated by the 73rd Amendment to the Constitution, passed in 1992, which paved the way for decentralized governance by setting up *panchayati raj* (local governance) institutions.

The lowest, most grassroots tier of these institutions is the deliberative village forum, the *gram sabha*. These governmentally coordinated deliberative exercises, which are open to all voting-age adults in a village, have multiple decision-making tasks. They follow governmental criteria in selecting beneficiaries for government-subsidized private goods, determine the spatial location of public goods, arrive at common demands for public resources, perform oversight over government income and expenditures, and monitor the progress of public works. These initiatives are aimed at opening up spaces of dialogue between the state and citizens through the creation of "invited spaces" (Cornwall 2004) that bring publics and public officials face to face in deliberative forums. They have inaugurated an era of deliberative development and deliberative democracy.

Development deliberations are impressive in their global relevance, functional scope (public budgets and community-wide decision making on affairs that affect the entire community), and the magnitude of lives they affect. Following their worldwide diffusion and increasing appeal, academic attention has begun to focus on these deliberative forums. This interest follows a long hiatus since Habermas (1990) theorized on "communicative action" and its impact on moral consciousness. There is a significant body of literature on citizens' participation in participatory development (Cooke and Kothari 2001; Hickey and Mohan 2004) and a sizable body of theoretical literature on deliberative democracy. Neither pays attention to the possible role emotions might play in deliberative exercises, however.[3]

Development deliberations are a promising site for the study of public emotions. Wide differences in power are often evident among the parties to deliberations, which include poor, landless, illiterate villagers from scheduled castes and tribes[4]; villagers who are better off, educated, and from locally dominant caste groups; and elected leaders and public officials. This power divide in the *gram sabha* is a unique and important feature of the deliberations occurring in it. In such a setting, which is shot through with socioeconomic inequities and power inequalities, villagers use displays of emotion to get what they want from public officials and goad them into action.

This chapter describes instances in *gram sabha* deliberations in Indian villages in which emotions play expressive and instrumental roles. It uses them as a basis for empirically informed theorizing about the role of emotions—particularly some constructive roles and a cognitive role—in deliberations within institutions of deliberative democracy and decentralized development.

The chapter is organized as follows. The next section reviews the literature on emotions in deliberative democracy. The third section describes the data and methods underlying this study (analysis of transcripts of village meetings in four South Indian states). The fourth section outlines three broad roles that emotions appear to play in development deliberations in Indian villages. The last section summarizes the conclusions that emerge from the field research.

Emotions in deliberative democracy

Normative theories of deliberation for the most part do not acknowledge any role of emotions. Ideal deliberations are envisioned as reasoned argumentation among equals (Habermas 1984, 1990; Cohen 1989; Mansbridge 1990; Fishkin 1991; Bohman 1996; Dryzek 2000; Fung 2004; Gutmann and Thompson 2004). The moral community imagined is one in which its citizens, who are all free and equal, fully and autonomously accept the norms and practices of society. Social behavior is never agonistic, as among opposing entities with unequal means. Behaviors such as fighting, threat, attack, appeasement, submission, and retreat are not present. In this environment, the "ideal speech situation" (Habermas 1984) exists— discursive equality that guarantees fairness in deliberations.

Deviating from this classical view, a few deliberation theorists acknowledge the presence and role of emotions. Mansbridge argues that, in contrast to adversary democracy, which is designed to be emotion free, unitary democracy is informed by an array of sentiments. The need to operate in a consensus-forming manner under unitary democracy may generate more "angry" conflicts, because people may need to figure out the correct solution to a problem, a process that may be laden with acerbic arguments. But the process can also be full of love, so that democratic decision making is driven by "concern for others, we-feeling, and readiness to cooperate when cooperation does not serve self-interest narrowly conceived" (Mansbridge 1983, xi).[5] "Respect" and "pleasure of collective experience" also play important roles by subduing individual self-interests in favor of accommodating the concerns of others whose happiness matters to one's own well-being.

This initial acknowledgment of emotions in deliberations has been accompanied in the past decade by an acknowledgment of the use of personal narratives, or storytelling, in deliberative settings geared toward decision making on community development matters (Young 1996, 2000; Sanders 1997; Mansbridge 1999; Polletta and Lee 2006). Instead of viewing personal narratives as discursive infractions into "reflexive arguments" (Benhabib 1996, 70), some scholars argue that storytelling plays an equalizing role in the public sphere, especially for disadvantaged groups, by eliciting hearing and empathy from groups that have different life experiences (Sanders 1997; Young 2000). Because of their allusive and iterative characters, the "interpretive ambiguity" of stories that are narrated in the course of deliberations also allows for the introduction of alternative, minority points of view and compromises (Polletta and Lee 2006).

Although deliberative democracy theorists have come far in recognizing the presence and role of emotions in some forms of democratic arrangements and the equalizing and inclusive effects of personal narratives for disadvantaged groups and minority points of view, important areas remain unaddressed. One is how socioeconomically disadvantaged and relatively powerless groups use displays of emotion in their discursive encounters with more privileged groups and state functionaries to get what they want in deliberative civic settings. Particularly intriguing, but not yet well understood, is how emotions enter into reflexive arguments and rational debates, not just through the discursive medium of storytelling. The centrality of power and powerlessness also needs to be better understood to understand which groups and people are more prone to experiencing and expressing emotions in deliberative settings and the roles their emotions play.

Mouffe (1999) acknowledges these twin dimensions of power and emotions as playing prime roles in the political life of democracy. She proposes an alternative model of democracy—"agonistic pluralism" (1999, 754)—which acknowledges "the dimension of power and antagonism and their ineradicable character" (752). The conceptual frame underlying this model distinguishes between two types of political relations: "antagonism between enemies," in which the goal is to destroy the enemy, and "agonism between adversaries," in which an adversary is a "legitimate enemy," one with whom the subject shares adherence to the principles of democracy but disagrees in its meaning and implementation, resulting in antagonistic feelings. "Far from jeopardizing democracy, agonistic confrontation is in fact its very condition of existence," according to Mouffe (1999, 755–56). She argues that the aim of democratic politics is "domesticating hostility"—that is, transforming antagonism into agonism. In her model, the main goal of democratic politics is "not to eliminate passions nor to relegate them to the private sphere in order to render rational consensus possible, but to mobilize those passions towards the promotion of democratic designs" (1999, 755–56). What are these constructive roles into which passions ought to be mobilized within democratic political structures? This question is left unaddressed, leaving an important gap.

Elster highlights the capacity of emotions to "distort the cognitive appraisal that triggered them in the first place" (1994, 27). He argues that an emotionally aggravated state may reduce the capacity for making logical connections between the cause of emotions, the effect of hastily chosen actions, and the ultimate achievement of desired goals. Elster's argument opens up the question: What, if any, is the cognitive impact of emotions in development deliberations? This area remains unexplored.

Data, methods, and analytic approach

This chapter is based on an ongoing large-scale research project on deliberative democracy in which 290 *gram sabhas* in four South Indian states (Andhra Pradesh, Karnataka, Kerala, and Tamil Nadu) were visited and tape recorded. The recordings were transcribed into the local language and then translated into English. Each transcript includes information on attendance and some identifiable features of the speaker, including gender, caste (from name), official designation, and social position (elected representative, school principal, villager, and so forth).

Across states the average *gram sabha* meeting lasted 84 minutes and was attended by about 83 people, a small fraction of the village population. One-third of attendees were women and 37 percent were from scheduled castes (a majority from "other backward castes," the dominant castes in South India).[6] Issues that regularly came up for discussion included problems with the supply of drinking water and lack or disrepair of village roads, followed by concerns about village schools, electricity, housing, and health. Issues that came up less frequently but predictably included the legitimacy of paying taxes when service provision was unsatisfactory and the fairness of caste-based affirmative action as a principle of resource allocation.

A household survey was also conducted in these villages. Regression analysis of the household survey data conducted by Besley, Pande, and Rao (2005) reveals that, after controlling for household characteristics and village fixed effects, illiterate individuals, members of scheduled castes, the landless, and the poorer were more likely to attend the *gram sabha*. This effect is thought to be largely the result of one of the main functions of the *gram sabha*, which is to select beneficiaries for government-subsidized schemes for households below the poverty line and members of scheduled castes. This form of selection into participation was less marked in villages with higher literacy levels, where participation was more representative (Ban, Jha, and Rao 2012).

This chapter focuses on the discursive level of the deliberations in these meetings, in order to determine the influences of emotions on deliberation itself. Expressing their emotions is a way through which sub-altern publics exercise their power—their political power with respect to the local state and their social power with respect to their status superiors, who may be elected leaders and state-level bureaucrats.[7] The justification for associating the use of emotions as a medium of social and political power in *gram sabha* deliberations with subalterns is based on the fact that regression analysis of the household survey data shows that illiterate villag-ers, members of scheduled castes, the landless, and the poorer were more likely to attend these meetings, especially in villages with lower literacy.[8]

The view of emotions adopted in this chapter converges with the cul-tural view of emotions proposed by Goodwin, Jasper, and Polletta (2004, 414), whose study of the role of emotions in social movements and poli-tics emphasizes the cultural foundation of "how, when, and where to experience and express different emotions." It also converges with recent observations by sociologists that emotions may be put to strategic use. Sociologists have shown how politicians and political activists use dis-plays of emotion to signal information about themselves (Ng and Kidder 2010; Xu 2012). The distinction between the sudden arousal of emotions and their spontaneous expression on the one hand and the deliberate performance of feelings on the other is not a conceptually significant dis-tinction for this chapter. What is significant is the strategic role (intended or unintended) emotions can play in settings of deliberative development. Emotions do not always play a strategic or well-defined instrumental role in deliberative settings, but the fact that they may be disruptive, unruly, and dysfunctional does not undermine the importance of the ways and settings in which emotions do play an influential role in development deliberations. Emotions and reasons (or rationality) are not treated as opposed binaries or mutually exclusive. The data bear out that in a delib-erative setting such as a *gram sabha*, where local-level representatives of the state and the public deliberate over important private and public goods, a reaction that is a rational response can also be highly charged emotionally.

The role of emotions in deliberative development

Emotions as enforcers of accountability and justice

Indignation, or righteous rage, appears to play a consequential role as a governance tool in dealing with corruption, injustice, and discrimination. In the *gram sabha,* the frontline grassroots institution of deliberative democracy, this role seems to recur frequently and prominently. The reality of rural development in India is replete with instances of malpractice and corruption in public works (resource and infrastructure projects), public distribution systems, schools, primary health services, and many other government-sponsored services.[9] These unfair practices include the imbalanced or nepotistic allocation of public goods favoring some neighborhoods and villages while neglecting others, the habitual absenteeism by government-salaried teachers and doctors, the siphoning off of in-kind resources meant for public distribution (such as the mid-day meal program in schools), and petty bribe-taking. Black markets for government-subsidized grains, sugar, kerosene oil, and other basic supplies meant for distribution to poor households are thriving.[10] Poor villagers who confront unjust treatment like the unfair allocation of public resources are normally powerless to insist on their entitlements; village meetings open up a deliberative venue in which villagers can express their pent-up anger through vociferous complaints and protests against such discriminatory and nefarious practices. Righteous rage helps villagers disregard the fear of reprisal from powerful stakeholders against whom they make allegations of discrimination and corruption and whose unfair practices they expose in public forums. Consequently, emotions that are experienced and expressed in the context of development deliberations may influence official decisions regarding remedying public resource and infrastructure problems. This emotionally charged airing of these grievances may eventually improve a community's access to public resources and infrastructure.

In the following extract, the informal representative of the village's scheduled caste community, accompanied by another man from a "backward caste," erupts in angry allegations of caste-based discrimination in the village water supply. As a result of the emotionally charged complaint that the neighborhood was being deprived of water, the de facto *panchayat* president (the husband of the president) promises regular water supply to the neighborhood:[11]

> Jayaraman (male villager from other backward caste): There are 45 families in our village. None of us have any land. We work for meager daily wages. Whatever little we get we spend on our children's education. . . . Our whole area is dirty. Even the water is muddy, that's what we drink. . . . How many times we have requested for a road near the cremation ground and for the supply for clean water?! We can only request and apply. The rest is up to you.

> De facto *panchayat* president: If there are 20–25 houses in an area, a ward member should be appointed to represent the area. That ward member should listen to your problems and must do something to help you.

> Muniraj (male villager from scheduled caste): [In anger] That way [if they have a ward member], we will have the guts to enter this room. If the required ward members are not with us, to whom can we voice our woes? Who will represent us? . . . If the ward member belongs to another community, he won't even listen to our problems.

Earlier there was a time when a backward caste person was not even allowed to sit in the same area with others! The officers and leaders who come already have a preset plan about what to do and say. You come, sit on the chair, say something, decide among yourselves, and go away. What's there for us to do?! You've enjoyed power for all these years. Why don't you let us have a turn? . . . We don't want any problem at the communal level. For us, whether Subban or Kuppan [common names] comes, it is the same. We vote, but what happens later? While other people get water even before they ask for it, we have to ask endlessly, and even so, our demand is not fulfilled. . . . We don't want to fight with anyone. But at least there should be someone to listen to our problems. We've been without water supply for the past month. Even the president knows it. He has promised to send water. But the ward member is not allowing us to take water. The water is sent to all his relatives. We cannot do anything to stop it.

De facto *panchayat* president: You mean to say you still don't get water?

Muniraj: At present we get water supply, but the water we get is muddy.

De facto *panchayat* president: That is because it is a new bore pump. For 40 families, five pumps in public places will suffice. But you dig pits, and mud gets mixed with water supply. So in order to help you, a pump shall be installed at the center at the cost of Rs. 10,000. It will solve your present water problem. You talk a lot about community problems and misunderstandings. But water is a common problem for everyone. Just take care of the pipe when it is not in use.

Muniraj: How do you know that we don't do it? If you come and see it is not done, then you ask.

De facto *panchayat* president: In any competition it's a rule that one should win and the other should lose. There's no community-based discrimination or problem. . . . Today, among youngsters, the level of public awareness is very high. Anyone can become a leader.

Muniraj: We're not even allowed to stand for ward member elections. How can we become the *panchayat* leader?

De facto *panchayat* president: It depends on how you approach people. If you become a ward member depending only on those 45 families, find out why others are not voting for you. Change your approach. Why do they threaten you? Because you give in, and you allow them to do it!

Muniraj: When we're not even allowed to open our mouths, what can we do?

De facto *panchayat* president: You're afraid! You're scared to open up with them. I am asking you to be patient and not to increase the problem. You have told me what you want, and I will do it in the proper way.

Muniraj: OK. There should not be any caste discriminations. That is our request.

De facto *panchayat* president: Coming back to the pipe problem. How do you think it should be solved?

Muniraj: The number of pipes should be increased. Water should be distributed equally. You cannot stop our water supply.

Rajendran (second male villager from scheduled caste): When our supply is cut, the other side enjoys the full benefit of it. Why should they benefit, at our cost?

De facto *panchayat* president: OK, Rajendran. Five pipes will be fixed in each street, and I will see that it is done.

Rajendran: For one whole week, we did not receive any water. Even you know it. What little water we got was not usable. That, too, you know.

De facto *panchayat* president: OK. You won't face any water problem from now on.

Muniraj: Everyone should be treated equally. No one should be treated as inferior to others. We should also be given a chance to sit on the dais [where the leaders sit]. Why should we be denied that right? Just because I talk like this [in an aggressive manner and with raised voice], it doesn't mean that I fight with you or disrespect you. I am simply voicing my feeling.

This exchange reveals how an emotional outburst or calculated performance of anger (it is difficult to determine which) was effective in eliciting a concrete promise from the leader about rectifying a problem.

A study of nearly 300 village meetings across four South Indian states revealed numerous instances of explicit and implicit threats. Citizens angrily threatened political representatives and public officials to protest severe shortages of essential resources (often water or roads). Ward members threatened higher levels of elected officials, such as *panchayat* presidents and union collectors,[12] with unrest unless the demands they had made on behalf of their constituencies were fulfilled. Irate ward members spoke of experiencing feelings of shame and embarrassment in facing their constituencies because of their inability to deliver on their promises. *Panchayat* presidents and officials reminded agitating citizens of their habitual nonpayment of taxes and illegal actions (such as drawing unauthorized water connections), using these facts as justifications for the nonprovision of public goods and services. For their part, *panchayat* officials and members made conciliatory promises of fixing problems and rectifying shortages by delivering public goods or increasing their scrutiny of public works. Analysis of these meetings and examples reveals that public displays of emotions occurred frequently, that they were accompanied by verbal exchanges of hostility and appeasement, and that the exchanges were consequential for the means and ends decisions arrived at in these meetings.

In another village, villagers angrily complained about the doctor's chronic absence from the government health center. This segment of the deliberation ends with the *panchayat* president deciding to provide the village doctors with an ultimatum:

> Female villager 8: If we go to hospital, there is no doctor there and nor are there any medicines!
>
> Male villager 2: People are complaining! Who did you tell about this? . . . See, people are complaining directly. (To the *panchayat* president) You should also respond directly.
>
> Male villager 22: He (doctor) is never there! Whenever we go, he is never there!
>
> Male villager 2: What is going on? What do *gram panchayat* members have to say about this?
>
> Male *gram panchayat* member: I did not know about this. Only now I've come to know about this.
>
> Male villager 6: Whatever it is, the doctor is never there! Every time in the *gram panchayat* meeting this complaint is voiced.
>
> *Gram panchayat* president (male): We will give them one month's more time. . . . Within one month, if they do not change, then serious action will be taken against them. We promise! We will give them one opportunity. *Gram panchayat* members should observe these doctors, whether they come on time or not, whether they give treatment or not, for one month. After one month, if nothing has changed then let the *gram panchayat* bring it to my notice. I will take some serious action against them.

Strong public displays of indignation—a combination of anger and annoyance/exasperation—are a countervailing force against apathy and passive acquiescence. They play a fortifying role in driving citizens' demands for accountability in public service provision and just treatment from political leaders and public officials.

Another powerful segment shows a ward member in Tamil Nadu asking for an electric power line for his community of tribal people, who live on a forested hilly tract. He complains about government inaction and discrimination—other communities/villages being provided with electricity lines and water supply while his tribal community/village is passed over. In his complaint, which is emotionally charged, he makes a very important reference, to Veerappan, a fugitive bandit who symbolized the disaffection of tribal and poor rural people with local governments.[13] By making this reference, he is reminding the political authority of the deadly consequences of the pent-up collective feeling of frustration and anger over state negligence. As a finale to his passionate complaint, he compares the force of the tribal community's outrage with the ravaging force of a tsunami.

Mr. Ranga Sami (ward member, scheduled tribe): Keep one EB [Electricity Board] line exclusively for us [tribal families living in a hilly forest tract]. You are saying (we can get) only solar light. But, for us, we also want current bulb. "Electricity Board line cannot be installed in elevated areas like hills." [Speaks in anger] How can you say that?! You installed electricity line from Karamadai to Badrakaliamman temple and beyond Bavani river. So, why not in our area? If you make an effort, you can do it. The law is the same for all! How can you say it is not possible?!

Panchayat president: After the EB people visit and make a survey of your area, they will decide. It is possible only after taking license from the forest officials. There's a lot to clarify.

Mr. Ranga Sami: You always talk about solar, but when will we get electricity line? What help you want from the public, you tell me. Only if we try it is possible, boss. [Emotionally charged] [Otherwise] like how things happened with Veerappan, it will happen. Law is the same for all. When one village is getting Electricity Board line in the upper area, why not our village? Our children should get that facility. We are not educated, but for our children to be educated they need electricity light. Up to 10th standard only we are able to give education, so surely we need electricity line for us.

Panchayat president: If this becomes court issue, only then I can do something. Until then I cannot interfere in this regard.

Mr. Ranga Sami: For Mannar area alone there is water supply from the national Rajiv Gandhi drinking water scheme. But for Koraipathi area there is no water supply! Where is the justice? Like that, don't repeat the same thing with the solar light scheme and keep us in the dark. . . . If you want bribe, then also it will be given. Don't think we are naive. The speed in us is like the tsunami. . . . If our anger surges like the tsunami, that won't be tolerable.

When they can be induced in status-superiors through concerted criticism by status-subordinates in public forums, certain negative emotions (guilt, embarrassment, shame) have a potentially disciplining or punitive role. These emotions are a penalizing tool that ordinary citizens in democracies possess; they can sometimes help enforce justice and accountability.

Hossain (2009) studied frontline government service delivery (safety net programs, government-funded schools and health centers) in rural Bangladesh, where she witnessed poor female villagers rudely demanding accountability from doctors, nurses, and teachers. She argues that in the face of poor service delivery and the absence of formal means of complaints, "rude accountability" (which varied from "faintly impolite" to "downright abusive" to "plainly violent") reflected the annoyance, anger, and helplessness of the public. It became a tactical discursive tool that poor villagers used to seek their entitlements. Shame and embarrassment, the threat of violence, and concern about preserving status and reputation help explain how and why "rude accountability" was effective in inducing "rough responsiveness" to demands for services.

Emotions as cognitive impediments

Deliberative development requires that the participating public understand the often complex constraints and conditions of government budgetary allocations to development as well as the nature of development possibilities and problems. However, ordinary citizens' ability to understand these complex issues is, at times, affected by emotions. Examples from village meetings suggest that collective fury over the scarcity of essential resources may obfuscate the understanding of underlying problems, such as the fact that droughts and groundwater shortages cannot be remedied in the short run and water cannot be supplied to every household without charging a service fee. Anger focused on an external target may prevent communities from seeing the role they play in exacerbating problems by engaging in detrimental practices, such as digging additional pit holes or illegally tapping the water supply.

These issues come to the surface in the segment below, in which villagers angrily argue with elected leaders about water scarcity and accuse them of inaction. The villagers appear unwilling to grasp the facts that contributed to the water shortage, including illegal household tap connections, their own ward member's opposition to laying water pipes, his adamant insistence on obtaining a new motorized pump for which funds were not readily available from the *panchayat*, and the failure of monsoons. The villagers' emotionally charged accusation of negligence by the local government—an accusation which may be misplaced in this case—reflects the cognitive role of emotions in obscuring the deeper roots of the problem:

> Mrs. Akila (Villager): [Angrily] My name is Akila. I don't hold any post; I am a housewife. We have given lots of petitions to the village *panchayat* administrative office, to the collector, etc. but for Pattakapatti [village name] they have not done anything! Why have you not taken any action? [Angrily threatens] If you don't take action within three days, we don't know what will happen! You tell us whether you intend to do something or not.

> Mr. Marimuthu (*panchayat* president, member of other backward caste): You have the right to ask, so you can ask, but you mustn't talk so, like "We do not know what will happen if we don't get water within three days!" Government work will progress slowly.

> Other villager: In our place alone there have been no improvements.

> Other villager: We are not asking for anything except drinking water. Even if we go to different villages, they don't give us water. Our fasting days [Ramadan] have come; let us have drinking water. We are not asking for road facility, toilet facility, etc. We don't have any other facility.

> Other villager: For this village you have not done anything. What have you done for this village? Have you given road facility, toilet facility etc.? Why must I talk softly? [Shouts in anger] What have you really done for our village?

> Mr. Ganapathi (union councilor, member of other backward caste): In our village we have six (water) tanks. You are asking what we have done! Just because of fire to a Muslim person's house we spent Rs. 64,000. Just for a single person!

> Other villager: Is that the only thing needed? We are asking only for water facility. In your place, school is there, toilet facility is there, everything is there. So what've you done for our place?

> Mrs. Akila: [In anguish] Shall we take a jar of water from your house?!

> Mr. Ganapathi: Each year [the government] gives [funds] to each village. It cannot be given to all villages at the same time.

> . . .

> Mr. Ganapathi: We have had two bore-wells dug, spending Rs. 35,000 on each.

Mrs. Akila: Where is the bore-well for us?

Other villager: There is no water in the bore-well. If there is water available in the bore, we would not have to go in search of water to other villages.

Mr. Ganapathi: The whole of India is suffering without water due to failure of monsoon, so what can we do? . . . We tried our level best by laying pipes, spending Rs. 20,000. But your ward member refused to accept that and was adamant in fixing a new motor [motorized pump for bore-well]. He stopped the process of laying pipes and asked us not to fix the old motor.

Other villager (member of scheduled caste): It has been six months since the pipes arrived here. [Villagers shout together in anger] Why must we be quiet? You listen to us.

Mr. Ganapathi: Just listen to me and then talk! Only after doing the whole job, like laying the pipes and fixing the motor, if you still don't get water only then you can question the *panchayat.* . . . You all said, either you put new motor or don't put anything at all! *Panchayat* does not have the funds for buying a new motor, but if the old motor does not work, then definitely we would do what is needed to get a new motor. You even stopped the pipe-laying work. What is the dispute between us? Why must we fight with you all?

Mr. Marimuthu: OK, we'll put 500-foot depth with new motor.

Ward member: OK.

Mr. Ganapathi: If according to the member we have to fix a new motor, all the individual connections (household taps) must be removed or they must pay Rs. 1,000 per house.

Mr. Marimuthu: We'll fix up new motor. But all illegal connections must be removed. Not even one connection must be there.

Mr. Ganapathi: We'll fix up 10 taps in the center of village in a row, and we'll fix up new motor, but not even one illegal pipe connection must remain in the village; everything must be cut. [Formal resolution recorded in writing]

Babu (ward member): All the illegal taps must be removed right from the Head's [*panchayat* president's] village to all the villages.

Mrs. Lakshmi (ward member, member of other backward caste): Even in the beginning, when the water problem started, they had decided to remove all the illegal taps. In our place, a few said that they wouldn't cooperate. When I told them to pay the deposit, they refused to pay. Just don't blame the president alone.

Other villager (member of scheduled caste): All of them have pipes in their bathroom and in other places in their house. In the entire village they have. So let us have even in our village.

Other villager: Pattakapatti has more illegal connections than any other village.

Mr. Ganapathi: We'll fix a new motor, but only in the center of the village. There will be 10 taps, and not even one illegal connection must be there.

Another exchange highlights how extreme emotions can impede understanding of governmental principles of subsidy allocation. In this segment, a man loses his temper on being informed that the government housing grant received by the *panchayat* was earmarked exclusively for scheduled caste families.

Velusamy (male villager, member other backward caste): I have been residing in this village through several generations and I've been asking for a house to live in. They say "today, tomorrow," but so far, nothing's been done. . . . I am sitting here at the mercy of my fate.

Panchayat clerk: Until now houses have been allotted only for SCs [scheduled castes] . . . not for OBCs [other backward castes].

Velusamy: They say that it has come only for the SCs, only for them! Is it that only they are humans? And are we people not human beings? How can you say such a thing! What kind of a *panchayat* is this? We can't go directly and meet the officer. We can only make kind requests to our president, whom we believe in. Make some arrangements for me!

The above examples point to the unconstructive role of negative emotions in the *gram sabha*. Heightened negative emotions impede the public's ability to understand the constraints and conditions of government funding for subsidized schemes and impedes them from realizing their own responsibility. The government is made an easy scapegoat.

Emotions as regulators of relationship between publics and the state

Theorists of social exchange (Lawler 2001) argue that social exchange has emotional effects. Emotions, they claim, are linked to affective states, which in turn have consequences for cohesion and commitment of the parties involved in the exchange.

Deliberation is a form of discursive social exchange; development deliberations have public and private material outcomes. When deliberations occur in discursive spaces created by the state, such as the *gram sabha*, and include state representatives and functionaries, the state is viewed as a figurative participant in the deliberative exchange. Such state-led development deliberations are proximate exchanges in a long chain of exchanges between the government and the public. The emotions aroused in the course of these deliberations, therefore, have the capacity to affect the relationship between local government bodies and citizens and, in a broader sense, state-society relationships.

The excerpt below highlights the escalation of negative sentiments during the course of deliberations, which eventually led to the breakdown of the *gram sabha* and the casting of blame on *panchayat* officials:

Villager: But where are the health and forest department officers?

Secretary: We extended invitations to the officials and also called them over the phone personally. They may arrive at any time.

Villager: With whom shall we discuss our village problems?

Villager: [Agitated] What we say should come out in the newspapers. We want a bridge; we are saying this for a long time. You have not done that. We are asking for a good drainage system. That, too, you have not done. But you spend on other unnecessary things that are not needed. What will you do about this?

Secretary: I myself cannot go on for inspection and sanction the money. There is a procedure for it. First it has to be approved by the *panchayat*. Then the engineer will come for the inspection. I think you know about this. They [government officials] are also interested in the development of the village. . . .

Villager: You always say the same thing. First create good drainage system.

Secretary: I know your problem, and we are also fighting for justice. But we need your cooperation.

Villager: You are the ones not cooperating with us. To whom shall we go with our problems?

[Mass speaking]

Secretary: Let all the officers finish with their guidelines, then we will all go to the hospital and stage a protest over there. [Mass speaking] It is not right to protest at the meeting and then return home. That doesn't solve our problems. We shall discuss how to protest. Listen to me for a minute, give the president a chance to talk. He will make the decision. He is consulting with the nodal officer [government bureaucrat]. Please be seated. I am sure he will make a good decision.

Villager: We can't sit here until 2 PM.

Secretary: Even if we hold a protest here, it should reach them, that is the way we should plan it. . . . If the president and vice president themselves walk out, it means the meeting has not taken place.

Villager: We will also stage a walkout and protest!

. . .

President (member of scheduled caste): Simply boycotting the proceedings and returning home will not be a solution to the problem.

Villager: Then what is the solution?

President: The station inspector is here, I shall ask him what can be done. Otherwise, you only suggest a solution. We will not say no to your valuable suggestion. The best solution we have is to lodge a written complaint against the officer. Then we can go to higher officials and talk about it. There is no point in simply boycotting the meeting.

. . .

Villager: Why has [the health officer] not arrived? He is irresponsible!

Secretary: Since we have decided to boycott the meeting on the issue of the absence of the health officer, I wish that all of you will give us your cooperation.

Villager: [Angrily] Why have we given votes to the president and the vice president? Say that they were absent and cancel the meeting [this effectively puts the blame on *panchayat* officials]. All members: Leave the *gram sabha*!

Emotions play a regulatory role in setting the tone of the state-society relationship at the local level. This example is a negative one. Positive emotions could have a constructive effect in forging a relationship of cooperation.

Conclusions

Emotions are important in settings of deliberative development. They can play a constructive role by helping enforce accountability and justice. They can play an unconstructive cognitive role by impeding understanding of the parameters of governmental allocations and the limits within which *panchayats* and their elected functionaries operate. Emotions can also hinder citizens from understanding their own civic responsibilities. They can also regulate the relationship between citizens and the local state.

Socioeconomically disadvantaged groups and groups that are relatively powerless with respect to political and government functionaries use displays of emotion in their discursive encounters with local government and state functionaries to get what they want in deliberative civic settings. Emotions function as a medium of informal power over politically consequential people who have the authority in development deliberations to make and ratify decisions that affect a community's access to vital resources as well as its quality of life and general well-being.

The examples presented in this chapter show how emotion-laden exchanges between agitated villagers and *panchayat* functionaries led to concrete recorded decisions about the provision of public services. Whether the decisions would have been made without the displays of emotion is an open question. Based on the data, it is reasonable to assume that in some scenarios, emotions act as a catalyst in the distributive decisions that are reached and ratified.

Whether or not they yield a positive distributional outcome, emotions serve as a medium of informal political and social power for subaltern publics in deliberative settings. The people who participate in these forums are largely subaltern publics: marginal and landless farmers, below-the-poverty-line families, illiterate or barely literate villagers. Their villages are typically deficient in basic resources and facilities, such as regular and sufficient water supply, road connectivity, and electricity. Schools and health centers are inadequate, and corruption is rampant. Life is marked by daily hardships and contentious engagement with government institutions. These struggles are combined with long histories of caste-based discrimination in the allocation of resources and the denial of dignity. These objective conditions make certain publics more prone to emotional dispositions when they participate in development deliberations.

When emotions bubble up to the surface, negative emotions predominate. When anger and indignation impede understanding of practical constraints or trigger a noncooperative relation with the local government, the consequences can be negative. But such emotions can also have posi- tive effects, as they do when they enforce accountability and justice. When expressed publicly and powerfully in deliberative settings, negative emotions can move authorities to action. In the "invited spaces" of the *gram sabha,* the informal power of public collective emotions works discursively—by threatening, shaming, or challenging status superiors who have formal and authoritative power over development budgets and over public works.

Powerless citizens use emotions as a medium of social and political power to try to get their share of public resources and services and governmental attention in an intensely competitive distributional field. Expressive release or performance of anger and indignation as a discursive strategy is a "weapon of the weak" (Scott 1990) in the deliberative arena of the *gram sabha*. One might even think of the effective discursive expression of emotion as a consequential capability for subaltern publics.

Emotions are more frequently observed in their constructive, cognitive, and relational roles in states that have higher capacity in terms of a decentralized planning and development system (that is, the *panchayat* system [in Tamil Nadu and Karnataka, for example]).[14] Larger numbers of villagers attend these meetings expecting to get their demands fulfilled and their public resource complaints heard. Because the village meetings in these states are substantive, expectations are higher and there is a greater sense of entitlement to fair treatment and basic infrastructure and resources. Under these conditions, an open deliberative format results in a temporarily hierarchy-less discursive civic space for a public that is familiar with deliberative participation and various discursive strategies.

When expectations of efficient service delivery and problem redressal from the *panchayat* are substantial, disappointments can also be great; anger and indignation result. These emotions become channeled through discursive strategies for confronting the local government to enforce accountability and justice. When emotions are roused, they may cloud understanding and influence the relationship with the local state.

In states with low capacity in terms of the *panchayat* system (such as Andhra Pradesh, which deemphasized the *panchayat* system at the time of the data collection), we observed no similar displays of emotion in village meetings. *Gram sabhas* are irregular, empty, and perfunctory rituals without content. Consequently, villagers are not familiar with how to discursively navigate this public forum. The meetings are thinly attended; villagers tend to make brief matter of fact statements of demands. They do not appear to have a strong sense of expectation or entitlement behind their demands because of the vacuous, ceremonial nature of the meetings. Their demands are met with cursory responses from *panchayat* leaders, who typically promise to refer the matter to the higher authorities.

Displays of emotion are also rare in *gram sabhas* in Kerala. In Kerala, which can be considered very high capacity in terms of its *panchayat* system, the *gram sabhas* are used primarily to select beneficiaries and ratify decisions that have already been deliberated in smaller deliberative settings and previous participatory exercises (Gibson 2012).

This study of development deliberations also shows how emotions enter into reflexive arguments and rational debates—and not just through the discursive medium of personal narratives or storytelling. This crucial point challenges the false dichotomy between emotions and rationality in classical normative theories of deliberative democracy. In development deliberations of the kind studied here, emotions and rationality are not necessarily oppositional. In fact, one might flow from the other.

Deliberative development can be thought of as a sentimental economy. The term reflects the paradoxical relationship between the envisioned and observed roles of emotions. In the classical Habermasian sense, it refers to the economizing restraint that individuals are ideally expected to exercise over private emotions and sentiments while engaging in public deliberations. But people who regularly suffer deficiencies in important public services and infrastructure may be prone to impulsive disclosure of their feelings, even expressive excesses.

Sentimental economy also refers to the ways in which emotions work as levers in this redistributive economy that concerns the distribution and allocation of public and private goods to households and village communities. Development deliberations have both economic/material and social consequences in preserving or establishing dignity (Rao and Sanyal 2010), both of which can have immediate and far-reaching effects on life chances, conceived in a broad Weberian sense. Based on these insights, this chapter sounds a call for further exploration of the role of emotions in systems of deliberative development and other institutional forms of deliberative democracy.

Notes

1. Some scholars draw a distinction between sentiments and emotions. I use the two terms interchangeably.
2. Rational calculations and social norms are two other forces that direct human action.
3. A growing body of sociological literature addresses the role of emotions in social movements. See, for example, Snow and Oliver (1995) and Goodwin, Jasper, and Polletta (2001, 2004). I do not discuss this literature because the realm of social movements is distinct in significant ways from the realm of development deliberations.
4. These castes and tribes are referred to as scheduled because they are listed in a schedule of the Indian Constitution. They receive affirmative action benefits because they were historically marginalized.
5. Adam Smith made a similar point in *Moral Sentiments* (2010 [1759]), arguing that certain types of emotions—especially negative sentiments, such as pride, vanity, and ambition—pushed human action beyond the limits of pragmatic self-interest.
6. Affirmative action benefits afforded to schedules castes and tribes include reservation of positions in employment in public sector institutions and elected political bodies and preferential allocation of government subsidized benefits, many of which are distributed at the village level and discussed and ratified through the *gram sabha*.
7. Moon (2013) argues that emotions serve as a medium of symbolic power in struggles over classification by identity groups. I highlight emotions as a medium of social and political power for subaltern publics with respect to the local state.

8. A few important tasks have to be put aside for the future. One is identifying the preconditions under which emotions play these roles in development deliberations (for instance, does the level of literacy or poverty of participants or the nature of the state regime matter?). Another is examining the post-deliberation implementation of delivery of the decisions and promises in which emotions played a guiding role.

9. Staple grains and other commodities are supplied at subsidized prices through a vast national chain of fair price shops. This system is targeted to benefit people falling below the poverty line.

10. In January 2011 the kerosene mafia set on fire a collector in a district in Maharashtra when he confronted a group of men pilfering oil from a tanker. He burnt to death in an incident that shocked the nation and spurred protests from public servants. A BBC report ("India's Immense 'Food Theft' Scandal," Geeta Pandey, February 21, 2011) noted that in one North Indian state alone, "the micro-economy around the stolen supplies was estimated to be worth $7.45 billion in the year 2004–2005." A senior official in the food cell apparently admitted that nearly 40–70 percent of public distribution system supplies are stolen.

11. In Indian villages there is a pattern of residential concentration by caste and religion. The speaker's reference is to a neighborhood with scheduled caste households.

12. A union collector is an elected representative of a ward, the constituent part of a *panchayat*, usually consisting of 500–1,000 people.

13. Veerappan was an infamous Indian bandit who smuggled forest resources (sandalwood and ivory), poached hundreds of elephants, and abducted and murdered nearly 200 people, including government officials. He operated in forest hideouts spread across three Southern Indian states for several decades. Upset by government neglect, a sizable following of disaffected villagers and tribal people joined his informal army.

14. Higher capacity refers to states that take the mandate of decentralized development seriously and have regular and substantive village meetings in the presence of village-level public officials.

References

Baiocchi, Gianpaolo. 2005. *Militants and Citizens: The Politics of Participatory Democracy in Porto Alegre.* Stanford, CA: Stanford University Press.

Baiocchi, Gianpaolo, Patrick Heller, and Marcelo Kunrath Silva. 2011. *Bootstrapping Democracy: Transforming Local Governance and Civil Society in Brazil.* Stanford, CA: Stanford University Press.

Ban, Radu, Saumitra Jha, and Vijayendra Rao. 2012. "Who Has Voice in a Deliberative Democracy? Evidence from Transcripts of Village Parliaments in South India." *Journal of Development Economics* 99 (2): 428–38.

Barbalet, Jack M., ed. 2002. *Emotions and Sociology.* Oxford: Blackwell.

Benhabib, Seyla. 1996. "Toward a Deliberative Model of Democratic Legitimacy." In *Democracy and Difference*, ed. S. Benhabib. Princeton, NJ: Princeton University Press.

Berezin, Mabel. 2002. "Secure States: Towards a Political Sociology of Emotions." In *Emotions and Sociology*, ed. Jack M. Barbalet, 33–52. Oxford: Blackwell.

Besley, Timothy, Rohini Pandey, and Vijayendra Rao. 2005. "Participatory Democracy in Action: Survey Evidence from South India." *Journal of the European Economic Association* 3(2–3): 648–57.

Bohman, James. 1996. *Public Deliberation: Pluralism, Complexity, and Democracy*. Cambridge, MA: MIT Press.

Calhoun, Craig. 2001. "Putting Emotions in Their Place." In *Passionate Politics: Emotions and Social Movements*, ed. J. Goodwin, J. M. Jasper, and F. Polletta, 45–57. Chicago: University of Chicago Press.

Cohen, Joshua. 1989. "Deliberation and Democratic Legitimacy." In *The Good Polity: Normative Analysis of the State*, ed. A. Hamlin and P. Pettit, 17–34. London: Basil Blackwell.

Cooke, Bill, and Uma Kothari. 2001. *Participation: The New Tyranny*. London: Zed Books.

Cornwall, Andrea. 2004. "Spaces for Transformation? Reflections on Issues of Power and Difference in Participation in Development." In *Participation: From Tyranny to Transformation? Exploring New Approaches to Participation in Development*, ed. Samuel Hickey and Giles Mohan. London: Zed Books.

Delli Carpini, Michael X., Fay Lomax Cook, and Lawrence R. Jacobs. 2004. "Public Deliberation, Discursive Participation, and Citizen Engagement: A Review of the Empirical Literature." *Annual Review of Political Science* 7: 315–44.

Dryzek, John S. 2000. *Deliberative Democracy and Beyond: Liberals, Critics, Contestations*. Oxford: Oxford University Press.

Elster, Jon. 1994. "Rationality, Emotions, and Social Norms." *Synthese* 98 (1): 21–49.

———. 1996. "Rationality and the Emotions." *Economic Journal* 106 (438): 1386–97.

Fishkin, James S. 1991. *Democracy and Deliberation: New Directions for Democratic Reform*. New Haven, CT: Yale University Press.

Frank, Robert. 1988. *Passions within Reason*. New York: Norton.

Frijda, Nico H. 1986. *The Emotions*. Cambridge: Cambridge University Press.

Fung, Archon. 2004. *Empowered Participation: Reinventing Urban Democracy*. Princeton, Oxford: Princeton University Press.

Fung, Archon, Erik Olin Wright, and Rebecca Neaera Abers. 2003. *Deepening Democracy: Institutional Innovations in Empowered Participatory Governance*. London: Verso.

Gastil, John, and Peter Levine. 2010. *The Deliberative Democracy Handbook: Strategies for Effective Civic Engagement in the Twenty-First Century*. San Francisco: Jossey-Bass.

Gibson, Christopher. 2012. "Making Redistributive Democracy Matter: Development and Women's Participation in Gram Sabhas of Kerala, India." *American Sociological Review* 77(3): 409–34.

Gibson, Christopher, and Michael Woolcock. 2008. "Empowerment, Deliberative Development and Local Level Politics in Indonesia: Participatory Projects as a Source of Countervailing Power." *Studies in Comparative International Development* 43 (2): 151–80.

Goodwin, Jeff, James J. Jasper, and Francesca Polletta, eds. 2001. *Passionate Politics: Emotions and Social Movements.* Chicago: University of Chicago Press.

———. 2004. "Emotional Dimensions of Social Movements." In *The Blackwell Companion to Social Movements*, ed. David A. Snow, Sara A. Soule, and Hanspeter Kriesi. Oxford: Blackwell Publishing.

Gutmann, Amy, and Dennis Thompson. 2004. *Why Deliberative Democracy?* Princeton, NJ: Princeton University Press.

Habermas, Jurgen. 1984. *The Theory of Communicative Action.* Boston: Beacon Press.

———. 1990. *Moral Consciousness and Communicative Action.* Cambridge, MA: MIT Press.

Hickey, Samuel, and Giles Mohan, eds. 2004. *Participation: From Tyranny to Transformation? Exploring New Approaches to Participation in Development.* London: Zed Books.

Hirshleifer, Jack. 1987. "On the Emotions as Guarantors of Threats and Promises." In *The Latest on the Best*, ed. J. Dupre, 307–26. Cambridge, MA: MIT Press.

Hossain, Naomi. 2009. "Rude Accountability in the Unreformed State: Informal Pressures on Frontline Bureaucrats in Bangladesh." *IDS Working Paper* 319: 1–35, Institute of Development Studies, University of Sussex, Brighton, United Kingdom.

Lawler, Edward J. 2001. "An Affect Theory of Social Exchange." *American Journal of Sociology* 10 7(2): 321–52.

Mansbridge, Jane J. 1983. *Beyond Adversary Democracy.* Chicago: University of Chicago Press.

———. 1990. *Beyond Self Interest.* Chicago: University of Chicago Press.

———. 1999. "Everyday Talk in the Deliberative System." In *Deliberative Politics: Essays on Democracy and Disagreement*, ed. Stephen Macedo, 211–40. New York: Oxford University Press.

Mansuri, Ghazala, and Vijayendra Rao. 2004. "Community-Based (and Driven) Development: A Critical Review." *World Bank Research Observer* 19 (1): 1–39.

———. 2012. *Localizing Development: Does Participation Work?* World Bank Policy Research Report, Washington, DC.

Moon, Dawne. 2013. "Powerful Emotions: Symbolic Power and the (Productive and Punitive) Force of Collective Feeling." *Theory and Society* 42: 261–94.

Mouffe, Chantal. 1999. "Deliberative Democracy or Agonistic Pluralism?" *Social Research* 66 (3): 745–58.

Ng, Kwai Hang, and Jeffrey L. Kidder. 2010. "Toward a Theory of Emotive Performance: With Lessons from How Politicians Do Anger." *Sociological Theory* 28 (2): 193–214.

Polletta, Francesca. 2001. "The Laws of Passion." *Law and Society Review* 35: 467–93.

Polletta, Francesca, and John Lee. 2006. "Is Telling Stories Good for Democracy? Rhetoric in Public Deliberation after 9/11." *American Sociological Review* 71 (5): 699–723.

Rao, Vijayendra, and Paromita Sanyal. 2010. "Dignity through Discourse: Poverty and the Culture of Deliberation in Indian Village Democracies." *Annals of the AAPSS* 629: 146–72.

Sanders, Lynn M. 1997. "Against Deliberation." *Political Theory* 25: 347–76.

Scott, James C. 1990. *Domination and the Art of Resistance: Hidden Transcripts.* New Haven, CT: Yale University Press.

Smith, Adam. 2010 [1759]. *The Theory of Moral Sentiments.* New York: Penguin Books.

Snow, David A., and Pamela E. Oliver. 1995. "Social Movements and Conflict Behavior: Social Psychological Dimensions and Considerations." In *Sociological Perspectives on Social Psychology*, ed. Karen S. Cook, Gary Alan Fine, and James House, 571–99. Boston: Allyn and Bacon.

Xu, Bin. 2012. "Grandpa Wen: Scene and Political Performance." *Sociological Theory* 30 (2): 114–29.

Young, Iris Marion. 1996. "Communication and the Other: Beyond Deliberative Democracy." In *Democracy and Difference: Contesting the Boundaries of the Political,* ed. Seyla Benhabib. Princeton, NJ: Princeton University Press.

———. 2000. *Inclusion and Democracy.* Oxford: Oxford University Press.

CHAPTER 9

Global Institutions and Deliberations: Is the World Trade Organization More Participatory than UNESCO?

J. P. Singh

A comparative analysis of global governance institutions from a deliberation perspective is overdue. Global governance theory and practice have moved away from a preoccupation with how state power and decision making are refracted or shaped through global institutions. Instead, global governance and theorists and practitioners have now become discerning about the processes of governance, which include formal institutions and networks, the norms and rules they produce, and the collective or intersubjective contexts within which they operate (Rosenau and Czempiel 1992; Held and others 1999; Grewal 2008). Deliberation contexts in such governance can be understood as habits of participation, dialogue, and persuasion within these institutions, including formal negotiation processes (the ways an issue is imagined or represented within an institution through discursive practices) and dialogic problem-solving solutions. To paraphrase Mackie (chapter 5 of this volume), at a minimum deliberation involves the giving of public reasons.

The author thanks Archon Fung, Erin Gamble, Varun Gauri, Patrick Heller, Celestin Monga, Vijayendra Rao, and Katy Saulpaugh for comments on previous drafts. Earlier versions of the chapter were presented at the conference on Deliberation for Development: New Directions, held in Washington, DC, November 12–13, 2010, and at the International Political Economy Society Meeting, held at the University of Wisconsin-Madison, November 12, 2011.

The legitimacy of international institutions depends on leadership and inclusion, partly a result of political abilities to attract and persuade. Therefore, a comparative analysis of deliberation processes is crucial to assessing the effectiveness, quality, and longevity of global governance. Such an analysis is especially important for global actors who are aware that global institutions' intersecting and overlapping agendas provide them with opportunities to "venue shop" in order to meet their strategic interests. In order to ascertain the scope of deliberation in global governance, it is important to determine the extent to which global actors participate in institutions in which deliberation contexts allow only strategic interests to be realized. Prospects for democratic global governance also depend on analyzing internal decision making and participation in the deliberative context of global institutions.

This chapter provides a comparative analysis of the scope of deliberation within two international organizations, the World Trade Organization (WTO) and the United Nations Educational, Scientific and Cultural Organization (UNESCO). The WTO is often critiqued in intellectual and policy institutions, and in the popular media, as being nontransparent and undemocratic and fostering market liberalization policies that benefit only the developed countries or the developing world elite. Terms such as "a crisis of legitimacy" and "nontransparent" are often used to describe the WTO. In contrast, UNESCO is written about almost with veneration, as encompassing a moral agenda that reflects some of the highest ideals of humanity, from scientific cooperation to guarding the world's cultural heritage.

This chapter demonstrates that closer examination of the "issue structures" of these organizations leads to different conclusions. Issue structures encompass organizational goals and existing knowledge about an issue, the involvement of relevant actors and their interests, media and press coverage, and the institutional and social mobilization that the organization fosters from the grassroots to the international level. There appears to be far more participation at all levels of decision making, from the local to the international levels, for issues within the WTO than within UNESCO. Comparison of the two organizations can thus generate hypotheses based on issue structures rather than ideological alignments or popular critiques.

The WTO's goal is to liberalize trade. Member-states are intensely involved in this mission through important domestic mechanisms, including trade and other ministries, highly organized interest groups with transnational linkages, and expert debates of the pros and cons of trade liberalization measures and their incidence. The WTO fosters high degrees of participation in its rule making because of the need for preference alignment within and across states in the various issue-structures. Participation does not always lead to cooperative agreement, but the

WTO's decision-making processes are characterized by high degrees of scrutiny and participation by a wide variety of actor interests. Although inclusive participation in general is worthwhile, the WTO remains driven by the interests of its member-states; civil society interests are often represented only indirectly. All the same, in many cases WTO participation and negotiations can be characterized as deliberative, as state actors learn and take positions they may not have anticipated before deliberation.

UNESCO has more diffused and idealistic goals. The preamble to its constitution states that "since wars begin in the minds of men, it is in the minds of men that defenses of peace must be constructed." This statement, adapted by U.S. Librarian of Congress Archibald MacLeish from a speech given by British Prime Minister Clement Attlee, provides UNESCO with an encompassing agenda to foster peace through global norms that guide everything from digging for minerals below the Earth's surface to eradicating human inequalities on Earth and ensuring that global media in the skies above foster peaceful communications. At face value, UNESCO seeks to mobilize participation on this agenda through national commissions, interagency task forces, and networks around the world. In practice, beyond a few initiatives, UNESCO's work remains largely hidden from public scrutiny or media spotlight; it features elite decision making involving only representatives of member-states and expert groups.

This chapter is organized as follows. The first section provides a conceptual framework for understanding issue structures. It synthesizes institutionalist, constructivist, and deliberation analyses. The second section describes the contrasting issue structures in the WTO and UNESCO in broad strokes. Preliminary analysis suggests that the WTO, not UNESCO, is the better model of global deliberations. The analysis is meant to provide a comparative context for evaluating the quality of deliberations; by no means does it claim that the WTO is an exemplar of deliberation processes. The third section examines creative industries, such as films and television, an issue that is featured in the agendas of both organizations. The last section concludes that issue structures that feature high degrees of alignment of preferences and institutional strength are far more likely to be participatory than issue structures featuring diffused preferences and weak institutional involvement.

Issue structures and deliberation contexts

Global governance is patterned sets of interactions and collective understandings among relevant actors. Except for a few analyses of diplomacy and negotiations, the deliberative aspects of global governance interactions are often ignored.[1] Instead, two sets of interactions are studied. The regimes literature examines how domestic and international levels intersect and produce a convergence of expectations in global governance.

The norms formation literature examines how prescriptions and proscriptions for action arise at the international level and are then diffused to the "subsystemic" or domestic level.

Both bodies of literature point to issue structure analysis, but they are limited in providing a comparative context for understanding deliberations in international institutions. Either international institutions are merely nodes within which other actors play out their roles or institutions are posited as having limited agenda-making and implementation roles, without specifying the origins or scope of these roles. International institutions are often treated as black boxes, merely responding to external prerogatives; the "pulling and hauling" of their agenda or the problem solving within that agenda is ignored. This section briefly summarizes the literature and examines the burgeoning body of work on global governors.

Regimes and international institutions

Regimes help explain how global actors' expectations converge, explicitly or implicitly, to produce principles, norms, rules, and decision-making procedures in a given issue area (Krasner 1983). Although concepts of global governance are now replacing the regimes literature, a few enduring legacies are important.

First, the focus on issue areas, a concept coined by James Rosenau (1967), provides a micro-empirical basis for examining governance. This framework makes it somewhat easier to locate a set of actors (mostly states, international organizations, and groups of experts or epistemic communities) and their interests.

Second, depending on the theorist's worldview, these interests or preferences are generally taken to be given, articulated from the ground up (Putnam 1988), and either reflective of or consistent with great power preferences.

Third, the literature at times focuses on epistemic communities—groups of policy makers, experts, and relevant institutions—that share an understanding of how to address an issue. For example, the shift in international telecommunications from engineering to more market-based practices is traced to a new epistemic community of economists and trade practitioners that replaced the old epistemic community made up mostly of engineers (Cowhey 1990).

Negotiation and bargaining theories have tried to bridge the gap between interests and outcomes in the study of global governance, which the regime or international institutionalist literature is unable to address. Negotiators can improve on their alternatives in bargaining through the issue structure by fostering linkages or tradeoffs with other issues (Davis 2004); they can influence or shape outcomes and agendas through processes of coalition building or other strategies (Odell 2000, 2006); they can also solve issues together (Singh 2008). Steinberg (2002) also accords attention to decision-making structures themselves, arguing in the case of the WTO that great powers such as the United States wanted consensual decision making in the organization starting in the late 1950s, so that weak powers, especially the postcolonial countries, could not block their agenda. The great powers thus used their vast resources to set the agenda within these organizations to their liking.

The international institutions through which these diplomatic interactions are sifted remain relatively unexamined. Some attention has been paid to how international organizations are actors in their own right (Sandholtz 1992; Finnemore 1996; Slaughter 2004), but micro-level studies of how international institutions are calibrated to respond to particular demands are missing. This vacuum has two implications, especially when an institution does not respond to particular or generalized interests.

First, studies of venue or forum shopping show that states and other actors often take their agendas to the institutions where they are most likely to find a receptive audience. Thus, when developing world advocacy increased in importance for telecommunications at the International Telecommunication Union (ITU) or in patent regimes at the World Intellectual Property Organization (WIPO) and World Health Organization (WHO) in the 1970s, the United States switched venues and took the agenda to the General Agreement on Tarrifs and Trade (GATT), where it began to shape liberalized rules in its favor. Eventually, the ITU, WHO, and WIPO accepted the new rules that came out of the WTO. Although a great deal is known about the external pressures these organizations faced, relatively little is known about the internal decision making of these organizations or how their bureaucracies and member-states' conferences responded to the various agendas. In fact, as argued later, the WTO became deliberative in some issues. For example, it allows for leveled, law-based bargaining in dispute settlement or in cases such as the Doha Health Declaration, where weak states and civil society actors prevailed over great power interests.

Second, the failure of international institutions to respond to particular issues or agendas is blamed on actors outside the institution. The failed WTO negotiations in 1999 in Seattle are blamed on transnational civil society activism, and the gridlock in the Doha Round of trade talks is blamed on the domestic difficulties of major powers such as the European Union, the United States, Brazil, and India.

Although the networks of interests and global actors that affect an international institution are important, they do not sufficiently show how an international institution responds internally to them. Network analyses are especially deficient when agenda formation arises from within institutions or the effectiveness and legitimacy of an international institution are in question. Without accounting for how issues are discussed, debated, or contested in these institutions, one cannot a priori rule out the possibilities or ascertain the scope of deliberation in global governance.

Norm diffusion

The norm diffusion literature calls attention to two processes of global governance. First, it shows how agenda formation arises through international processes, often from international organizations. Second, as opposed to most of the regimes literature, which finds international outcomes to be reflective of "domestic" interests, the norms literature often shows how international actors, or norm champions, go about socializing domestic and other actors.

Finnemore (1996) shows that national interests in science in the postwar era came about at the behest of UNESCO. Its bureaucrats championed the cause of science to national governments and persuaded or "taught states the value and utility of science policy organizations" (566).[2] Finnemore and Sikkink (1998) document a value chain of norms formation from the time of "norm emergence" in international organizations to "norm cascade" or diffusion to states through norm champions to "norm internalization." Their theory is similar to other theories of the social construction of interests, whereby socialization leads to the internalization of social constructs (Berger and Luckmann 1966).

The norms literature has begun to address particular types of deliberative practices used in global governance. Naming and exposing labor infringements may lead to compliance by states (Weisband 2000). "Reflexive discourse" from an international organization encourages action, as it awakens a country to what it believes about itself (Steele 2007). Norms themselves may emerge at an international level from a process of contestation among actors (Wiener 2008; Dubash 2009). What this literature lacks—but scholars are slowly moving toward—is an understanding of the internal prerogatives of international organizations and the deliberative practices that describe them. The social construction of norms also reveals little about the comparative effectiveness of contending actors in constructing a norm in similar issue areas. Legitimacy in these bodies of literature is described as involuntary and habitual practice (Hurd 1999) rather than based on Pareto-optimal and discursively effective perspectives. In fact, as this chapter seeks to show, even when they succeed in socializing domestic actors, many of the norms arising from agencies like UNESCO are expert driven and do not include deliberative practices that might make one question their legitimacy. For example, culture and heritage agencies in the developing world often complain that UNESCO acts like a paternalistic global ministry of culture in implementing its conventions on natural and world heritage.

A new institutionalism and deliberations

The lacunae in the literatures described above are the subjects of consider-able scrutiny. One strand of literature examines rules and resources within international organizations and the networks in which they are embedded. Another describes types of deliberative practices that go far beyond diplo-macy and negotiations. This section describes this work in terms of its relevance to this chapter.

An important place to start is the literature on "global governors," as one volume calls the nexus of global governance institutions and their internal processes. Global governors *"create issues, set agendas, estab-lish and implement rules or programs, and evaluate and/or adjudicate outcomes"* (Avant, Finnemore, and Sell 2010, 2; italics in original). Since the 1980s, the historical institutionalist tradition opened up the black box of the state to examine its resources, capacity, autonomy, and ideals in a historical context. Similarly, a new institutionalism in global gover-nance leads to scrutiny of international organizations. The examination of international organizations is rooted in the ever-expanding globalization and practical concerns about decision making at the global level. Instead of merely positing international organizations as nodes in a network or as being able to influence a few agendas here and there, the organizations now provide both a point of entry to examine processes of governance and ways in which they become central to it. This role of international organizations neither takes away from domestic-level influ-ences on these institutions nor minimizes their role in the socialization of other actors.

These analyses examine the internal machinery and decision making within these organizations in order to locate the mechanisms for change. The Global Institutions series published by Routledge provides "in-depth treatments of prominent global bodies and processes," in the words of its editors, Thomas G. Weiss and Rorden Wilkinson. The journal *Global Governance* has led the way in identifying the institutions and their inter-nal contexts.

Institutionalist analyses are sensitive to both the structure of the institu-tion, or the specific issue, and the processes of deliberation within it. Smith (1999) proposes a set of hypotheses to explain the degree of consensus at the UN General Assembly over specific issues in order to show that a formal institutional mapping of goals and procedures must be combined with sets of strategic interactions and informal networking to examine these deliberations. The formal aspects point to the broad predications of an institution; the informal elements detail the specific sets of interactions, often deliberative, within them. Dubash (2009) examines the representa-tive make-up and deliberative contestation within the World Commission on Dams to show that norm formation is neither unproblematic nor merely reflective of some form of global corporatism.

The new institutionalist traditions are less discerning in noting the presence or absence of deliberative traditions. In terms of bureaucratic procedures, deliberation often begins when the agendas have been set and organizational resources already allocated to them. Most studies describe whether the goals were fulfilled rather than examine the scope of deliberation in fulfilling them. When they do focus on deliberation, studies tend to outline or isolate a single aspect of it. Steele (2007), for example, shows how "reflexive discourses" from international institutions act upon states' narratives about themselves. Use of the word *stingy* by UN humanitarian official Jan Egeland to describe U.S. foreign aid after the 2004 Indian Ocean tsunami goaded the United States to offer far more aid than it had promised earlier. At the other extreme, idealized theories of communicative action show that in situations where strategic calculations are minimized, global institutions can foster problem solving (Risse 2000; Farrell 2003).

In terms of formal aspects of institutions, this chapter focuses on the salience of issues and agenda, the known discursive and information boundaries of the issue, and the organizational resources and mobilization of actors accorded to them—that is, the issue structure. Instead of assuming away strategic interactions and the formal institutional constraints within international organizations, it views them as a set of first-order conditions for examining these organizations. A set of second-order conditions reflects forms of deliberation but departs from the ideal type posited for deliberation; these conditions are reflective of the institutional context in which deliberation operates. The ideal type, drawing mostly on theories of communicative action and dialogic communication (Freire 2000; Habermas 1976, 1985; Taylor 1994; Dryzek and Niemeyer 2008), includes the degree of inclusion of various participants, the transparency of their interactions, the level of trust among them, and the degree to which they empathize with, or listen to, one another. Ideally, deliberation assumes equality of participants, inclusion of relevant voices, and the giving of reasons—qualities that are often lacking in everyday politics. Deliberation must thus be assayed through the institutional constraints through which it operates. Global actors' interests matter; international interactions may transform them, but political processes such as negotiation and bargaining are as likely to tame and modify them (Singh 2008; Mansbridge and others 2010).

As global governance is unlikely to meet the ideal criteria of deliberation, it is especially important to think of deliberation in a plausible and feasible fashion, operating within the constraint of available institutional alternatives (Fung 2007; Fung, Gilman, and Shkabatur 2013). Although global governance can feature reasoned and informed argumentation, it is unlikely to feature any minimal criteria for democracy, such as direct elections involving the global public. Deliberation in global governance institutions must thus be viewed using other criteria. Depending on the qualities of inclusion, transparency, empathy, and trust, the governance of an issue structure can result in problem solving that often benefits all participants or a form of strategic manipulation (or monologue) that benefits particular actors. Discursive engagements, especially where they result in problem solving, provide an opportunity for participants to take ownership. They are therefore considered more legitimate in producing voluntary compliance (Hurd 1999).

This set of first- and second-order conditions that focus on abstract institutional features and deliberative processes provides a preliminary comparative framework for assessing international institutions and their agenda formation and implementation. To the extent that these norms are expertise driven or top down, their deliberative and democratic parameters are not particularly strong, as shown below. This framework moves beyond regime theory's characterization of international institutions as black boxes, beyond constructivist analyses that are more interested in showing how international actors socialize domestic actors than in how these agendas arise and the extent to which they are deliberative. If anything, the norms literature tends to assume that norms that do not reflect great power interests must be democratic.

The World Trade Organization and UNESCO: Creation, philosophy, and context

Both the GATT (the precursor of the WTO) and UNESCO are post–World War II organizations. The GATT was a timid leftover from the original postwar trade institution that was proposed. Its successor, the WTO, stays close to its original goal of international trade liberalization. UNESCO was created with high idealism. It makes a high moral claim for trying to resolve humanity's greatest problems.

The two institutions' subsequent history followed a similar path. The WTO is devoted to a single issue: a trade agenda that many view as benefiting only elite actors. In contrast, UNESCO cast a wide net, with an agenda encompassing its five "sectors" (education, the natural sciences, the social and human sciences, culture, and communication and information). Table 9.1 summarizes the issue structures in the two institutions to show the ways in which the domestic, national, and international levels intersect.

The World Trade Organization: Issue structures and deliberative context

There was high-minded philosophy behind the creation of the GATT, but neither its staff nor outside observers cite it frequently. The GATT preamble exhorts states toward "reciprocal and mutually advantageous arrangements directed to the substantial reduction of tariffs and other barriers to trade and to the elimination of discriminatory treatment in international commerce" (GATT 1986).

TABLE 9.1 Issue structures at the World Trade Organization and UNESCO

Item	WTO	UNESCO
Main issue	Trade liberalization	Global education, science, communication, and culture
Official annual budget	Less than $200 million	More than $300 million
Staff	634 full-time staff from 78 member-states, hired in extremely competitive processes	2,000 staff, hired in process that is frequently not merit based
Relevant national ministries	Trade and finance; WTO generally a top issue	Education, culture, external affairs; UNESCO generally a low priority
Links with industry	Strong	Weak
Links with civil society	Dual links: direct consultations with labor and agricultural groups and advocacy through media or protests	Maintains network of professional or civil society organizations; civil society represented through UNESCO National Commissions, but in practice links are weak
Media involvement	Close scrutiny of deliberations	Weak scrutiny of deliberations, except salient issues, such as the November 2011 vote granting Palestine member-state status
Knowledge production	Global trade salient concern for think tanks, academic institutions, research organizations, and trade officials; findings often publicly debated and covered in media	Brings together experts and intellectuals to produce reports; some reflection in academia of similar issues
Status of international treaties	Treaties often subject to intense domestic and international review and domestic ratification	Most treaties not reviewed widely; only a few are subject to intense debates in ratification

GATT grew out of both World War II and the tariff escalations that followed the Great Depression, such as the enactment of the Smoot-Hawley tariffs in the United States in 1932. But the philosophy of a postwar trade organization goes back to Western ideas of exchange and reciprocity (part of enlightenment humanism), to Adam Smith's moral philosophy of exchange and division of labor, and to the ideas of 19th and 20th century intellectuals correlating trade and exchange with peace. Cordell Hull, Franklin Delano Roosevelt's Secretary of State, who championed the cause of Bretton Woods and a trade organization, noted, "I have never faltered, and I will never falter, in my belief that enduring peace and the welfare of nations are indissolubly connected with friendliness, fairness, equality and the maximum practicable degree of freedom in international trade" (cited in Narlikar 2005, 10).

What won the trading states of the postwar world over to the cause of the proposed International Trade Organization (ITO) was the prospect of tariff reductions and their connection with economic prosperity. Even as negotiations were proceeding for a new trade organization, negotiations on tariff reduction were underway in multilateral trade rounds (in London in 1946, Geneva in 1947, and Annecy in 1949). In 1947 trade ministers and delegates met in Havana to give final shape to the ITO; they also negotiated a few general agreements on tariffs and trade to guide countries while the ITO was getting ratified. President Truman never submitted the ITO charter to Congress, fearing that it might not pass, and the GATT became the de facto organization for trade.

The GATT's legal articles are straightforward and deal with rules for trade reductions. Nothing is stated in terms of overall prospects for peace or even economic development. Article I deals with the most favored nation principle, Article II with schedules for tariff reductions on particular products, Article III with national treatment of products, Article X with transparency of trade law and rules, Article XXVIII with reciprocity, and so forth. In the 1947 Geneva Round of trade talks, 123 bilateral negotiations on 50,000 trade items were conducted. These talks eventually provided for a multilateral agreement (Odell with Eichengreen 2000, 163).

The GATT was folded into the WTO, which came into being on January 1, 1995, after the conclusion of the eighth round of trade negotiations, known as the Uruguay Round (1986–94). It had 160 members in 2015. Many member-states maintain special diplomatic delegations to the WTO in Geneva. Most of the WTO delegations are drawn from or directly linked to their capitals' trade, finance, and external affairs ministries. The staff of these ministries are usually among the top cadres of any administration; the ministries' policies are regularly the subject of public debate and discussion through the media and other processes. The networks with which these ministries work generally include manufacturers, industry, and labor organizations. Leaders of these organizations often accompany official trade delegations to Geneva and other places. Many countries have formal processes and frameworks set up for soliciting input into trade policy positions. Trade agreements are also likely to be subject to legislative scrutiny and ratification.

These processes notwithstanding, there is considerable evidence that the GATT and the WTO have been opaque and provide benefits only to a rich club of countries (Narlikar 2003; Jawara and Kwa 2003). Negotiations are secretive, with considerable pressures on weak countries to cave in. At least until the Uruguay Round, the primary option given to the developing world was a take-it-or-leave-it type of trade text (Singh 2000). The United States is fond of making high moral statements and giving foreign aid and side payments to the developing world rather than making trade concessions, which reveals some duplicity of purpose (Singh 2010).

Over time, however, deliberations have become ever more inclusive, and concessions do not accrue to the rich and powerful countries alone. The WTO often engages in problem solving and persuasion that allow for new positions to be adopted. A few processes and issue areas are summarized here to highlight the process of deliberation at the WTO.

First, state-driven participation continues to be broadened. The ultimate metaphor for the GATT's secrecy and exclusion was the "Green Room" process, named after the room adjacent to the Director-General's office, where great powers (usually the European Union, the United States, and Japan) met to hammer out trade texts to the exclusion of other countries. Things have changed. Green Room meetings now generally include a variety of players, depending on the issue in question, also almost always including a host of developing countries. The G4 meetings during the Doha Round included the United States, the European Union, Brazil, and India. Brazil and India traditionally provided leadership to the developing world but were often excluded from the inner circle. They, along with several other developing countries, are now in that circle. The fact that the WTO itself must now work closely with other global forums, such as the G20, is also indicative of broadened participation. Although such coordination contributes to gridlock, it means that developing countries can no longer always be coerced into signing agreements.

Second, the deliberation processes themselves have changed multilaterally to allow more and weaker powers and civil society to be included and for these voices to persuade the powerful to change their positions. Civil society is represented through member-states. Large nongovernmental organizations such as Oxfam have only observer status, but WTO member-states find it hard to ignore civil society concerns even if their representatives are not sitting at the table. The global media often spotlight these issues, making it harder still for member-states to put civil society concerns aside.

The list of issues that were discussed at the WTO because of pressures from, or inclusion of, civil society includes sustainable agriculture, genetically modified crops, global climate change, labor issues, trade capacity building, and public health. The Doha Health Declaration and subsequent intellectual property negotiations are exemplars of civil society advocacy leading to issues being addressed at the WTO. The opening of the Doha Round of trade negotiations was held up in November 2001 until the North made crucial intellectual property concessions on public health in response to pressures from global civil society and the developing world (Odell and Sell 2006; Sell 2003). Paragraph 6 of the Doha Health Declaration instructed member-states to find a solution for countries requiring medicines for public health emergencies but lacking the capacity to manufacture them by allowing them to break patents (compulsory licensing). Initially, countries like the United States sought to restrict the number of diseases that would be covered and the terms under which medicines could be imported from cheaper sources ("parallel imports"), but pressures from civil society and legal challenges to big pharmaceutical manufacturers in countries such as Brazil, India, and South Africa led to a comprehensive revision of the framework covering public health measures by the December 2005 Hong Kong WTO ministerial meetings.

Article 31 of the WTO's Trade-Related Aspects of Intellectual Property Rights (TRIPS), upon which Para 6 negotiations were based, was also based on tough persuasion from India and other countries during the Uruguay Round. It allowed for exceptions to TRIPS provisions under emergency circumstances. Negotiation and diplomacy are ultimately about persuasion. The Paragraph 6 case is illustrative of the weak making effective use of these processes. However, in order to examine negotiation and diplomacy in a deliberative context, one must broaden the scope of actors and issues at the table and the means by which actors not at the table are able to influence them.

Third, the great powers have brought some issues to the table that were adopted by the weak powers willingly and voluntarily as their interests changed during the deliberations. Steinberg (2002) notes that the very inclusion of services and intellectual property on the trade agenda of the Uruguay Round reveals that the powerful still dictate agendas. What he does not show is that over time the services issue took into account the interests of the developing world and allowed big countries like India and small ones like Costa Rica to take ownership of the services agreement and emerge as net service exporters. In this sense, processes in Geneva served as learning processes for countries like India to envision a future for themselves in exports of services. India led the developing world in its opposition to inclusion of services on the Uruguay Round agenda. But in 1986—three years after the start of the Uruguay Round, when the General Agreement for Trade in Services (GATS) was more or less ready—India and countries like it applauded the agreement, while the Coalition of Service Industries in the United States denounced it as too weak. Crucially, India and the developing world worked through the GATT processes to enshrine an approach to making liberalization commitments in sectors of their own choosing (the "positive list" approach) rather than having to make commitments in all sectors unless they skillfully excluded some sectors (the "negative list" approach) that the United States favored (Singh 2008). As services represent half to three-fourths of the national income of all countries, the benefits of selecting particular sectors for liberalization and the ability to liberalize them slowly cannot be underestimated for the developing world. The services negotiation example showcases persuasion, learning, and problem solving during a deliberation leading to a voluntary change of interests.

Fourth, the WTO is a rule-based organization that allows for some leveling of the playing field. The concessions on intellectual property and services are examples of learning to work within the WTO's negotiation context to persuade others. But there are also legal practices in the WTO that are important and structure deliberations in a fair fashion. The WTO charter put in place a formal dispute settlement mechanism (DSM), in which adjudication follows the spirit of the law rather than power. Although it remains expensive for small countries to fight cases through the DSM, it is not impossible for them do so. In fact, almost a third of all cases have come from the developing world, which has won almost half of those cases. At more informal and general levels, WTO delegations acquaint themselves with the structured way in which proceedings take place, from preparation of texts and communiqués to informal processes such as coalition-building, tradeoffs/linkages, and information dissemination. The WTO represents a form of multilateralism that is obviously driven by state interests and power, but the resulting multilateral outcomes also reflect the legal, bureaucratic, rule-based, and professional culture of the organization itself.

Within the WTO, its secretariat of 639 full-time staff, from 70 member-states, is hired through an extremely competitive process. They produce technical reports and provide technical guidance and trade capacity assistance to member-states. The WTO's budget is less than $200 million a year (WTO 2014). The organizational culture is cordial and collegial; in-fighting between divisions or departments is rare. The institution is hardly ever characterized as an incompetent bureaucracy, and former staff members generally provide glowing reports of their experiences there.

Fifth, the indirect representation of civil society and the media in WTO processes is widespread, because WTO issues are of importance to people's livelihoods. The deadlock in the Doha Round and earlier rounds was caused by objections to trade concessions, usually from domestic constituencies, indicating that they are indirectly involved in the trade process. India has been unable to make concessions in agriculture at the Doha Round because of pressures from its domestic agriculture constituencies. A particularly symbolic move came in September 2003 from the cotton-producing countries in West Africa (the C4), whose trade ministers asked the United States to cut its subsides to cotton, which hurt the livelihoods of millions of farmers in Benin, Burkina Faso, Chad, and Mali. The images of the C4 in global media during the Cancun ministerial perfectly symbolized an ongoing discursive shift at the WTO in which the concerns of small countries can no longer be ignored. One should not, however, overestimate this shift: the United States did not make the concessions the C4 requested.

It is fair to characterize the lists of participants in the WTO—governments, trade and labor associations—as elite actors. However, it is equally fair to say that transnational social movements and media outside the WTO provide considerable balance and scrutiny to the WTO processes. O'Brien and others (2000, 109) offer a useful summary of how global social movements contest dominant global governance: "Although the [World] Bank and the WTO are intergovernmental organizations with a membership comprising sovereign governments, not only are their activities the subject of intense scrutiny by nonstate actors, but the membership and administration of these organizations have to varying extents become engaged in dialogue with groups representing diverse interests." In order to ascertain whether organizations like the WTO meet the qualities of democratic global governance, one needs to account for the processes through which interests from various constituencies are articulated at the negotiation tables in Geneva and, once articulated, the ways in which representatives are persuaded to adopt new positions.

UNESCO: Issue structures and deliberations

The idea for UNESCO arose from the Conference of Allied Ministers (CAME), which, starting in 1942, began to meet in London to consider creating an organization that would counteract the Nazi agenda through education. These meetings led to the creation of an international organization that would assist postwar reconstruction with a philosophy rooted in scientific humanism.

UNESCO's founders called upon intellectual antecedents such as Emmanuel Kant's ideas for perpetual peace (1775), Jan Amos Comenius' (1592–1670) idea of a world assembly of nations, and Auguste Comte's (1798–1850) religion of humanity rooted in scientific thinking. Although this idealism had to be balanced against the tug of war among even the allied powers to endow the organization with their own prerogatives, idealism won over power battles. UNESCO's preamble notes that "wars begin in the minds of men" and that "ignorance of each other's ways and lives has been a common cause, throughout the history of mankind. Of that suspicion and mistrust between the peoples of the world through which their differences have all too often broken into war."

To carry out its mandate for creating a culture of peace, the organization soon launched projects. Interdisciplinary teams studied arid zones around the world. African historians published a multivolume history of Africa, written to give Africans voice and representation. "Tension studies" investigated the bases of human prejudice (especially racism). Campaigns were launched to save cultural heritage sites. Hajnal (1983, 57) notes that UNESCO is "easily the least specialized of the specialized agencies" of the United Nations. The list of philosophers and intellectuals who aided UNESCO's endeavors—which includes Julian Huxley, Claude Levi-Strauss, Sarvepali Radhakrishnan, Jean-Paul Sartre, and Wole Soyinka—reads like a who's who of 20th century thought.

UNESCO was founded amidst several controversies: the United Kingdom and France battled over alternative visions for its creation; the Soviet Union and many of its allies refused to join until 1954 because of their objections to U.S.-led propaganda about media and press freedoms and trickle-up McCarthyism; the institution faced budgetary battles and shortfalls from its inception and subsequent internal wrangling on how to divide its resources across issue areas. The cultural theorist Richard Hoggart, who served as an assistant director-general of UNESCO in the 1970s, later described an organization that was marred with wars among its sectors, a faux cold war among the great powers, a feisty political battle in which the Arab states sought to isolate Israel, a culture of incompetence among its bureaucrats, and a grueling agenda of meetings involving its Secretariat in Paris, with little time to follow up on the numerous recommendations, declarations, and conventions in the member-states themselves. In 1986, amidst calls for a New World Information and Communication Order, the United States, the United Kingdom, and Singapore left UNESCO. As a result, UNESCO's funding was cut by almost half. The organization struggled to stay afloat in the 1990s. The United Kingdom rejoined in 1999 and the United States in 2003. However, the United States stopped paying its dues in 2011, after UNESCO voted to admit Palestine as its 195th member.

Despite internal dysfunction, even UNESCO's worst critics applaud the organization for its agenda. Hoggart himself touts the organization's highly idealistic missions (1978, 59):

> In spite of all such disappointments, there are occasionally moments which remind one dramatically of what UNESCO is about. I remember Pablo Neruda, in poor health and only a few months from death, standing before the Plenary Meeting of the General Conference and reminding the delegates about UNESCO's fundamental commitment to the poor and deprived of the world, to them as whole human beings not simply as units who have to be made literate and given more money. It was as if the poor of his native Chile, of all Latin America, of the whole world, walked sadly and in silent reproof through that elegant hall, evoked by Neruda's passion and poetry.

As a UN specialized agency, UNESCO receives contributions that rank it among the top four recipients of member-state contributions (the other organizations are the Food and Agriculture Organization, the World Health Organization, and the International Labour Organization). Its annual budget of about $300 million in 2011 is supplemented with nearly $500 million of extrabudgetary resources, largely from UN funding agencies, including the United Nations Development Programme and the World Bank. These resources are used to meet biennial goals through a budgetary process that often features intersectoral fights and member-state pressures. Efforts over the years to introduce intersectoral cooperation or to narrow the goals have failed, leaving the organization with encompassing agendas but meager resources.

To implement its programs, UNESCO relies on the goodwill of national ministries or the vast networks of experts/intellectuals and civil society organizations it fosters. In practice, except for a few success stories, the norms from UNESCO are weak and do not find resonance among the national governments. For example, UNESCO's biggest budget item is education (it is the leading UN agency for education). But until the 1990s, UNESCO could point primarily to reports and conferences on education rather than implemented initiatives (Mundy 2006, 2010). The Delors Commission's 1996 report *Learning: The Treasure Within* is an almost philosophic meditation on what it means to be human. It provides no clear set of recommendations on what steps need to be taken. Starting in the 1980s, other agencies, such as the World Bank, began to implement an education agenda that seemed to be far more realistic. UNESCO stood to lose its premier place among UN organizations for education. Two world conferences on education, one in Jomtien, Thailand, in 1990 and another in Dakar, Senegal, in 2009, sought to "rescue" UNESCO's agenda in education. Before the Dakar conference, however, Oxfam wrote (Gutman 2000):

> We are worried that Dakar is going to turn into another talking shop where everyone reaffirms things already agreed, sets new targets and then, as after Jomtien, goes home, cuts the aid budget and allows debt problems to continue undermining education systems of Third World countries. For these conferences to work, you need to create a public perception that there is a serious problem which people have to tackle. And you have to come up with solutions.

Another problem is the issue structures themselves. UNESCO has such a broad agenda that finding a place for all of it in national delegations is difficult. National delegations in Paris often find it hard to connect UNESCO with various ministries and civil society actors in their home countries. As a result, the natural and human sciences sectors find themselves marginalized because national delegations to UNESCO may not include scientists. The ministries affiliated with UNESCO from national governments are mostly education in the developing world (102 national governments) and external affairs in the developed world (57 national governments). Only seven countries specify culture in the lead role, and two designate science and technology as the lead ministries affiliated with UNESCO (Singh 2011b).

Beyond governments, UNESCO can lay claim to a network of international, intellectual, and other organizations that it has fostered. The origins of organizations such as the International Council of Science (ICSU), the World Wildlife Fund (WWF), the International Union for the Conservation of Nature (IUCN), the International Political Science Association (IPSA), the International Social Science Council (ISSC), and the International Council on Monuments and Sites (ICOMOS) can be traced back to UNESCO. These organizations represent meeting places of the world's finest minds on particular issue areas and provide links to national governments and important agencies.[3] These organizations are expert driven, however; they lack input from people whose lives are most affected by the issues they address. For example, UNESCO's best-known initiative is probably the World Heritage Sites, which numbered 1,007 in 2014. The prioritization of how these sites are chosen is subjective and expert driven (Brianso 2010). Frequent complaints are heard in the developing world that once added, these sites are cleansed from local practices and alienate communities whose input was not taken into consideration (De Beukelaer, Pyykkönen, and Singh 2015).

A former staffer provides this resounding critique of UNESCO (Lengyel 1986, 93):

> When I look back on the hours and hours I spent listening to experts who had never actually dealt with a juvenile delinquent, never had been party to the negotiation of a labor dispute, never tried to cope with problems of a mother of 11 in a *favela* or the dilemmas of small business in precarious situations talking airily about applied social science I must wonder where I have been these 30 years.

In an earlier era, Herman Hesse wrote the following, with UNESCO's ideals and intellectuals in mind (quoted in Hoggart 1978, 59):

> I must confess that I have no faith whatever in the concerted action of intellectuals or in the good will of the "civilized world." The mind cannot be measured in terms of quantity, and whether 10 or a 100 "leading lights" appeal to the mighty to do or not to do something, such an appeal is hopeless.

It is hard to critique the nobility of purpose with which UNESCO was founded or its engagements with creating and deepening intellectual ties around the world. However, UNESCO's norms remain top down and expertise driven; if they take place at all, deliberations are limited to elite agencies. Structurally, the agenda is so broad that UNESCO lacks the capacity to include all relevant actors in its decision making, and national governments have no framework or motivation for implementing this agenda for UNESCO.

Audio-visual, cultural exception, and cultural diversity

One of the most colorful issues to arise from the GATT/WTO and later "venue-shopped" over to UNESCO is that of creative industry exports and imports and their connections to cultural identity. Cultural identity is one of the most important issues of contemporary globalization. Assessment of this issue in the two organizations provides some clues to global deliberations over cultural identity. It also provides an opportunity to examine how the two organizations deliberated a similar issue.

Creative expressions are not just market commodities, they are also vessels of cultural identities. In the 20th century the valuation of these expressions increased in economic and cultural terms through parallel processes in cultural politics that raised the stature of arts and entertainment in public deliberations. Hollywood and Bollywood provide metaphors for cultural identities not just in the United States and India but also, depending on their reception, in groups and diasporas worldwide. French cinematic identities are often constructed in direct opposition to Hollywood's norms. Freedom Music from apartheid South Africa, telenovelas from Latin America, and animé from East Asia have now entered the lexicon of cultural identity expressions and shaped the understanding of what cultural voices mean. As these expressions have moved from what early Enlightenment thinkers called "frivolous activities" to become more central to cultural and economic global deliberations, institutions associated with these activities also gained in stature (Goodwin 2006). Not only the WTO and UNESCO but also many other international organizations—the World Intellectual Property Organization (WIPO), the United Nations Conference on Trade and Development (UNCTAD), the World Bank, the European Union, and regional development banks—now have creative industry or cultural policy programs. National ministries of culture that were often relegated to the backburner are now becoming ever more prominent in national decision making.

GATT and audio-visual issues

The issue of audio-visual, as it is known at the WTO, galvanized global public debates about cultural identity during the Uruguay Round. The case analyzed here involves mostly the United States and the European Community, in particular France, during that round. From the late 1940s onward, Western Europe successfully argued that cultural industries, especially the films industry, needed special protections, such as quotas. During the Uruguay Round of trade talks (1986–94), the need for a "cultural exception" supplemented the language of quotas. As a result, the European Union took the most favored nation (MFN) exemption that allowed it to preserve its cultural industry policies.[4]

The main issue concerned the 51 percent programming quota for television (which came out of the European Commission's Television without Frontiers directive), which went into force in 1992, just as the Uruguay Round headed into its endgame. Very few states implemented this quota, but the EU position was to try to enshrine it formally through the evolving General Agreement on Trade in Services (GATS). A related issue was the EU position that content restrictions apply to all of the 300-plus channels that had emerged as a result of satellite and cable technologies. The United States wanted the exemption restricted to 50–70 percent of all channels. Inasmuch as U.S. films and television programs dominate in Europe, and taxes on box office receipts often subsidize domestic films and television, the Motion Picture Association of America argued that the United States was subsidizing the European industry and objected to the agreement sought by the Europeans at the Uruguay Round. The European Union and the United States fiercely opposed each other in these negotiations, which came to be called the *guerres des images* (war of images) in France.

Transnational cultural industry coalitions among the Europeans resulted in the MFN exemption that allowed the European Union to make no commitments regarding liberalizing its audio-visual sectors. This "cultural exception," as it became known in the European Union, underscored the firm belief that cultural industries were nonnegotiable and directly linked to cultural identity.[5]

Justification for the cultural exception emphasized the importance of the ("aesthetically superior") audio-visual industry to European identity and unity and the harmful effects of the ("aesthetically inferior") American industry. Every statement by French officials evoked the loss to French or European identity. France's former culture minister Jack Lang, an important force behind the Television without Frontiers directive and the European Union's GATT position, famously declared that "the soul of France cannot be sold for a few pieces of silver" (Washington Times 1994).

The European Union's framing and coalition-building moves emphasized the importance of films and television to cultural identity. The people seen in the media speaking for this issue—such as French actor Gerard Depardieu —were well known throughout Europe. Goff (2007) presents a comprehensive analysis of the way the elite in Europe used the dispute to endow meaning to their borders, deepening national identities and helping create the momentum for a European identity. From the negotiation side, this framing exercise, which pointed out threats to European culture, began to serve as a glue for creative industry lobbies in the European Union. The framing exercise helped build a sense of European cultural identity through the need for quotas, although in practice the European identity was a poor cousin to national identities, which states promoted. In the French case, the two were sometimes confounded. The European Commission as well as French officials now regularly espouses the historical links between states and culture in Europe.

There is an important contradiction in the position the European Union took. The audio-visual issue was singled out for protections and labeled a cultural exception, but the European Union asked for no such exceptions for other industries, which can also be taken to be symbolic expressions of cultural identity. Table 9.2 provides a summary list of the number of countries that made market liberalizations in sectors that are equally creative or important for culture. Why, one might, ask, is French identity less threatened by the 85 million international tourists who come to France each year

TABLE 9.2 Number of countries making market commitments in creative industry subsectors

Subsector	Number of countries
Professional services (including architectural services)	94
Other business services (including advertising, photography, printing, publishing)	90
Audio-visual	29
Tourism	131
Recreational, cultural, and sporting	45

Source: Singh 2011a.

than by the 100 or so Hollywood films that enter its markets? France also remains one of the top exporters of cultural and creative products worldwide. Thus the argument often used by civil society and member-states in Europe that the WTO made them cave into a market-driven global order is only partially correct, because these actors use the same markets to realize their own goals. Furthermore, the GATS framework allows for several exceptions and flexibilities in balancing these commitments with national regulatory and moral objectives, further diluting the claim that all WTO commitments are only market driven.

It would be hard to call the audio-visual negotiations during the Uruguay Round nondeliberative.[6] The European Union was able to ward off intensive U.S. pressures through discursive rule-based practices at the WTO. That these deliberations were fraught with emotional intensity as well as reason is emblematic of the quality of deliberations in general, which are often feisty and contentious.

UNESCO and culture

The decade since the Uruguay Round ended featured a progressive hardening of the European position on cultural industries. Europeans continued to frame the issue in cultural identity terms but also shifted the focus from cultural exception to cultural diversity. Canada and France led an international coalition of governments to switch the cultural industry issue from the WTO over to UNESCO.

The efforts resulted in a Declaration on Cultural Diversity in 2001 and a Convention on the Protection and Promotion of Diversity of Cultural Expressions in 2005 at the 33rd General Conference of UNESCO. The preamble to the text starts by "affirming that cultural diversity is a defining characteristic of humanity." Its 35 articles affirm the rights of nations to formulate cultural policies that promote cultural diversity and protect indigenous cultures. Taken collectively, these articles outline a legal rationale against liberalization. Article 20 then establishes the relationship to other international treaties: "mutual supportiveness" is mentioned as the underlying principle, but the convention cannot be subordinated to other treaties. Trade versus cultural protection issues thus have to be resolved in the spirit of mutual supportiveness without subordinating the UNESCO Convention.

In moving toward a convention, the French and the Canadians created a network of cultural ministers from around the world, with funding from the Canadian Council for the Arts. This International Network on Cultural Policy (INCP) now includes more than 70 cultural ministries (see www.incp-ripc.org). INCP was also instrumental in creating a parallel nongovernmental network of international cultural industry workers and artists that in September 2000 coalesced into the International Network for Cultural Diversity (INCD; www.incd.net). People who later formed the INCD were in Seattle for the failed WTO Ministerial in December 1999, in an effort to bring cultural issues to the meetings and to organize protests against them. INCD is headquartered in the Canadian Council for the Arts, the leading arts advocacy group in Canada. INCD and INCP annual meetings and agendas run parallel to each other. INCD had drafted an International Convention on Cultural Diversity, which was similar to that of the INCP in its aims and philosophy, except that it was more emphatic in keeping audio-visual negotiations out of the WTO.

While Canada and France frame INCD as a global network of nongovernmental organizations, the imprint of the Canadian and French governments is ubiquitous. Canadian trade economists Acheson and Maule (2004, 246) note, "The official side has kept a tight rein on the 'grassroot' input through funding its liaison office and various research initiatives, holding the INCD meetings concurrently with its own, and providing consultants or staff that develop themes, suggest speakers, write background papers and summary reports and proselytize."

It seems that as they proceeded, UNESCO's deliberations on cultural diversity and convention became more and more about commerce, to the exclusion of other perspectives, including anthropological and sociological ones. UNESCO's thinking about culture in the 1990s was often framed in terms of the 2005 annual *Our Creative Diversity* report (Peréz de Cuéllar 1995), but that report often emphasized the syncretic, hybrid, and exchange features of cultures. By the time the UNESCO cultural convention was adopted, the complexity of these anthropological arguments had been lost, to make way for national cultural policies and economic protections for culture.

The program for drafting a convention was presented at the 32nd General Conference of UNESCO, in September–October 2004. UNESCO appointed a 15-member committee of independent experts to examine the issue. After several meetings and drafting sessions, they presented a preliminary draft in May. The draft was presented at the 33rd General Conference in October 2005; it passed, with 148 votes in favor and 2 (the United States and Israel) against. The resulting treaty is known as the Convention on the Protection and Promotion of Diversity of Cultural Expressions.

A look at its articles shows that although it is supposed to be framed for the broader purpose of ensuring cultural diversity, its main focus seems to be preserving and protecting (from trade) a few cultural industries in national terms. Thus "cultural industry" seems to be coterminous with national identity, even if it leaves open the possibility to governments to define cultural identities. The case of France is especially ironic because, like many other European states, its government does not collect any data on any identity except national identity. Its ethnic minorities see themselves as excluded from socio-political-economic life. Just as the ink was drying on the 2005 convention, riots broke out in several French cities over police brutality, leading President Jacques Chirac to declare a state of emergency that lasted from November 8, 2005 until January 4, 2006.

The issue of cultural diversity does not seem to follow from earlier moves within UNESCO, which were leading the organization toward broad anthropological definitions of culture. UNESCO officials note that the cultural diversity declaration and convention followed from the 1993 *Our Creative Diversity* report by the UN- and UNESCO-appointed World Commission on Culture and Development and from the 1998 and 2000 *World Culture Report*. However, these reports were on culture and development (or culture broadly defined). The purpose of the 2005 convention is altogether different. In fact, while the convention found some support in the developing world, it also halted the momentum toward an anthropological conception of development and thinking of culture in development terms.

The convention succeeded in ending any further moves to seek audiovisual liberalization through the WTO. Thus the most important issue in UNESCO in the past decade came in opposition to another organization's agenda and effectively killed its own agenda on cultural development. People like Claude Levi-Strauss in the 1950s and the authors of UNESCO's 1993 *Our Creative Diversity* report emphasized cultural hybridity and the growth of cultures through openness. However imminent Hollywood's threat to cultural growth may have been, the convention did not strike any balance between openness and hybridity.

Most important, UNESCO seemed to exclude voices in the framing of the convention. Anthropologists, who might have been expected to support it, criticized the focus on cultural industries. Trade ministries from the countries who signed the convention, including Canada, condemned their cultural ministries for supporting the convention. Latin American and West African countries noted that EU countries had bullied them into signing the convention by threatening to cut off their market access and production subsidies. China; Hong Kong SAR, China; Taiwan, China; Japan; and Mexico presented a communication in the WTO on June 30, 2005, indirectly criticizing the moves and noting that "trade in audio-visual services results in cultural exchange, the best way to promote cultural diversity" (WTO 2005).

Conclusion

UNESCO is often perceived as a champion of humanity's noblest ideals, a symbol of universal notions of justice, whereas the WTO is often viewed as an organization that furthers the interests of the rich and the powerful. But examination of the deliberative practices at the institutions reveals a very different reality. The WTO is a streamlined organization with a focused agenda, institutional focus, and a convergence of interests from the global to the domestic levels. From its formal negotiation processes to its involvement, in protest or otherwise, of civil society and various other actors, it is a far more deliberative body than UNESCO, an institution that lacks focus and suffers from infighting. UNESCO's deliberative processes are haphazard and seldom undergo the kind of scrutiny accorded by the WTO.

The audio-visual and cultural diversity issues allow examination of an issue area the two organizations share (table 9.3). As on other trade issues,

TABLE 9.3 Treatment of creative industries at the World Trade Organization and UNESCO

Item	World Trade Organization (WTO)	UNESCO
Main issue	Audio-visual liberalization	Protection and promotion of cultural expressions
Secretariat staff	Two people work on audio-visual issues	Cultural division and several subdivisions
Relevant national ministries	Trade, finance, culture, and tourism; generally a top issue among national ministries	Ministries of culture
Links with industry	Strong	Weak
Links with civil society	Heavy involvement through national (or EU) representatives and advocacy through media or protests	Work through International Network for Cultural Diversity (INCD)
Media involvement	Close scrutiny of activities and deliberations	Weak scrutiny of activities and deliberations
Knowledge production	Economists show links between cultural industries and growth or impact of specific cultural policy instruments on industry	Reports such as *Our Creative Diversity* and *World Culture Reports* sought interdisciplinary, but mostly anthropological, understanding
Status of international treaties	GATS commitments on audio-visual heavily scrutinized; EU most favored nation exemption contentious	2005 convention weak and not effectively enforced

pro-trade and anti-trade interests within and across national borders mobilized and got involved. This issue also raised passions and interests situated around cultural identity and politics.

The issue has been one of the most prominent issues ever debated at UNESCO. Its salience owes something to its link with the WTO. At UNESCO the issue has taken on characteristics that have departed from the institution's own understanding of cultural diversity. A variety of political manipulations and contradictions have marred deliberation of this issue, in which a few global actors have been mobilized but many more excluded. In contrast, the WTO has moved toward an appreciation of cultural diversity issues, adopting a flexible framework that allows for minimal or no commitments from member-states.

To say that the WTO embodies a better deliberative process than UNESCO is not to claim that it is an exemplar of deliberations at the global governance level. The WTO engages in processes that are rule- and reason-based and that are accountable to the scrutiny of a global public. Its texts, treaties, and rules can often be traced back to notions of justice and fairness or in notions such as special and differential treatment for products from the developing world. That said, the WTO does not constitute itself through direct representation, and it is often not inclusive of all relevant voices in its decision making. Concentrated and powerful interests can also lead to outcomes that are not deliberative at all.

The WTO represents deliberation and debate around principles that are market-based. Some political thought takes deliberations that create markets to be outside of deliberative political thought altogether because of disagreement about the welfare-enhancing effects of markets. This notion is not universally shared. Cotton farmers in Mali and sugar farmers in Brazil believe that the WTO is the place for them to seek a sense of redress. Their sense of justice is rooted in, not anathema to, market principles (the desire to cut U.S. subsidies for cotton or sugar).

Deliberation theory at the global level can learn from empirical exercises such as the ones presented here, which scholars such as Fung (2007) take to be important for providing a sense of "feasible institutional arrangements." Even if the WTO is anathema to some quarters of political thought, there is still value in learning from it in terms of the kinds of institutional structure and processes that can foster reason-based argumentation.

In providing a comparative framework for deliberations in international organizations, scholars and practitioners need to accord attention to the issue structure as well as the deliberative context. This chapter hypothesizes that streamlined or focused interests around issue structures are far more likely to be participatory than issue structures featuring divided interests and weak institutions. The everyday scrutiny and controversies that neoliberal institutions such as the WTO generate may be their greatest deliberative strengths.

Notes

1. Because of their strategic nature, diplomacy and negotiations are sometimes taken to be nondeliberative (Keohane 2001). Inasmuch as diplomacy can also feature problem solving and actors involved are held accountable, it is a deliberative process (Niemann 2006; Singh 2008).
2. As this chapter details later, this process was top down and expert driven rather than progressive and deliberative.
3. They also reveal the influence of the French preference for an intellectual organization in the CAME negotiations. The United Kingdom and the United States won the battle in making UNESCO member-state driven.
4. MFN in international trade means that no nation is to be discriminated against in the application of trade measures. An MFN exemption allows Europeans to discriminate against any nation, in this case the United States.
5. The European Union negotiates as a single entity at the WTO. However, its single position often reveals fissures. The United Kingdom, the biggest exporter of cultural products in the European Union, and countries such as Denmark and Netherlands are reluctant to go along with protectionist measures
6. As such, they may belong to the category of deliberations that the anthropologist Arjun Appadurai calls "failed performative" in this volume to bring attention to how failed deliberations are as instructive for future successes of deliberations

References

Acheson, Keith, and Christopher Maule. 2004. "Convention on Cultural Diversity." *Journal of Cultural Economics* 28 (4): 243–56.

Avant, Deborah D., Martha Finnemore, and Susan K. Sell. 2010. *Who Governs the Globe?* Cambridge: Cambridge University Press.

Berger, Peter L., and Thomas Luckmann. 1966. *The Social Construction of Reality: A Treatise in the Sociology of Knowledge.* New York: Anchor Books.

Brianso, Isabelle. 2010. "Valorization of World Cultural Heritage in Time of Globalization: Bridges between Nations and Cultural Power." In *International Cultural Policies and Power*, ed. J. P. Singh, 166–80. Basingstoke, U.K.: Palgrave Macmillan.

Cowhey, Peter F. Spring. 1990. "The International Telecommunications Regime: The Political Roots of Regimes of High Technology." *International Organization* 44 (2): 169–99.

Davis, Christina L. 2004. "International Institutions and Issue Linkage: Building Support for Agricultural Trade Liberalization." *American Political Science Review* 98 (1): 153–69.

De Beukelaer, Christiaan, Miikka Pyykkönen, and J. P. Singh, eds. 2015. *Globalization, Culture, and Development: The UNESCO Convention on Cultural Diversity.* Basingstoke, U.K.: Palgrave Macmillan.

Dryzek, John S., and Simon Niemeyer. 2008. "Discursive Representation." *American Political Science Review* 102 (4): 481–93.

Dubash, Navroz K. 2009. "Global Norms through Global Deliberation? Reflections on the World Commission on Dams." *Global Governance* 15 (2): 219–38.

Farrell, Henry. 2003. "Constructing the International Foundations of E–Commerce: The EU–U.S. Safe Harbor Arrangement." *International Organization* 57 (2): 277–306.

Finnemore, Martha. 1996. *National Interests in International Society*. Ithaca, NY: Cornell University Press.

Finnemore, Martha, and Kathryn Sikkink. 1998. "International Norm Dynamics and Political Change." *International Organization* 52 (Autumn): 887–917.

Freire, Paulo. 2000 (1970). *Pedagogy of the Oppressed*. New York: Continuum.

Fung, Archon. 2007. "Democratic Theory and Political Science: A Pragmatic Method of Constructive Engagement." *American Political Science Review* 101 (3): 443–58.

Fung, Archon, Hollie Russon Gilman, and Jennifer Shkabatur. 2013. "Six Models for the Internet + Politics." *International Studies Review* 15 (1): 30–47.

GATT (General Agreement on Tariffs and Trade). 1986. Text of the General Agreement on Tariffs and Trade. Geneva.

Goff, Patricia M. 2007. *Limits to Liberalization: Local Culture in Global Marketplace*. Ithaca, NY: Cornell University Press.

Goodwin, Craufurd. 2006. "Art and Culture in the History of Economic Thought." In *Handbook of the Economics of Art and Culture, Handbooks in Economics 25*, ed. Victor A. Ginsburgh and David Throsby. Amsterdam: North-Holland.

Grewal, David Singh. 2008. *Network Power: The Social Dimensions of Globalization*. New Haven, CT: Yale University Press.

Gutman, Cynthia. 2000. "A Global Campaign." *UNESCO Courier*, March.

Habermas, Jürgen. 1976. *Communication and the Evolution of Society*. Boston, MA: Beacon Press.

———. 1985. *The Theory of Communicative Action, Volume 1: Reason and the Rationalization of Society*. Boston: Beacon Press.

Hajnal, Peter I. 1983. *Guide to UNESCO*. London: Oceana Publishers.

Held, David, Anthony McGrew, David Goldblatt, and Jonathan Perraton. 1999. *Global Transformation: Politics, Economics and Culture*. Stanford, CA: Stanford University Press.

Hoggart, Richard. 1978. *An Idea and Its Servants: UNESCO from within*. New York: Oxford University Press.

Hurd, Ian. 1999. "Legitimacy and Authority in International Politics." *International Organization* 53 (2): 379–408.

Keohane, Robert O. 2001. "Governance in a Partially Globalized World." *American Political Science Review* 95 (1): 1–13.

Krasner, Stephen D., ed. 1983. *International Regimes*. Ithaca, NY: Cornell University Press.

Jawara, Fatoumata, and Aileen Kwa. 2003. *Behind the Scenes at the WTO: The Real World of International Trade Negotiations*. London: Zed Books.

Lengyel, Peter. 1986. *International Social Science: The UNESCO Experience*. New Brunswick, NJ: Transaction Books.

Mansbridge, Jane, James Bohman, Simone Chambers, David Estlund, Andreas Føllesdal, Archon Fung, Cristina Lafont, Bernard Manin, and José Luis Martí. 2010. "The Place of Self-Interest and the Role of Power in Deliberative Democracy." *Journal of Political Philosophy* 18 (1): 64–100.

Mundy, Karen. 2006. "Education for All and the New Development Compact." *Review of Education* 52: 23–48.

———. 2010. "'Education for All' and the Global Governors." In *Who Governs the Globe?* ed. Deborah D. Avant, Martha Finnemore, and Susan K. Sell. Cambridge: Cambridge University Press.

Narlikar, Amrita. 2003. *International Trade and Developing Countries: Bargaining Coalitions in the GATT and WTO*. London: Routledge.

———. 2005. *The World Trade Organization: A Very Short Introduction*. Oxford: Oxford University Press.

Niemann, Arne. 2006. "Beyond Problem-Solving and Bargaining: Communicative Action in International Negotiations." *International Negotiation* 11 (3): 467–97.

O'Brien, Robert, Anne Marie Goetz, Jan Aart Scholte, and Marc Williams. 2000. "Contesting Global Governance: Multilateralism and Global Social Movements." In *Contesting Global Governance: Multilateral Economic Institutions and Global Social Movements*, 1–23. Cambridge: Cambridge University Press.

Odell, John S. 2000. *Negotiating the World Economy*. Ithaca, NY: Cornell University Press.

———. 2006. *Negotiating Trade: Developing Countries in the WTO and NAFTA*. Cambridge: Cambridge University Press.

Odell, John S., with Barry Eichengreen. 2000. "Changing Domestic Institutions and Ratifying Regime Agreements." In *Negotiating the World Economy*, ed. John S. Odell. Ithaca, NY: Cornell University Press.

Odell, John S., and Susan K. Sell. 2006. "Reframing the Issue: The WTO Coalition on Intellectual Property and Public Health, 2001." In *Negotiating Trade: Developing Countries in the WTO and NAFTA*, ed. John S. Odell. Cambridge: Cambridge University Press.

Peréz de Cuéllar, Javier. 1995. *Our Creative Diversity: Report of the World Commission on Culture and Development*. Paris: UNESCO Publishing.

Putnam, Robert D. 1988. "Diplomacy and Domestic Politics: The Logic of Two-Level Games." *International Organization* 42 (3): 427–60.

Risse, Thomas. 2000. "Let's Argue! Communicative Action in World Politics." *International Organization* 54 (1): 1–39.

Rosenau, James N., ed. 1967. *Domestic Sources of Foreign Policy.* New York: Free Press.

Rosenau, James N., and Ernst-Otto Czempiel. 1992. *Governance without Government: Order and Change in World Politics.* Cambridge: Cambridge University Press.

Sandholtz, Wayne. 1992. *High-Tech Europe: the Politics of International Cooperation.* Berkeley: University of California Press.

Sell, Susan. 2003. *Private Power, Public Law: The Globalization of Intellectual Property Rights.* Cambridge: Cambridge University Press.

Singh, J. P. 2000. "Weak Powers and Globalism: The Impact of Plurality on Weak-Strong Negotiations in the International Economy." *International Negotiation* 5 (3): 449–84.

———. 2008. *Negotiation and the Global Information Economy.* Cambridge: Cambridge University Press.

———. 2010. "Development Objectives and Trade Negotiations: Moralistic Foreign Policy or Negotiated Trade Concessions?" *International Negotiation* 15: 367–89.

———. 2011a. *Globalized Arts: The Entertainment Economy and Cultural Identity.* New York: Columbia University Press.

———. 2011b. *United Nations Educational, Scientific and Cultural Organization: Creating Norms for a Complex World.* London: Routledge.

Slaughter, Anne-Marie. 2004. *A New World Order.* Princeton, NJ: Princeton University Press.

Smith, Courtney B. 1999. "The Politics of Global Consensus Building: A Comparative Analysis." *Global Governance* 5 (2): 173–202.

Steele, Brent J. 2007. "Making Words Matter: The Asian Tsunami, Darfur, and 'Reflexive Discourse' in International Politics." *International Studies Quarterly* 51 (4): 901–25.

Steinberg, Richard H. 2002. "In the Shadow of Law or Power? Consensus-Based Bargaining and Outcomes in the GATT/WTO." *International Organization* 56 (2): 339–74.

Taylor, Charles. 1994. "The Politics of Recognition." In *Multiculturalism: Examining the Politics of Recognition*, ed. Amy Gutman. Princeton, NJ: Princeton University Press.

UNESCO (United Nations Educational, Scientific and Cultural Organization). 1945. "Constitution." http://portal.unesco.org/en/ev.php-URL_ID=15244&URL_DO=DO_TOPIC&URL_SECTION=201.html. Washington Times. 1994. November 24.

Weisband, E. 2000. "Discursive Multilateralism: Global Benchmarks, Shame and Learning in the ILO Labor Standards Monitoring Regime." *International Organization* 44 (4): 643–66.

Wiener, Antje. 2008. *The Invisible Constitution of Politics*. Cambridge University Press.

WTO (World Trade Organization). 2005. Communication from Hong Kong, China; Japan; Mexico; the Separate Customs Territory of Taiwan, Penghu, Kinmen, and Matsu; and the United States. Joint Statement on the Negotiation of Audiovisual Services. TNS/S/W/49, June 30. Geneva.

———. 2014. *Annual Report 2014*. Geneva: WTO. http://www.wto.org/english /res_e/booksp_e/anrep_e/anrep14_e.pdf.

CHAPTER 10

The Judicialization of Development Policy

Varun Gauri

Over the past three decades, courts around the world have become increasingly involved in what were previously considered purely political matters; in other words, politics in general has become more "judicialized" (Tate and Vallinder 1995; Hirschl 2008). In some settings, judicial interventions can improve the quality of deliberation over development policies.

"Social rights constitutionalism" has emerged in policy domains that were previously the exclusive provenance of the other branches of government (Brinks, Gauri, and Shen forthcoming). In Colombia the courts hear and largely support tens of thousands of cases a year on demands for medications and health care services (more than 140,000 in 2008 alone). In 2008 the Colombian Constitutional Court issued a landmark ruling, finding that the government's system for health finance was unconstitutional, and directing the government to develop a more equitable scheme (Yamin and Parra-Verra 2010). The Brazilian courts are also very active in health care policy. In the state of São Paulo alone, more than 10,000 patients were receiving drugs ordered by courts in 2005, and the numbers have only increased since then (Ferraz 2009). The South African courts famously challenged the HIV/AIDS policies under President Mbeki, directing a reluctant state to begin to provide antiretroviral drugs (Berger 2008; Roux 2009; Forbath 2010). The Indian Supreme Court and High Courts annually rule on thousands of fundamental rights and public interest litigation cases related to social and economic policies. In a series of orders beginning in 2001, the Indian Supreme Court directed states to universalize the midday meals scheme in schools in 2001. In 1998 it ordered the Delhi municipal government to convert public commercial vehicles to a cleaner emissions technology. It is (at least) a co-equal to the executive branch in the management of national forest policy (Sathe 2002; Shankar and Mehta 2008; Gauri 2011; Khosla 2011). Beginning in 2005, a series of cases before the Indonesian Constitutional Court demanded that the government comply with a constitutional requirement that specifies that it devote 20 percent of its expenditures to education. These cases contributed to a debate between Indonesian civil society organizations and the state regarding the appropriate level of educational spending. Indonesian educational expenditures as a share of total expenditures went from 7 percent to nearly 12 percent in the next few years (Susanti 2008). The Hungarian Constitutional Court struck down a structural adjustment loan agreement that the executive had made with the International Monetary Fund and the World Bank (Scheppele 2003). The judicialization of development policy is apparent in many other countries, including Costa Rica, the Arab Republic of Egypt, the Philippines, and Poland, as well.[1]

For some observers, judicializing development policy necessarily improves the quality of public deliberation. Rawls, for instance, held that the role of courts "is part of the publicity of reason and is an aspect of the wide, or educative, role of public reason" (Rawls 1996, 236–37). For Habermas, courts involve a kind of deliberation in which adversarial parties can genuinely come to understand one another. "The perspectives of participants and the perspectives of uninvolved members of the community (represented by an impartial judge)," he writes, "come to be transformed into one another" (1996, 229).

But this is really an empirical question. Some courts, particularly those in developing societies in which the consciousness of rights is underdeveloped and a competitive electoral system is absent, do not exhibit high-quality deliberation. And in every society there are many instances in which courts attempt to enforce development policy peremptorily. For instance, the large majority of cases on the provision of medications in Latin America are resolved without elaborated or reasoned justification. In other instances, courts do not include all relevant interests in their orders (one example is the failure of the Indian Supreme Court to include the interests of auto-rickshaw drivers when it forced commercial vehicles to convert to compressed natural gas [Rajamani 2007]).

Yet over time it is common for courts to come under moral and political pressure to include relevant interests and develop procedures for public communication. For instance, after watching judges grant tens of thousands of individualized remedies in medication cases over the years, Brazil's highest court, the Supreme Tribunal Federal, decided that a public dialogue was crucial. It held six days of televised public hearings on a case in April and May 2009.[2]

Courts involved in development policy can offer three deliberative benefits (Gauri and Brinks 2012). First, they can provide a forum in which information regarding the feasibility of development policies and the cost of meeting them is made public. The South African courts helped adjudicate the government's claim that new AIDS treatments would be too difficult, dangerous, or costly; they brought HIV/AIDS policies in line with a general commitment to public health measures and commonly accepted scientific knowledge. In a series of orders on the right to food, the Indian Supreme Court reviewed government food distribution schemes. It agreed with petitioners that inefficiencies, rather than a lack of funds, prevented wider coverage. During its cases on the potential conversion of commercial vehicles in Delhi to compressed natural gas, the Court supported the use of nonpartisan, scientific knowledge to assess the technical feasibility of conversion, which was opaque to outsiders. Indian and South African cases and on the pricing of pharmaceuticals involved the examination of claims that producers and distributors were charging excessive prices.

Second, by bringing a number of parties into dialogue, allowing socially marginal individuals and groups into the courtroom, and using procedural rules to establish a level playing field among parties with unequal social and political power, courts improve the quality of deliberation by including previously excluded points of view. The Indian courts developed new procedures in public interest litigation, a process that loosens rules of standing and strictures on writ petitions in order to give individuals and groups who have difficulty representing themselves to have a voice.[3] The Constitutional Chamber of the Costa Rican Supreme Court dramatically lowered procedural obstacles to access, as well. As a result, the number of habeas corpus and unconstitutionality (*amparo*) claims filed by poor individuals jumped sharply (Wilson 2009).

Third, judicial deliberation can facilitate the reciprocal exchange of public reasons, which is a hallmark of high-quality deliberation. By design (if not always in practice), public interest litigation moves the judicial process away from an adversarial model to one in which all parties attempt to find a joint solution to a pressing human problem (Fredman 2008; Gauri 2011; Gauri and Brinks 2012). In such contexts, courts often impose requirements that parties argue in good faith; they reserve their harshest admonitions and penalties for communication that is not "serious" or information that is inaccurate. In its landmark cases on health financing (Decision T-760, of 2008) and displaced persons (Decision T-025, of 2004), the Colombian Constitutional Court required state officials to explain their policies and report back with new plans at defined intervals. The Indian courts routinely ask the state to give reasons for social and economic policies, and their (non-)implementation, and to present reforms to programs in areas such as pollution control, the right to food, employment, prison conditions, and women's rights (Desai and Muralidhar 2000). Writing about U.S. courts, Sabel and Simon (2003, 1056, 1062), describe the role of modern courts in policy making as a process of "destabilization" that triggers deliberation:

> Destabilization induces the institution to reform itself in a process in which it must respond to previously excluded stakeholders. . . .

In the typical pattern of the new public law suit, a finding or concession of liability triggers a process of supervised negotiation and deliberation among the parties and other stakeholders. The characteristic result of this process is a regime of rolling or provisional rules that are periodically revised in light of transparent evaluations of their implementation.

Courts are increasingly active in formulating development policy; in many settings, judicial interventions can improve the quality of deliberation over development policies. Although the academic literature has traditionally expressed skepticism regarding the effectiveness and value of judicial interventions in policy making, recent analyses of "social rights constitutionalism" suggest that it is an increasingly widespread phenomenon, with significant and often progressive effects on the distribution of national resources and the quality of public deliberation. (Dugard 2013; Brinks and Forbath 2014; Brinks and Gauri 2014).

Notes

1. Summary assessments of the role of courts in social policy in developing countries include Gauri and Brinks (2008), Langford (2009), Tushnet (2009), and Yamin and Gloppen (2011).
2. Transcripts are available at http://www.stf.jus.br/portal/cms/verTexto.asp?serv ico=processoAudienciaPublicaSaude&pagina=Cronograma.
3. There is a sense in India that public interest litigation has been used to dress up private disputes. The government and the courts are formulating criteria to screen "motivated" and "frivolous" claims and to sanction litigants in such cases.

References

Berger, Jonathan. 2008. "Litigating for Social Justice in Post-Apartheid South Africa: A Focus on Health and Education." In *Courting Social Justice: Judicial Enforcement of Social and Economic Rights in the Developing World*, ed. V. Gauri and D. M. Brinks. New York: Cambridge University Press.

Brinks, Daniel M., and William Forbath. 2014. "The Role of Courts and Constitutions in the New Politics of Welfare in Latin America." In *Law and Development of Middle-Income Countries*, ed. R. Peerenboom and T. Ginsburg. Cambridge: Cambridge University Press.

Brinks, Daniel M., and Varun Gauri. 2014. "The Law's Majestic Equality? The Distributive Impact of Judicializing Social and Economic Rights." *Perspectives on Politics* 12 (2): 375–93.

Brinks, Daniel M., Varun Gauri, and Kyle Shen. Forthcoming. "Social Rights Constitutionalism: Negotiating the Tension between the Universal and the Particular." *Annual Review of Law and Social Science*.

Desai, A. H., and S. Muralidhar. 2000. "Public Interest Litigation: Potential and Problems." *Supreme but Not Infallible: Essays in Honor of the Indian Supreme Court*, ed. B. N. Kirpal and others. New Delhi: Oxford University Press.

Dugard, Jackie. 2013. "Courts and Structural Poverty in South Africa: To What Extent Has the Constitutional Court Expanded Access and Remedies to the Poor?" In *Constitutionalism of the Global South: The Activist Tribunals of India, South Africa, and Colombia*, ed. Daniel Bonilla Maldonado. New York: Cambridge University Press.

Ferraz, O. 2009. "Between Usurpation and Abdication? The Right to Health in the Courts of Brazil and South Africa." *Social Science Research Network*. http://papers.ssrn.com/sol3/papers.cfm?abstract_id=1458299.

Forbath, William (with assistance from Zachie Achmat, Geoff Budlender, and Mark Heywood). 2010. "Cultural Transformation, Deep Institutional Reform, and ESR Practice: South Africa's Treatment Action Campaign." In *Stones of Hope: How African Activists Reclaim Human Rights to Challenge Global Poverty*, ed. Lucie White and James Perelman. Stanford, CA: Stanford University Press.

Fredman, S. 2008. *Human Rights Transformed: Positive Rights and Positive Duties*: Oxford: Oxford University Press.

Gauri, Varun. 2011. "Fundamental Rights and Public Interest Litigation in India: Overreaching or Underachieving?" *Indian Journal of Law and Economics* 1 (1): 71–93.

Gauri, Varun, and Daniel M. Brinks, eds. 2008. *Courting Social Justice: Judicial Enforcement of Social and Economic Rights in the Developing World*. New York: Cambridge University Press.

Gauri, Varun, and Daniel M. Brinks. 2012. "Human Rights as Demands for Communicative Action." *Journal of Political Philosophy* 20 (4): 407–31.

Habermas, Jurgen. 1996. *Between Facts and Norms: Contributions to a Discourse Theory of Law and Democracy*. Cambridge, MA: MIT Press.

Hirschl, R. 2008. "The Judicialization of Mega-Politics and the Rise of Political Courts." *Annual Review of Political Science* 11: 93–118.

Khosla, M. 2011. "Making Social Rights Conditional: Lessons from India." *International Journal of Constitutional Law* 8 (4): 739–65.

Langford, M. 2009. *Social Rights Jurisprudence: Emerging Trends in Comparative and International Law*. New York: Cambridge University Press.

Rajamani, L. 2007. "Public Interest Environmental Litigation in India: Exploring Issues of Access, Participation, Equity, Effectiveness and Sustainability." *Journal of Environmental Law* 19 (3): 293–321.

Rawls, John. 1996. *Political Liberalism*. New York: Columbia University Press.

Roux, T. 2009. "Principle and Pragmatism on the Constitutional Court of South Africa." *International Journal of Constitutional Law* 7 (1): 106–38.

Sabel, C. F., and W. H. Simon. 2003. "Destabilization Rights: How Public Law Litigation Succeeds." *Harvard Law Review* 117: 1015–101.

Sathe, S. P. 2002. *Judicial Activism in India: Transgressing Borders and Enforcing Limits*. New Delhi: Oxford University Press.

Scheppele, K. L. 2003. "A Realpolitik Defense of Social Rights." *Texas Law Review* 82 (7): 1921–61.

Shankar, Shylashri, and Pratap Bhanu Mehta. 2008. "Courts and Socioeconomic Rights in India." In *Courting Social Justice: Judicial Enforcement of Social and Economic Rights in the Developing World*, ed. V. Gauri and P. G. Brown. New York: Cambridge University Press.

Susanti, Bivitri. 2008. "The Implementation of the Rights to Health Care and Education in Indonesia." In *Courting Social Justice: Judicial Enforcement of Social and Economic Rights in the Developing World*, ed. V. Gauri and D. M. Brinks. New York: Cambridge University Press.

Tate, C. Neal, and Torbjörn Vallinder. 1995. "The Global Expansion of Judicial Power: The Judicialization of Politics." In *The Global Expansion of Judicial Power*, ed. C. N. Tate and T. Vallinder. New York: New York University Press.

Tushnet, M. 2009. *Weak Courts, Strong Rights: Judicial Review and Social Welfare Rights in Comparative Constitutional Law*. Princeton, NJ: Princeton University Press.

Wilson, B. 2009. "Institutional Reform and Rights Revolutions in Latin America: The Cases of Costa Rica and Colombia." *Journal of Politics in Latin America* 1 (2): 59–85.

Yamin, Alicia Ely, and Siri Gloppen, eds. 2011. *Litigating Health Rights: Can Courts Bring More Justice to Health?* Cambridge, MA: Harvard University Press.

Yamin, Alicia Ely, and Oscar Parra-Verra. 2010. "Judicial Protection of the Right to Health in Colombia: From Social Demands to Individual Claims to Public Debates." *Hastings International and Comparative Law Review* 33 (2): 101–29.

CHAPTER 11

Technology for Democracy in Development: Lessons from Seven Case Studies

Archon Fung, Hollie Russon Gilman, and Jennifer Shkabatur

Claims regarding the positive and negative effects of information and communication technology (ICT) on democratic deliberation and development are overblown in both developing and developed countries (Rheingold 2002; Shirky 2008; Noveck 2009; Global Voices 2010; O'Reilly 2010; Morozov 2011; Sifry 2011). The deployment of various ICT projects to enhance governmental accountability, political participation, and public deliberation is at an early stage. It is therefore too early to identify patterns or principles with confidence. Instead, this chapter reviews several efforts to use ICT platforms to improve accountability and democratic engagement and draws lessons about the interaction between technology and politics.

Study of the social and political dynamics surrounding these efforts reveals some patterns that depart from the expectations of observers who expect technology to midwife a new era of dramatically enhanced political accountability or public participation. Some ICT use may produce such revolutionary shifts in the fullness of time, but such changes are not (yet) discernible from the cases we examined.

Between July and September 2010, our small research team examined seven cases of ICT interventions that aimed to enhance political or private sector accountability through transparency and greater public engagement with organizations (Fung, Gilman, and Shkabatur 2010). The cases span five countries (Brazil, Chile, India, Kenya, and the Slovak Republic) and diverse issues, including municipal problem solving, consumer products and services, public budget monitoring, election integrity, tracking

TABLE 11.1 Case studies of information and communications technology platforms used to improve accountability and democratic engagement

Project	City	Issue
Budget Tracking Tool	Nairobi	Budget monitoring
Cidade Democrática	São Paulo	Citizen participation in local government
Fair Play Alliance	Bratislava	Watchdog, citizen journalism, advocacy
Kiirti (Ushahidi)	Bangalore	Complaint resolution
Mumbai Votes	Mumbai	Legislative agenda setting
Reclamos	Santiago	Consumer complaints
Ushahidi and Uchaguzi	Nairobi	Election monitoring

and disclosure of political candidates and representatives, public service complaint resolution, and political journalism and advocacy (table 11.1). Investigation of the political and social dynamics these cases set into motion yields tentative insights into the character and success of technological innovations in the governance arena.

Why are communication technologies not used more to improve governance?

There are many reasons to think that new ICTs will increase accountability. ICTs allow the decentralized spotting and reporting of incidents and abuses by governments and organizations to be shared in centralized and viral ways (think of the ubiquity of cell phones and messaging). ICTs lower communication costs and should therefore allow citizens to coordinate with one another in their efforts to call leaders to account (Shirky 2008; Howard 2010). ICTs can create many decentralized forums in which individuals can share information and develop their political ideas and perspectives.

Many critics have cast doubt on the capacity of ICTs to enhance accountability or improve the quality of politics. ICTs engage citizens for public discussion at the penumbra of political activity instead of at the core of where political decision-making takes place (Schlozman, Verba, and Brady 2010). Furthermore, instead of unifying citizens, they may fragment them into like-minded enclaves (Sunstein 2009). People who publish in the brave new media of blogs and web pages may be even more elite than the mainstream media (Hindman 2009). Clever authoritarians and fascists may be able to outwit democrats in their control and use of ICTs (Diamond 2010; Morozov 2011). The jury on the macroscopic impact of ICT on democratic politics and political accountability is thus still very much sequestered. The debate will rage on for some time.

The picture comes into focus more clearly as one descends from considering ICT broadly as a social force or undifferentiated new media extension of the abstract public sphere to examining particular platforms and

ICT initiatives. At the level of platforms, there is a curious divergence between the political realm on one hand and the social, media consumption, productive, and commercial realms on the other. Several platforms have arguably revolutionized the way in which hundreds of millions of individuals interact and communicate socially. The past two decades have seen technology produce extraordinary levels of "creative destruction" (Schumpeter 1942)—think of Facebook, Twitter, YouTube, Flickr, Tencent in China, and even World of Warcraft and Second Life. The search engines of Google and Baidu, together with online publications, large and small, have disrupted the news industry and profoundly altered the ways much of the Earth's population finds all manner of information. Open-sourced cooperative platforms such as Wikipedia and the Linux project have created novel and powerful ways to produce knowledge, software, and even some consumer products (Raymond 2001; Weber 2004; Von Hippel 2005; Benkler 2006; Reagle 2010). Companies such as eBay, Amazon, Craigslist, Orbitz, Netflix, and iTunes have dramatically altered the pattern of commercial transactions.

In contrast, when it comes to governance—how people make public decisions and policies, address public problems, and hold leaders accountable—no platform is in the same league as these companies.

ICT has not yet transformed politics in the same way it has altered other areas of social, informational, productive, and commercial lives for at least four reasons. First, platforms such as Facebook, Twitter, iTunes, and Netflix provide social or commercial services to individuals (finding out what a friend from high school is up to or making snarky comments about him; finding a movie and beginning to watch it in 30 seconds). ICT cannot improve most citizen experiences in the political governance and decision-making realm in this individual and immediately gratifying way, because political processes are essentially collective or aggregative.

Second, massively parallel, collaborative, and typically volunteer production (see Benkler 2006), enabled by platforms such as Wikipedia and Linux, is a fundamentally novel mechanism. Much activity in the political decision-making realm is strategic and competitive. There, parties share no common goal. The dynamics of collaborative production therefore do not apply.

Third, citizens would like influence over decisions or policies; if political ICTs conferred influence, more people would use them. Political authorities are often reluctant to share power in this way, however.

Fourth, ICT success in the commercial or social realm confers only benefits—primarily financial success—to founders and sponsors. In contrast, ICT success in the governance and accountability realm has costs as well as benefits, as increased political accountability would presumably hurt some politicians. An ICT platform that creates massive public deliberation may yield policy recommendations that are at odds with policy makers' preferences. ICTs that advance democratic values produce ambiguous costs and benefits for the officials who are called upon to sponsor them.

For all of these reasons, the rate of ICT platform innovation is much lower in the political, public realm than in the commercial or social sectors. Instead of relying on analogies to apply insights from, say, the Wikipedia experience to a public agency's rule-making process, one should instead be attentive to the differences between governance and these other realms.

This is not to say that appropriate technologies cannot or will not dramatically improve democratic politics and governance. Someone someday, perhaps soon, may invent an app or platform that improves the quality of public engagement in governance and accountability. No one can predict the incidence or shape of such transformative platforms much before they actually appear. The iPhone was originally a closed platform with no third-party apps. Jimmy Wales first envisioned Nupedia as an online encyclopedia with articles written by experts, rather than the open and collaborative Wikipedia (Reagle 2010). However, the factors that make the political governance realm different from social and commercial realms reduce the rate of innovation by creating distinctive and fundamental challenges. Therefore, transformative ICT platforms in the political arena will likely be a long time coming.

How can technology improve governance?

These factors notwithstanding, ICTs can improve the quality of democratic governance and deliberation. In the seven cases we examined, these contributions occur incrementally. Rather than setting in motion fundamentally new dynamics of popular engagement and mobilization, technology can amplify existing strategies of civic or governmental organizations, thereby affecting the balance of political forces.

ICTs enhanced three strategies used in the cases examined below: truth-based advocacy, political mobilization, and social monitoring. These three mechanisms are not mutually exclusive; ICT-based accountability efforts sometimes combined two or three of these mechanisms.

Truth-based advocacy

Many efforts to increase political accountability and the quality of deliberation seek to assert and establish particular facts about the world—for example, the level and location of corruption or violence. These efforts gain traction as the truths they assert are substantiated and become more broadly and deeply acknowledged.

Well-designed and -implemented ICTs can enhance truth-based advocacy by facilitating the collection of relevant information, increasing the trustworthiness of information, and making information accessible.

Truth-based advocacy relies on both centralized and decentralized mechanisms of information collection.

The Kenyan budget tracking tool is an example of a centralized mechanism. It makes detailed information about financial allocations for local development projects publicly available. Corruption has prevented much of the allocated money from reaching poor and rural areas. Official governmental data made available by the tool have allowed activists and nongovernmental organizations (NGOs) to show that funds often fail to reach their intended recipients. The tool thus helps close evidentiary gaps and create common knowledge about corruption among NGOs, community groups, government, and interested publics.

In Mumbai Votes in India and the Fair Play Alliance in the Slovak Republic, watchdog organizations used ICT platforms to collect and disseminate information about government officials. Mumbai Votes collects information about the personal and political history and legislative records of candidates for political office. The Fair Play Alliance aggregates many kinds of political information using a variety of sources. It used the Slovakian Freedom of Information Act to build a database of financial flows between private sector actors and politicians. The data offered by both Mumbai Votes and the Fair Play Alliance are publicly available through websites.

Both Mumbai Votes and the Fair Play Alliance have turned out to be very useful resources for political reporting. These sites function in part as subsidies to investigative reporting, doing the time-consuming work of gathering information. They also seem to be regarded as credible. Their informational legitimacy stems partly from the care they take in gathering information and the fact that all of the data are available and thus in principle accessible by anyone with an Internet connection. Through these sites, journalists have discovered and publicized politicians' criminal histories, police malfeasance, and governmental corruption.

Kenya's Ushahidi ("testimony" in Swahili)—perhaps the most celebrated ICT platform in the political accountability domain—relies on decentralized (crowd-sourced) information collection. Launched by political bloggers in 2008 to map postelection violence, it aggregates reports citizens of human rights violations submit over the web or mobile phones and tags them on a publicly available Google map, according to predefined categories. The success of the original Ushahidi platform was unprecedented: it attracted more than 45,000 users in Kenya alone and exposed events that Kenyan mainstream media were reluctant to report and international media were not fully aware of. It also served as a catalyst for dozens of similar experiments around the world, in particular in the field of election monitoring in Mexico and the Philippines in 2009, Brazil and India in 2010, and Liberia in 2011.

Building on the Ushahidi experience, learning from its mistakes, and engaging its core team members, Uchaguzi was deployed to monitor the constitutional referendum in Kenya held on August 4, 2010. Its main innovation was to develop deep connections with election authorities and civil society organizations. These partnerships improve the accuracy of information and channel it to organizations that can act on it.

Political mobilization

ICT platforms can facilitate political mobilization by reducing the costs of communication between organizations and potential supporters. Cidade Democrática enables citizens, organizations, and government institutions to report problems in São Paolo and propose solutions. It covers a wide range of municipal issues, from environment and health to transport, education, and planning.

The platform is a collaborative social network that allows people interested in similar political causes to find one another, collaboratively develop ideas, express support of ideas suggested by other participants, spread information, and follow topics of interest. The best way to understand Cidade Democrática is not as a political spot market that connects citizens to one another but as a tool that allows NGOs, civil movements, and loosely structured groups of volunteers to mobilize support from interested citizens. Civil activists and organizations use the platform for their own advocacy needs, promoting their political causes, finding supporters, and allowing citizens to identify the political causes in which they are most interested.

Social monitoring

A central challenge to improving public and private services is the collection of information necessary for effective monitoring and accountability. Customers and clients who use those services are a potentially potent source of such information. This social monitoring dynamic is used in consumer review platforms, such as Amazon.com and TripAdvisor.com. The experiences of thousands of customers, if made widely available, could help others know whether products and services are safe and reliable. It is often beyond the capacity of a public agency or watchdog organization to cumulate such knowledge. ICT platforms can help solve this information problem by mobilizing individuals to monitor these problems in a crowd-sourced way.

Reclamos ("complaints" in Spanish) is a Chilean consumer complaint platform. It provides an open forum for consumers to monitor the activities of public and private service providers by sharing their experiences and complaining about bad customer care practices. The website has also evolved into an informal discussion forum in which users recommend or criticize products and help one another with helpful consumer advice. Journalists often follow up on complaints on the website, putting pressure on corporations and compelling them to change controversial practices. Ushahidi and Uchaguzi employ crowd-sourced social monitoring methods to reveal election violence and corruption.

Conclusion

Someone soon may invent an ICT platform that revolutionizes political accountability or democratic deliberation. A third political party in the United States, or more likely Brazil, could embrace an ICT that made party leadership much more transparently responsive to constituent interests, became massively popular, and as a result displace one of the existing parties—a political analogy to Netflix or Amazon displacing brick-and-mortar video rental shops.

Such technology has not yet emerged. We hope that it will. But today's governance ICTs operate in a more incremental, less revolutionary, way. They can improve political accountability and public deliberation by supplementing the efforts of civic and governmental organizations to establish and disseminate facts, mobilize constituencies, and monitor their socio-political environments.

References

Benkler, Yochai. 2006. *The Wealth of Networks: How Social Production Transforms Markets and Freedom.* New Haven, CT: Yale University Press.

Diamond, Larry. 2010. "Liberation Technology." *Journal of Democracy* 21 (3): 69–83.

Fung, Archon, Hollie Russon Gilman, and Jennifer Shkabatur. 2010. "An Examination of Several Experiences from Middle Income and Developing Countries." Draft report.

Global Voices. 2010. *Technology for Transparency: The Role of Technology and Citizen Media in Promoting Transparency, Accountability, and Civic Participation.* Available at http://globalvoicesonline.org/wp–content/uploads/2010/05/Technology_for_Transparency.pdf, accessed on February 25, 2010.

Hindman, Matthew Scott. 2009. *The Myth of Digital Democracy.* Princeton, NJ: Princeton University Press.

Howard, Philip N. 2010. *The Digital Origins of Dictatorship and Democracy: Information Technology and Political Islam.* Oxford: Oxford University Press.

Morozov, Evgeny. 2011. *The Net Delusion: The Dark Side of Internet Freedom.* New York: Public Affairs.

Noveck, Beth Simone. 2009. *Wiki Government: How Technology Can Make Government Better, Democracy Stronger, and Citizens More Powerful.* Washington, DC: Brookings Institution Press.

O'Reilly, Tim. 2010. "Government as a Platform." In *Open Government: Collaboration, Transparency, and Participation in Practice,* ed. Lathrop Daniel and Ruma Laurel. Sebastopol, CA: O'Reilly Media.

Raymond, Eric S. 2001. *The Cathedral and the Bazaar: Musings on Linux and Open Source by an Accidental Revolutionary.* Sebastopol, CA: O'Reilly Media.

Reagle, Joseph Michael Jr. 2010. *Good Faith Collaboration: The Culture of Wikipedia.* Cambridge, MA: MIT Press.

Rheingold, Howard. 2002. *Smart Mobs: The Next Social Revolution*. New York: Basic Books.

Schlozman, Kay, Lehman Sidney Verba, and Henry E. Brady. 2010. "Weapon of the Strong: Participatory Inequality and the Internet." *Perspective in Politics* 8: 487–509.

Schumpeter, Joseph. 1942. *Capitalism, Socialism, and Democracy*. New York: Harper and Row.

Shirky, Clay. 2008. *Here Comes Everybody: The Power of Organizing without Organizations*. London: Penguin Press.

Sifry, Micah L. 2011. *Wikileaks and the Age of Transparency*. Berkeley, CA: Counter Point.

Sunstein, Cass R. 2009. *Republic.Com 2.0*. Princeton, NJ: Princeton University Press.

Von Hippel, Eric. 2005. *Democratizing Innovation*. Cambridge, MA: MIT Press.

Weber, Steven. 2004. *The Success of Open Source*. Cambridge, MA: Harvard University Press.

CPSIA information can be obtained
at www.ICGtesting.com
Printed in the USA
FSOW02n1203091216
28372FS